W9-CPE-464

AGENTS UNLEASHED

A Public Domain Look at Agent Technology

LIMITED WARRANTY AND DISCLAIMER OF LIABILITY

ACADEMIC PRESS, INC. ("AP") AND ANYONE ELSE WHO HAS BEEN INVOLVED IN THE CREATION OR PRODUCTION OF THE ACCOMPANYING CODE ("THE PRODUCT") CANNOT AND DO NOT WARRANT THE PERFORMANCE OR RESULTS THAT MAY BE OBTAINED BY USING THE PRODUCT. THE PRODUCT IS SOLD "AS IS" WITHOUT WARRANTY OF ANY KIND (EXCEPT AS HEREAFTER DESCRIBED), EITHER EXPRESSED OR IMPLIED, INCLUDING, BUT NOT LIMITED TO, ANY WARRANTY OF PERFORMANCE OR ANY IMPLIED WARRANTY OF MERCHANTABILITY OR FITNESS FOR ANY PARTICULAR PURPOSE. AP WARRANTS ONLY THAT THE MAGNETIC DISKETTE(S) ON WHICH THE CODE IS RECORDED IS FREE FROM DEFECTS IN MATERIAL AND FAULTY WORKMANSHIP UNDER THE NORMAL USE AND SERVICE FOR A PERIOD OF NINETY (90) DAYS FROM THE DATE THE PRODUCT IS DELIVERED. THE PURCHASER'S SOLE AND EXCLUSIVE REMEDY IN THE EVENT OF A DEFECT IS EXPRESSLY LIMITED TO EITHER REPLACEMENT OF THE DISKETTE(S) OR REFUND OF THE PURCHASE PRICE, AT AP'S SOLE DISCRETION.

IN NO EVENT, WHETHER AS A RESULT OF BREACH OF CONTRACT, WARRANTY OR TORT (INCLUDING NEGLIGENCE), WILL AP OR ANYONE WHO HAS BEEN INVOLVED IN THE CREATION OR PRODUCTION OF THE PRODUCT BE LIABLE TO PURCHASER FOR ANY DAMAGES, INCLUDING ANY LOST PROFITS, LOST SAVINGS OR OTHER INCIDENTAL OR CONSEQUENTIAL DAMAGES ARISING OUT OF THE USE OR INABILITY TO USE THE PRODUCT OR ANY MODIFICATIONS THEREOF, OR DUE TO THE CONTENTS OF THE CODE, EVEN IF AP HAS BEEN ADVISED OF THE POSSIBILITY OF SUCH DAMAGES, OR FOR ANY CLAIM BY ANY OTHER PARTY.

Any request for replacement of a defective diskette must be postage prepaid and must be accompanied by the original defective diskette, your mailing address and telephone number, and proof of date of purchase and purchase price. Send such requests, stating the nature of the problem, to Academic Press Customer Service, 6277 Sea Harbor Drive, Orlando, FL 32887, 1-800-321-5068. APP shall have no obligation to refund the purchase price or to replace a diskette based on claims of defects in the nature or operation of the Product.

Some states do not allow limitation on how long an implied warranty lasts, nor exclusions or limitations of incidental or consequential damage, so the above limitations and exclusions may not apply to you. This Warranty gives you specific legal rights, and you may also have other rights which vary from jurisdiction to jurisdiction.

THE RE-EXPORT OF UNITED STATES ORIGIN SOFTWARE IS SUBJECT TO THE UNITED STATES LAWS UNDER THE EXPORT ADMINISTRATION ACT OF 1969 AS AMENDED. ANY FURTHER SALE OF THE PRODUCT SHALL BE IN COMPLIANCE WITH THE UNITED STATES DEPARTMENT OF COMMERCE ADMINISTRATION REGULATIONS. COMPLIANCE WITH SUCH REGULATIONS IS YOUR RESPONSIBILITY AND NOT THE RESPONSIBILITY OF AP.

AGENTS UNLEASHED

A Public Domain Look at Agent Technology

Peter Wayner

AP PROFESSIONAL

Boston San Diego New York
London Sydney Tokyo Toronto

This book is printed on acid-free paper. ∞

Copyright © 1995 by Academic Press, Inc.
Software agent copyright © 1995 by Peter Wayner

All rights reserved.
No part of this publication may be reproduced or
transmitted in any form or by any means, electronic
or mechanical, including photocopy, recording, or
any information storage and retrieval system, without
permission in writing from the publisher.

All brand names and product names mentioned in this book
are trademarks or registered trademarks of their respective companies.

AP PROFESSIONAL
1300 Boylston St., Chestnut Hill, MA 02167

An Imprint of ACADEMIC PRESS, INC.
A Division of HARCOURT BRACE & COMPANY

United Kingdom Edition published by
ACADEMIC PRESS LIMITED
24–28 Oval Road, London NW1 7DX

Wayner, Peter, 1964-
 Agents unleashed : a public domain look at agent technology / Peter
Wayner.
      p. cm.
  Includes bibliographical references and index.
  ISBN 0-12-738765-X
  1. Computer software. I. Title.
QA76.754.W39 1995
005.3--dc20   95-109
                                                     CIP

Printed in the United States of America
  95 96 97 98 IP   9 8 7 6 5 4 3 2 1

Contents

Preface

When I was writing this book, I relied upon the help of many people. BYTE magazine started this effort by sending me to write about software agents and they continued to support the effort by assigning more pieces for them. The editors at the magazine continue to surprise me with their depth of knowledge, force of intellectual curiosity and their command of the technological wave that grows taller and broader each day.

The strongest influence on the content of the book were the contributors to the cypherpunk mailing list (`cypherpunks-request@toad.com`). They became interested in the details of building a secure agent realm long before I did. The discussions on the list probed many of the topics with careful attention to detail. They taught me plenty and there are too many of them to thank by name.

There were also many people who opened up their minds to me. The representatives from the various companies described in here provided detailed information. Thank you.

Bruce Schneier deserves thanks for sharing an electronic copy of his bibliography with me. This saved me the trouble of typing it in myself.

Chuck Glaser, Mary Treseler and Mike Williams at AP Professional helped me through many details and provided the support that writers need.

The only person left to thank was my wife, Diana, who endured the long hours I spent on this book with good humor and devotion.

Peter Wayner
Baltimore, MD
January 1995
`pcw@access.digex.com`
`http://access.digex.net:/~pcw/pcwpage.html`

Book Notes

The copy for this book was typeset using the LaTeX typesetting software. Several important breaks were made with standard conventions in order to remove some ambiguities. The period mark is normally included inside the quotation marks like this "That's my answer. No. Period." This can cause ambiguities when computer terms are included in quotation marks because computers often use period marks to convey some meaning. For this reason, my electronic mail address is "pcw@access.digex.com". The periods are left outside.

Hyphens also cause problems when they're used for different tasks. LISP programmers often use hyphens to join words together into a single name like this Do-Not-Call-This-Procedure. *Unfortunately, this causes grief when these longer words occur at the end of a line. In these cases, there will be an extra hyphen included to specify that there was an original hyphen in the word. This isn't* hyper-compatible *with the standard rules that don't include the extra hyphen. But these rules are for readers who know that* self-help *is a word that should be hyphenated. No one knows what to think about* A--Much-Too-Long-Procedure-That-Should-Be-Shortened-For-Everyone.

Chapter 1

Off the Coast of Cannes

The SWAT trucks roll into position. The helicopters thump overhead. The news media trucks screech to a halt and start to extend their satellite antennas to the sky. The SWAT police scramble to surround the building.

Newscaster:

Police are gathering outside of Washington's largest and most prestigious McDonalds—the one that bears the distinction of being the Big Mac supplier to the President. We've received reports that major terrorists are inside, threatening the customers and making unknown demands.

In the White House, two aides walk briskly down a hallway and enter the President's Cabinet meeting. They whisper in his ear.

President:

We can put aside the rest of the agenda until the next meeting. Something pressing demands my attention.

More squad cars arrive. A helicopter buzzes low over the building. A terrorist looks out the window and recognizes the news media is filming. Suddenly, the front window of the McDonalds shatters as the terrorists discharge a hail of bullets to let the world know they are serious.

1

The President reaches the Oval Office.

President:

So we don't know who they are or what they want?

Aide:

No sir.

President:

Dammit. What can we do?

Aide:

The DC police have their special weapons squad there now, sir. The Secret Service always maintains two agents there to act as tasters, but we're not sure if they're still alive or being held as hostages. They might be able to act from inside, sir. The Army has its Delta Force on standby awaiting your command.

President:

No. I want someone who can sneak in there and get the job done without destroying the place. The Army and the police will go in with their guns blazing. The restaurant must be saved whole.

Aide

What other choices are there?

President:

Get me MI5 in Britain. I want that Bondo. 007. [1] He can get the job done.

---

[1] Object-Oriented Seven

Aide:

Yes sir.

South of France. Bondo is relaxing in Cannes racing a speedboat. At this point, his boat is just off of the leader. There is only one more lap to go. Bondo has to make a move if he's going to win. Suddenly, a cellular wrist watch rings. Bondo answers.

Bondo:

Bondo here.

Bondo nods several times. Shuts off his watch. Then turns to the Brunette and offers the wheel.

Bondo:

Take the wheel. Duty calls.

Bondo hauls out a waterproof portable computer and begins typing. He pauses and hits Return. Then he returns to the wheel.

A digital software agent leaves the computer on the boat and calls for airtime with the Slotted Aloha protocol controlling the local wireless network. When it reaches land, it hits the European phone network and then heads across the bottom of the Atlantic on a fiber optic channel running SONET. At the other end, it speeds through the DC net until it reaches the McDonald's central computer.

The central computer accepts the software agent, finds that Bondo programmed it with the correct access codes, and initializes it. The agent begins to send commands to the different appliances in the restaurant. Suddenly, the atmosphere in the restaurant starts to heat up. The grills and ovens have mysteriously turned themselves on to high. The terrorists stare in disbelief and try to shut it down. No amount of clicking on the controls makes a difference. The ovens and grills are locked in to a crazy, demented effort to create hell.

A message starts to flash on the computer monitors that normally keep track of the pending orders: IF YOU CAN'T STAND THE HEAT, GET OUT OF THE KITCHEN.

Back on the boat, Bondo's computer beeps. He has guided his boat into a narrow opening on the inside of the turn. He's practically running neck and neck with the leader.

Bondo:

Excellent. Take the wheel again and hold it steady through this turn. We'll pass them on the last corner.

Bondo returns to his computer. The software agent he sent to the MI5 computers has just returned with important information about the terrorist. Bondo had asked the agent to search for all known terrorists operating in the Washington, DC area. The agent then cross-checked the list with airport arrival information from the U.S. Customs computers. This narrowed the list to a few. A final pass through the alumni computers of Oxford found a direct hit. One of the men spent the same years at Oxford with the President. A psychological profile showed a strong animus for the man. Bingo.

The software agent's final task was accessing the national health computers for the medical records of the alumnus. Bondo scans this and whistles. Bondo clacks the keys some more. Then he returns to the wheel of the boat as they enter the final turn. The other boat had gained ground while Bondo typed and now Bondo's boat is being squeezed into the inside.

In Washington, the police helicopters swarm lower. The DC police begin to unload a tank from a special flatbed truck. They're taking no chances.

In the meantime, Bondo's latest agent screams through the fiber optic channels until it comes knocking on the door of the McDonald's computer. Again, it gains access and begins to issue commands to the machines. Suddenly the light bulbs start to flicker at about 3 flashes per second.

A terrorist begins to crumple. Bondo guessed right. The terrorist still suffers from epilepsy. The flashing of the lights was set to the right frequency to start a seizure. As the terrorist falls, one of the Secret Service agents grabs his gun and shoots the other two henchmen. The Big Mac is saved.

Off of Cannes, Bondo revs the motor and tries to elude the other boat that is cutting him off. Bondo scans the waves ahead and notes that the pattern will dramatically shift. The other pilot doesn't notice this because he is too busy grinning and waving to Bondo. The boats hit the waves seconds apart and the rogue wave almost knocks the leader upside down. Bondo is prepared and sails through to victory!

Chapter 2

Why Agents?

_____ The Hype _____

*Agents are like slaves, psychologists, mothers, and friends rolled
into one wonderful package. They'll do your bidding, read your
mind and help keep you sane in a world of ever-increasing choice.*

_____ Political Cynicism _____

*Agents are just another evil extension of the capitalist system de-
signed to increase consumption and destroy the souls of the work-
ers. Our minds and our hearts will be replaced by programmatic
automatons that will make all of our decisions for us. Eventually, we will cede control to the machines as our minds devolve
into agents.*

_____ The Buzzwords _____

*Agents are interoperable, hyper-compatible programs running in
a fault-tolerant, object-oriented, secure memory space linked to a
high-speed, ubiquitous network infrastructure.*

Good science fiction doesn't begin with gizmos— it just ends up there. The best stories start with dreams, needs, wants and worries, and then the writers come up with plausible ways that new technology can satisfy these goals. Science fiction writers came up with concept of agents long ago because they realized that we wanted to live in a world where every switch, appliance, window or wall came with a mind of its own. Computers wouldn't just churn out numbers for the bookkeepers in banks— they would liberate us by creating little slaves that would do everything right.

Now these dreams are becoming more real. The information super-highway is not just a sci-fi buzzword, but also a political goal embraced by those outside of Silicon Valley. But despite all of the relentless progress and excess attention, there is plenty of noise that clouds the dream. Computers can talk to each other over networks, but many people make a good salary keeping networks running because the machines still have a habit of crashing. Software can be shrink-wrapped and sold without customization, but companies still spend a fortune on support to help customers deal with non-standard configurations. Companies are exploring offering on-line services, but they're still grappling with many different business and legal problems.

If the world is actually going to enjoy many of the pleasures of ubiquitous computing, software developers must solve these problems. "Software Agents" is a buzzword that covers a number of different software solutions that will bring us one step closer. None of the ideas are new— in fact many of them were developed years ago. But now, the market is ready to absorb them into the software used by everyone. The hardware is available to link up the world, and now the programmers must develop software that can successfully negotiate these networks and do everyone's bidding.

This book explores some of basic technology that might be needed to develop a network where agents can flourish. At the basic level, it is about how to allow computers to set up links with other computers and get work done without opening up the channel to mischief and mayhem. At another level, it is about how to program for distributed networks. At a deeper level, it is about how to build and design an economy so people and their computer agents can interact successfully. And at the deepest level, it is about getting computers to do a better job of reading our minds. Each of these facets are important parts of an agent realm and each of them are touched upon in some way in this book.

2.1 What Is an Agent?

The term "agent" is already overused. Practically every program on the market today is said to include "agent technology". Word processors that have flexible, built-in spell-checking programs that alert you when you type a misspelled word have "agents" that correct the spelling. [1] Text search engines that use more sophisticated matching algorithms to find documents in large collections often refer to themselves as "agents". The advanced research labs of many companies put together computer prototypes that have all-knowing "agents" that are able to do whatever you want.

The scope of ideas that live under the rubric of "agent" is large and multi-faceted. Some of the different ways that I've seen people use the word "agent" are as a synonym for:

A Good Virus If Oz has a good witch, then there is nothing impossible about a good virus. Of course, no one is going to sleep tight if a software company's help line says, "I'll just ship over a virus to patch up your software and fix the bug." So, they use a nicer word. But the distinction isn't just a euphemism. A well-designed network for agents can defend itself against malicious attack. Agents are controlled versions of viruses.

A Time Saver Networks are great ways to find data, but they can often be too successful. Imagine you want to read a particular speech by President Clinton discussing health care. If you log into the White House's FTP server, you would need to download all of the speeches until you

---

[1] Will word processing companies start advertising their programs as "typesetting agents"? Will installation programs become "initialization agents"? Will the power switch become an "Empowering Agent"?

found the one that you wanted. This might take quite a while. [2] If you were lucky, the titles might give you some clues, but there could be plenty of discussion about health care. An "agent" could go to the White House's file server and search through the archives locally, saving the time it takes to transfer all of the information across the network. Network bandwidth would be conserved by allowing people to bundle some intelligent capabilities into their requests for information.

A Personal Shopper Wouldn't it be ideal if something could find its way through the network, choose the perfect little gift to pick up our spirits, accent our wardrobe or brighten up the family room? It would if you're in the marketing business. Agents will be able to bundle all of our preferences into a decision-making algorithm and then go off in search of the objects of our dreams. In most cases, these will revolve around making simple but necessary distinctions such as deciding between smoking and nonsmoking, but agents may grow to make more complicated judgments about taste.

A Butler Of course, butlers are supposed to read our minds and know what we want before we're through making up our minds. People routinely discuss the fact that agents could help our computers read our minds and create programs on their own. These agents would watch what we do with our computers and begin to mimic it. Naturally, this might make matters worse if you, like I, start off life with a new system by deleting something crucial to save disk space. The agent that learns from this example will be certain to cause havoc. Still, there is plenty of room for an active presence in computers that attempts to make life easier by noting patterns and adapting to them.

A Little Person Some books on raising children teach parents to treat their kids like "little people." The term "agent" is quite popular in the artificial intelligence community, which is continually trying to capture

---

[2]Network speeds may increase significantly in the future, but the amount of information provided by people like politicians who are intent on self-documentation could increase faster.

human, or at least intelligent, qualities in a machine. This is largely because some philosophers have pointed out that agency is one of the differences between humans and rocks. That is, the agent has the ability to get up and go somewhere and do something. The difference, though, between a potato and a couch potato will take much deeper thinking.

A Prodigy After parents raise their children past the "little people" stage, they move into the "you're old enough— figure it out for yourself" stage. Some researchers attempt to make "agents" learn for themselves. This usually involves some mixture of algorithms designed to pull a signal or a pattern out of a sea of noise. Genetic algorithms, computational learning theory and classification theory are just part of the past work in artificial intelligence that is being recast into agents.

A Power Librarian Everyone knows a librarian who can not only help you find the material but also help you straighten out your thinking. I knew one librarian in a math library who could give you the information without looking it up. There is plenty of active research in making computer programs that will search through the terabytes of data floating around the networks today. Everyone hopes that this software will be smart enough to parse the text, translate it from other languages and suss out ambiguities in the language. You'll be able to request articles about the head of Libya and get results that are filed under all of the different transliterations like *Kaddafi* or *Quadaffi*.

An Actor Or in computer-speak, an "emotion server". Some people are actively mining the world of animation to find ways to create little creatures in the computer that express their emotions. This could be used by an advanced operating system to tell its owner that it isn't happy because the disk is too full. Or it might express that there are too many programs running concurrently and the work is thrashing the disk. In any case, emotions could be produced at whim to convey a message when words aren't enough.

A Dancing Mailman Why stop at someone who just delivers the electronic mail? Why not let the electronic mail include diverse instructions that interact with the recipient? Many people are proposing that standards be developed that will let enhanced mail present pictures, diagrams and entire user interfaces with buttons, sliders and other gadgets so the recipient can interact with the program. At the most basic level, this would be used to send out more and more forms to people for them to fill out. At its most sophisticated we may stop to make the distinction between software and electronic mail. Everything will come delivered by the network ready to do some work.

These are all wonderful ideas and notions. Each of these has a place in the world. This book, though, will concentrate on the technology for creating seamlessly integrated networks that allow programs to move from machine to machine without leaving a trail of havoc. This is because the technology for creating flexible networks is much more grounded in reality than many of the ideas people express about artificial intelligence agents.

Defending machines on a network against a rogue virus or a poorly written agent may not be simple, but it does have a straightforward and well-defined solution.

On the other hand, creating agents that read minds or interpret your actions intelligently are difficult propositions. None of the artificial intelligence techniques that exist today are even close to accomplishing what we want them to do. They are much more realistic today than they were in the past, but there are still many computer cycles to burn before the solution is found to creating a combination of power librarian, actor and student.

So, for most of the book, the word "agent" will be used as shorthand for a software program that can roam a network, interact with its host, gather information and come home.

2.2 Why Agents?

Before attacking the technological problems of letting software loose on the Net, it might be a good idea to examine some of the advantages of this approach. Fancy artificial intelligence algorithms may be zippy, but there are clear economic advantages to developing even the simplest agent technology. Why? Current network transactions are too basic to be efficient. If you are going to do anything beyond make a simple request of a distant file server, you must often exchange several rounds of information before achieving the goal. These exchanges take time and consume network resources. In many cases, a request might spend more than 99% of its time communicating. This is fat that is ripe for cutting.

A good example of this is making a reservation for a flight. Although you have a vague idea of when you want to go, the only time you can encode these preferences in a simple message is if you know the exact flight number you wish to fly. But most of the time you won't know this information. So you need to first request a list of flights to your destination at certain times. Then after comparing time and availability, you would request a seat on a particular flight. Then you would need to choose among the seats available. What if there are no aisle seats left? You might want to switch flights if this is an important concern. What if you don't want to fly on a prop plane? You've got to switch again.

Each of these details complicates the process. Imagine you wanted to write a program that would allow your home computer to access a reservation system like American Airline's SABRE and make the reservation for you. Your preferences are simple: Aisle seat, nonsmoking, departing Baltimore between 7 and 9:30 a.m. and arriving in Austin before noon. No more than one connection. No changes in Chicago O'Hare.

Consider the network traffic in a world without agents. First you would make a simple request for a list of all flights leaving between 7 and 9:30 a.m. The list of these might include 200 different flights and take up thousands of bytes. The length would depend upon how much information was bundled in the list of each flight. If it just listed the departure and arrival times, then your local software could cut down the list to the flights that arrived before noon.

Then it would request a list of the connections and narrow the search more. This interaction would continue back and forth until the selection was made. Each transaction would often contain plenty of extraneous information that your software used to narrow the selection. This would clog up the

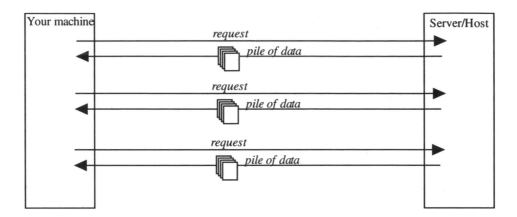

Figure 2.1: In a world without agents, the network carries many large lists of data back and forth between the user and the distant server.

network and be very inefficient.

Now imagine that you could find a way for a program encapsulating a flowchart to satisfy your requests to travel through the network, arrive intact and begin to send its queries to the database locally. There would be no need for long-distance communication. The request could be finished much faster because there would be no delays for communication. It could also be much cheaper because many future networks may charge by the byte they carry.

More pragmatic or short-sighted people may wonder if it would be easier to enhance the reservation system to take more complicated requests. You could expand its language so it would understand demands like, "Departing between 7 and 8 a.m. on a jet with at least three engines with no more than 32% of the seats sold. Also, a seat not near children." Constructing such a system would be possible and it would avoid many of the security problems discussed in this book, but it would have limitations. There would be no problems if the system architects could anticipate all possible demands. What if a customer wanted to leave in the morning but did not want to be in the air at a particular time when his religion asked him to be in prayer? If the reservation system didn't allow segmented departure windows, then it

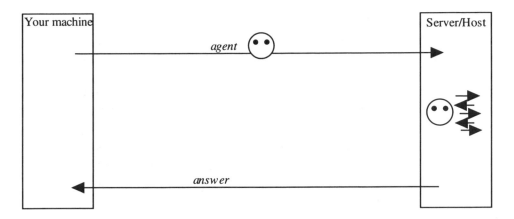

Figure 2.2: Agents add flexibility and efficiency by performing much of the work locally on the server. There is no need for excessive network load.

wouldn't be able to handle this request.

A reservation system that welcomes programs and gives them the possibility to churn away locally could easily handle this problem. The software for the reverent passenger's request could be expanded to include extra if-then-else clauses to avoid these times. It could even be expanded further to take into account time zones and flight changes so that the passenger could take one route if it would leave him on the ground changing flights at the right time.

Flexibility and reprogrammability are always great assets. They may be confusing to some people, but they are the foundation for good software that adapts to its users. Network information servers that allow software agents to arrive and execute code locally are the best way to allow systems to grow and serve the needs of the customers. At the same time, they save network resources and often work faster.

2.3   The Underlying Technology

If many of the dreams of computer slaves are to become real, we must build a network that allows programs to roam wherever they need to go to satisfy our whims. This sounds simple at first, but it isn't the same as simply grabbing the software, decompressing it and setting it running. Although anyone would find it easy to distribute a program through stores and a network, it is an entirely different matter to create software that moves itself through the world.

Giving the software the means and the power to control its location—agency if you will—sends shivers up some people's spines. Rogue software running amok through the network is a dangerous image and people have every reason to be scared of it. Crazed software deleting and destroying information could be caused by either a bug or a malicious programmer, but in either case the damage could be serious. Everyone is well aware of computer viruses and the potential they have for causing damage. Although viruses weren't officially created as agents, they illustrate what can go wrong when a program has the ability to move about at will and has access to the major files on the system.

The goal is to develop a way for software to live in a controlled environment where it can do no harm. If an agent is going to travel through a network, there are many different problems that will confront the agent on its journey. The major challenges are:

Transportation How will an agent get from place to place? How will it pack up and move?

The agents described in this book will presumably move about as ASCII-encoded, MIME-compatible e-mail messages on the Internet. There are many other networks and file formats, but this is the most common and the most widely accepted. The technology in this book can be adapted to other networks and file transmission protocols with a few simple modifications.

Authentication How do you know a message comes from someone else? How you know that a piece of software is making a request on behalf of a particular individual? How do you know that the agent being presented to you made it through the network without being infected by a virus?

Each of these questions can be solved by using some of the popular public-key technology. This allows computer programs to construct digital signatures of a particular file that guarantee that the file is unmodified and definitely from the computer of a particular person.

Secrecy How can you be certain that your agents maintain your privacy? How can you be sure that the network administrator doesn't read your agent and fire it up locally to satisfy some curiosity? How can you protect your interests?

These problems can also be solved with public-key and private-key encryption. In this case, the agent can have its contents encrypted so that no one but the rightful addressee can decrypt them and start them running.

Security How can you protect against viruses? How can you protect against bugs that run amok and destroy the system? How can you prevent the incoming agent from entering an endless loop and consuming all of the CPU cycles?

These problems can be solved by creating a special, limited language that will not allow the agent to access arbitrary parts of the system. The implementation will keep track of the execution and stop it if a program runs too long.

Cash How will your agent pay for things? Will it run amok and start running up an outrageous credit card bill?

There are many layers of solutions to this problem. The simplest use public-key encryption to produce certificates guaranteeing that you will pay bills up to a certain size. More sophisticated technology actually produces digital cash that can be spent anonymously like regular cash. Either of these approaches allows agents to leave home with some money to pay for what they need.

Each of issues in the last list dealt specifically with providing security for the agents or their cash in transit. They are large issues that have been confronted by many people in many different contexts. The concept of software agents is just a unifying goal for these technologies.

When the agents arrive at a host, the host must protect itself. What will the host need to do? Here are some important issues:

Resource Allocation How does the agent act politely in a local environment? Will it consume all of the available memory and lock up the machine? Will it try to fill up a local disk with endless copies of itself?

The operating system that runs the agent must prevent these occurrences. It must be able to bound the consumption of memory or other valuable resources and shut down the agent safely. Then it must return the agent home so that the problem can be fixed.

Host Resources When an agent goes to some machine, it is looking to interact with some of the databases or information services available there. How can a machine make services available in an manner that is easy to use?

The host operating systems must develop a standard format for publishing their interface to the network so that everyone can use it. The format should also include several general queries that will be supported on all hosts.

Access Privileges Should a host open its door to anyone? How can it keep out the riff-raff or limit its services to an exclusive group?

The host must publish these parameters so people can determine whether this service is interesting enough for them to send agents that way.

Resource Verification How can a host make certain that the cash offered by an agent is real? How will it check the credit of an incoming agent?

The programmer of the host will be responsible for determining the credit-granting privileges of the host. Different people will want to handle this in different ways. The verification of cash and the structure of how it can be used is covered in detail in Chapters 15 and 16.

The list of these problems is not all-inclusive, but it does touch upon all of the challenges that will be addressed by the book. There are many problems that may confront someone trying to set up a host for agents on the Net. Should they offer guarantees? How should they enforce copyright? What is the best way to advertise the product? These are all important challenges, but they lie outside the scope of determining the best way to let programs roam about the Net without causing damage.

2.4 The Goal of this Book

There is little doubt among many people that agents can save plenty of network resources. There is also little doubt that agents can go awry and damage everything in their path if the network that holds the agents is not well designed. The challenge is to maximize the power of the languages and technologies used by agents to roam successfully while keeping them from causing any damage.

This book will set out many of the technical principles that must be used to create a digital realm where agents can exist, work, play and prosper. The most important features will be covered on an abstract level that tries to explain everything in a language-independent fashion. The structure and purpose of the agent and its hosts are discussed in abstraction. The technical theory behind the cryptography that is used to provide many of the assurances of authenticity and secrecy is also covered in enough depth to ensure that anyone could implement the algorithms.

High-level discussions are fine, but the real proof of any computer science is the implementation. This book will provide an extended toy example that uses the LISP language. The language offers flexibility, extendibility and source code. More importantly, it is also easy to learn quickly because it has a very simple, almost primitive structure that is also the basis of its power. The different chapters of the book will discuss the various features or jobs for the different positions in the agent realm and then it will give a part of the example implemented in LISP.

There is no reason why the information in this book cannot be revised and extended to apply to other languages. It would be nice, in some respects, to use C or C++ as the central language for this book. This is hard to do, however, because of the limitations of the language that are discussed later in the book. Someone will no doubt come up with a very C-like language that solves many of problems without confusing the average C programmer, but this book is not the time or the place to do this.

The problem with creating a new language is that everyone who reads the book will need to learn it if they want to examine the technical details. LISP is relatively easy to learn. It also solves the problems successfully. The syntax is poor and annoying. I hate the endless parentheses as much as anyone. But why reinvent the horse? There is plenty of LISP code that can be used in the system if it is built around LISP.

The book also includes several chapters that center about a relatively new language known as TCL. This is a creation of John Ousterhout of Sun Microsystems who intended it to be a meta-language for linking together different tools written in a base language like C. Hence TCL stands for "Tool Command Language". The language provides many of the important features that make LISP desirable, and source code is also available. The most compelling reason for covering the topic in this book, though, is that Nathaniel Borenstein and Marshall Rose have already converted it into a rudimentary agent system.

2.5   How To Read this Book

There are many different ways to read this book. Some people might want to learn everything here, but many others might be interested in finding certain classes of information. To help the picky readers and to whet the appetite of the others, I'm offering these different suggested subsets of the book.

A Broad Overview

If you want to learn something about the structure of agent systems, their uses and the potential challenges that must be overcome during their design, then you'll want to do this:

1. Read the introductions to the chapter on agents (Chapter 3), hosts (Chapter 4) and resources (Chapter 8). These will present some of the problems and roles for each of the types. After the introduction, the chapters lay out the foundations for an experimental agent system.

2. There is a description of other agent languages in Chapter 9 that includes a high-level discussion about the essential features of an agent language.

3. Read the description of other languages in Chapter 13. This includes a short discussion of Telescript and SmalltalkAgents, two commercially available languages for experimenting with agents.

4. Chapters 17 and 19 include plenty of speculation on how the arena will develop. These chapters are intended to inspire the reader to create this technology.

Technical Guts

Many programmers attempting to create agent projects or add some of the important features to their existing work will want to know more technical details about how to construct these worlds. If you want to know this, then:

1. If you are unfamiliar with either LISP or TCL read the short descriptions of the LISP and TCL languages in Chapters 10 and 11 respectively. This will allow you to play with the experimental agent system described in the chapters.

2. Skip over the easier introductions at the front of each chapter. Skim chapters like Chapter 9 which are written at an introductory level.

3. Concentrate on the description of the guts of the agent (Chapter 3), hosts (Chapter 4) and resources (Chapter 8). The second half of each chapter describes an experimental implementation in XLISP.

4. If you want to know the details of how to check the owners of agents and enforce a pattern of authenticity, read Chapter 14.

5. Information on secure forms of digital cash can be found in Chapters 15 and 16.

6. Ideas for future implementations of agents can be found in Chapters 17 and 19.

The Bibliography in Chapter 21 is filled with many other sources that will allow you to investigate the topics in detail. Sources of information on the network can be found in Chapter 21. Anyone who wants to seriously use the information in this book will need to go deeper and investigate the areas in depth. This book is only an introduction to a burgeoning field. The examples in it are useful, but they are only toys that make it easy to experiment.

Chapter 3

A Basic Agent

_____ The Hype _____

Strong, lithe, supple, fluid, stylish, savory and smooth. Those are the ideal qualities for a modern agent.

_____ Political Cynicism _____

The state, if it is ever to wither away, must still maintain the ability to act upon the world and defend itself against the capitalistic impulses still smoldering in the hearts of the greedy.

_____ The Buzzwords _____

An object-based, dynamically linking program.

Ideally, an agent will be all things to all people. This is is a great dream that will never be realized with the current nature of computer intelligence. In reality, agents will be able to be programmed to do anything that computers can do. This means there are the natural limits that constrain any machine-based intelligence, but these bounds can be quite large.

What constitutes an agent? This question rings with the self-reflection that occurs in everyone's Hamlet period. The deep philosophical meaning of this question is fun to ask in a late-night cafe when you're smoking clove cigarettes, but it is best to forget about this glitzy anthropomorphism during the light of day and realize that agents are just programs. They do exactly what they are told to do and nothing more.

Agents may be programs, but they are programs with several additional features. They must be able to negotiate the network and ask for permission for everything they do. They must be ready to prove who they are and show that they have the authority to act for their masters. Upon arrival, they must be ready to negotiate credit for the host's services and, in the event that credit isn't available, the agent must be able to pay up front. Digitized chocolates or bottles of wine won't cut it.

Here are some elements that make up an agent :

State The agent must bring the state of all of the important variables and constants along with itself. This must be bundled in one list.

Functions These are all of the functions built into the agent. This is what it knows how to do.

Initialization Functions These are the routines or functions that must be run when the agent first arrives at the host.

Main Function This is the main function to be called upon arrival. It is equivalent to the `main` function in a C program.

Cleanup Functions What is done at the end to complete the exchange. These functions must package the agent and send it to its next destination.

Authorization Who sent the agent? Under whose authority does it operate? Who gets the bill?

Return Address Where will the results go? Where will reports about errors go?

Spending Limits How much computational time can the agent spend? How much money? How many other computational resources can it consume?

Cash Supply What if the agent must pay to play? If credit isn't available, then the agent needs to be able to offer something to the host.

This list of the major elements that constitute a computer-based, network-ready digital agent is not necessarily complete. Some agents might carry multimedia presentations with them to be offered to someone on the Net. Other agents might carry digital representations of contracts for negotiation with a host. The implementation of Safe-TCL, described in Chapter 12, includes functions for displaying information on the screen and interacting with the user so it can offer some smart mail. There are thousands of possible uses for agents that require different functions and capabilities. For now, these details are left as part of the initialization and main functions built into the agent. This book will concentrate on the technical details of how an agent will move through the network, prove its identity and execute its code without endangering the host.

Which language should be used? Any language could be used to assemble all of these elements in some shape or fashion, but some are better than others. Some offer good ways to segregate the information owned by the agent from the information and the files owned by the host. Some suffer the restriction brought about by this partition with more style because they were designed to help the programmer by constraining their access to the data. An overview of the issues of designing a language are given in Chapter 9. The rest of this chapter will concentrate on introducing a LISP-based example for a basic agent.

3.1   A LISP Agent

LISP is an easy language to use to build an agent because there are a number of built-in functions that are quite flexible and tuned to the process of maintaining lists of objects with embedded functionality.

The basic LISP agent will be a text file that will be evaluated when it arrives. The file can contain almost anything, but it must define certain required variables and functions. Each of these items will begin with the prefix FA to make their heritage clear. The required variables and functions are:

FA-Resource-Requests Which resources the agent will demand.

FA-Return-Address Where to send the final state if it doesn't go somewhere else.

FA-Agent-Identity This contains the identity of the agent. The fields in this structure include owner, date of birth, serial number, mission statement, and open fields for digital signatures.

FA-Error-Function error-type] What to do if there is an error.

FA-Resource-Negotiator This is executed before the main function to arrange for the right resources. If it does not succeed, then the **FA--Main-Function** won't run.

FA-Initialization-Function This runs at the beginning of the operation.

FA-Main-Function This is the main function. It must initialize what needs to be initialized, do the work and clean up at the end.

FA-Clean-Up-Function This runs when the main function terminates. It should be responsible for packing everything up and sending it to the correct destination.

FA-Report-Me-In-Errors This is a list of variables that should be mailed back to the owner in the event of an unrecoverable error. It is useful for debugging and is discussed in depth in Chapter 5.

FA-Burn-Some-Cycles This function is used only in the local debugging process. It will calculate for a fixed amount of computation for the purposes of debugging an agent before it leaves for the host.

FA-State-Info What the agent considers important. These are what will be packed up and moved with the agent.

The LISP file is evaluated upon arrival. Then the host executes **FA--Initialization-Function**, **FA-Resource-Negotiator**, **FA-Main-Function** and **FA-Clean-Up-Function**, in that order. Figure 3.1 shows the execution progression. Although all of these could be compressed into one function call, they are kept separate at this time to allow for future expansion. It may be desirable to create a type of resident agent that arrives at a host and sets up shop. The main function, in that case, will be executed every time the agent should be activated. The initialization and clean-up functions are only used to set up the state when it arrives.

The details of the resource negotiation process are discussed in Chapter 8. The resource negotiator is responsible for making sure that the **FA--Main-Function** will have everything available for it to run. In almost all cases, this will be a trivial exercise. People will know what they want their agent to get when it goes to a location and they will make sure it has the cash or whatever resources are necessarty to pay for it. The more complicated resource negotiation procedure described in Chapter 8 is designed to offer agents and hosts the flexibility to barter their way into agreement. It is quite possible that this will be used for souk-like brinksmanship, but it can also be used for the more mundane task of dealing with incongruities. An agent can ask for bananas and if they're not available, it can ask for pears.

When the agent and the host are satisfied that all of the agent's requests for resources can be fulfilled, then the host starts the function **FA-Main--Function** that runs until it is completed. In many cases, the agent might ask to be bundled up and shipped to another location before it finishes. This absolves the host from any responsibility. In other cases, it will simply end and the host must bundle up the state and send it back to the return address.

The variable **FA-State-Info** lists the names of all the variables and

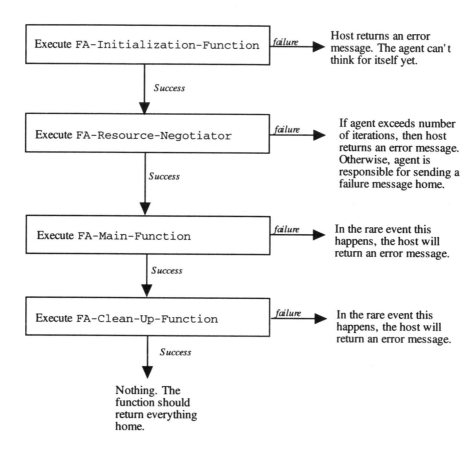

Figure 3.1: The execution flowchart of what happens to a basic agent when it arrives at a host.

functions that should be preserved when the agent moves. In some cases, this will be a long list. In others, it might be just a single atom with a name like **answer**. The agent programmer can tune the amount of state that is kept along with the agent in order to maximize the efficiency of the network travels. If only an answer is needed, then only an answer will be returned. This allows an agent to create temporary variables and not worry about them staying attached.

In the case of an error, the agent must be prepared to recover from the problem. The error function, **FA-Error-Function** , is called with information about the type of error. Chapter 5 describes the requirements of this function in detail and also defines some of the basic error codes recognized by all agents and their hosts.

There are also a number of different variables or functions that almost every agent will want to carry. Some will need to carry cash to pay for items along the way. Others will need specific instructions for returning themselves home with a minimum amount of baggage. The programmer should anticipate these needs and include them in the basic code.

3.2   An Airline System

This section will describe a small agent that will head off to a distant host to make an airline reservation. The structure of the host offering the reservations is described in Chapter 4 and the complete LISP text for the host can be found in AIRHOST.LSP. You might want to read that chapter before proceeding with this one. The text for the agent described here can be found in the AIRAGENT.LSP file.

The first job for the agent that arrives at a host is to establish a means of paying for the job. That means the host will execute **FA-Resource--Negotiator** so the agent will be able to interact with the host and make sure that it can pay for everything that it wants. This is described in section 8.4 in the chapter on resource negotiations.

The second job is to run **FA-Initialization-Function**. This will initialize everything the agent will need to do the job. In this case, the only job for the agent is to set up an information block that will be used to make

reservations. This includes all of the information about the customer. The
structure for this would be obtained from the host by executing `FH-Give--`
`Host-Description`.

```
(defun FA-Initialization-Function ()
   (setq LA-Info-Block (make-info-block
    :first-name "Peter"
    :last-name "Dogstar"
    :credit-card-number 01023414223234
    :address "1000110 Whim Drive, Sim, NY 41201"
    :month 'Jun
    :date 14
    :year 1995))
  t)
```

The flights stored in the host database are kept in a separate LISP list
of records defined by a `defstruct` command. The individual parts of each
record can be accessed with functions like `flight-day`, which returns the
day of the flight, or `flight-Coach-Window-Seats-Available`, which lists
how many window seats are available in the coach section.

The host will prevent the agent from accessing this list directly because
the agent could screw up the database for any number of malicious or inno-
cent reasons. So the host provides two main functions to allow the agent to
look for the right flight: `LH-Flights-By-Item` and `LH-Flights-By-Item-2`.
The first will only look for direct matches. The second accepts lists of three
items of this form:

```
(time less-than 1200)
```

which means find all flights that depart at a time before 1200 hours.

The agent can string together several of these requests to narrow down
the list of acceptable flights. When it finds one, it can make a reservation by
calling the host's function `LH-Make-Reservation`. The structure for these
functions looks like this:

```
(defvar LA-Triple-List
  '((time greater-than 900) (time less-than 1200)))
    (start-city equal charm) (end-city equal circuit)
    (day equal tue)))
(defvar LA-Info-Block nil)
(defun LA-Make-Res (flt)
;; Make a reservation.
  (LH-Make-Reservation (flight-number flt)
    'first-aisle LA-Info-Block))
(defun LA-Declare-Success (flt)
;; We found a flight.
  (print "Reservation Made Successfully.")
  (LH-Print-Flight-Info flt))
(defun FA-Main-Function ()
  (let ((answer nil))
    (setq answer (LH-Flights-By-Item-2 (car LA-Triple-List)))
  ;;;  (setq *time-left* (+ 1000 *time-left*))
    (do ((l (cdr LA-Triple-List) (cdr l))) ((null l))
        (Format t "Starting ~a" (car l))
      (setq answer (LH-Flights-By-Item-2 (car l) answer))
      (Format t "After ~a there are ~a possible flights.~%"
          (car l) (length answer)))
    (cond (answer ;; There is a flight!!
        (do ((l answer (cdr l))) ((null l))
          (cond ((LA-Make-Res (car l))
              (LA-Declare-Success (car l))
              (setq l nil))))))))
  ))
```

The main function of the agent, **FA-Main-Function**, feeds a list of triples to the host's function **LH-Flights-By-Item-2**. If there is a flight available at the end of this list of requests, then it makes the reservation by calling **LA--Make-Res** and returning. The function **LA-Declare-Success** was provided to include different ways that the information could be reported.

3.3 Summary

This Chapter provided a basic structure for an agent. An Agent must be able to negotiate for resources, trade the right resources, initialize itself, run through its interaction with the host and deal with errors. It should do all of this without overstepping its bounds at a host. There isn't much more to an agent.

Although there are many different ways that the resource negotiation process described in Chapter 8 can be extended, and many better ways to add standard functionality to a host, there aren't many ways to extend an agent. This is largely because an agent is just a program that interacts with a host.

Future definitions might add more structure for popular types of agents. There might be basic agents that come with the ability to pay a fixed amount for a service. Others might be constructed that go to one place and return. Standard types like this may emerge if people begin to use the agent systems frequently.

Any standard system, though, should be viewed with suspicion. Extreme flexibility is the attraction of any agent system. New features that handle basic chores can be confining if they can't be circumvented when it is necessary.

Chapter 4

A Basic Host

—————————— The Hype ——————————

*"Be our guest ...be our guest ...put our magic to the test."—
Walt Disney World commercial. Also from the movie "Beauty
and the Beast".*

—————————— Political Cynicism ——————————

*Hospitality may seem gracious and unselfish, but it is often the
most highly organized form of suppression and domination.*

—————————— The Buzzwords ——————————

*A C2-security grade system that can evaluate and instantiate in-
coming code while preventing unauthorized function evaluation.*

When an agent arrives from the network, the host must welcome the agent into the fold while defending itself from attack. The host must be able to check the authenticity of the incoming software, start it running, negotiate access to the local resources and bundle everything up when it is ready to leave. Figure 4.1 shows the flow of this process. Once the agent starts running, the host must be able to satisfy the agent with whatever the host promised to the Net. Some hosts might offer airline reservations. Others might provide a special database. Whatever the host offered, it must be available. These are stiff requirements, but they can be handled successfully with some planning.

The first step will be to check the authentication and strip off the encryption. This guards the incoming agent against tampering and eavesdropping while providing the host with some proof that the agent represents who it says it does.The agent will arrive as a text file. The digital signature is appended at the end of the file. The encryption key, if encryption is used, is also bundled at the end of the file, encrypted with the host's public key. The text of the file must be decoded and then the digital signature will be verified. The results of this are passed to the host. The details of this process are described in Chapter 14.

When the host receives the agent that is now in clear text, it must first prepare itself by loading in a clean set of the host's functions. This is because the host itself is also a LISP program. These functions include the required functions for negotiating resource allocation, handling requests for local data as well as any other functions that might be necessary to satisfy requests. The details for this are kept in a personality file. This is a set of LISP functions for a LISP host.

The host must now evaluate the agent's personality file. This file includes all of the basic definitions expected of an agent. This is when the host must be most wary. The agent may try to define functions that pierce the host's security and run rampant on the system. The host must scrutinize each definition to ensure that the agent only can operate upon its own variables and defined objects.

When the host starts executing the agent, it must be prepared to respond to the agent's requests for local information or processing. This is, after all,

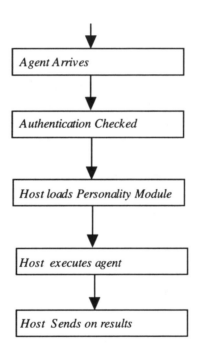

Figure 4.1: A high level view of the organization of the host's work processing an agent.

why an agent is dispatched for services or data. The host must respond to the requests that it has publicly announced will be available. Although this book won't go into the details of marketing or customer satisfaction, anyone who intends to run a host in an agent domain must recognize that they're running a business, even if they're not charging anything. Good service is important in an agent world because the agents aren't as reliable as people. Agents only can react as they are programmed to react. There are many unexpected occurrences and the good host programmer will try to anticipate all of them.

The host also has other obligations to the incoming agent. It must deal with errors. In some cases, the errors will emerge because the agent's programmer made a mistake. But the host could also be at fault. The interface it offers to the world might not be well defined. The agent might pass in parameters in what it thinks is an incorrect format. In any case, the host must be able to recover from errors, pack up the agent and send it home.

The host must also be ready to forward the agent when it asks to go. This may happen for any reason, but in most cases the agent will be returning with the answer it came to find. The agent defines the important parts of its internal state that should be forwarded and the host should use this packing list.

Life is substantially more complicated for the host because it must execute the agent software and guard against attack at the same time. If the proper precautions are taken, though, the host can operate efficiently and smoothly.

The major elements of a host can be summarized as follows:

Network Interface This handles moving the agents around the network. It's responsible for deciphering addresses and moving the files to and from these addresses. In most cases it will be an SMTP class mailer using IP addresses. This is just a convenient way to structure the system. This is not discussed in detail in this book because computers use different systems. Almost all operating systems, though, are moving toward a scriptable convention that will allow programs to call each other and pass information back and forth. The details of this are still far from standardized and are not central to the security discussion in this book.

Authentication and Encryption This unbundles the incoming file, decrypts it and checks the digital signature for veracity. This process is described in Chapter 14.

Execution Unit This evaluates the incoming message as a program. It might be a TCL interpreter or an LISP interpreter. Many details about constructing an XLISP-based host are described in Chapter 10. The details of a safe version of TCL are in Chapter 12.

Main Unit This is responsible for gluing everything together. It checks the incoming mail, calls the authentication and decryption unit to clear it, executes the file, encrypts the answers and sends them back out. It is described in this chapter.

4.1 The Execution Unit

Design the execution unit is a tricky task. It would be difficult enough to do in a safe environment, but it is all the more complicated in a world populated by potentially dangerous agents. Any extra feature added to the mixture must be scrutinized to ensure that it isn't inadvertently opening a back door for trouble.

The basic details for the execution unit can be found in the chapters on LISP (Chapter 10) and TCL (Chapter 11). They describe how to build a language that offers all of the basic features of a programming language while avoiding all of the dangerous side-effects and security holes. The chapters describe how to construct the interpreter so that it will not allow any incoming agent to execute functions it isn't allowed to touch.

The linguistic foundation of the execution unit on the host, though, is just half of the solution. The host must also offer information services to the incoming agent. The rest of this chapter explores the process of adding these features to an XLISP interpreter. First I'll define the structure of the Host Personality file. Although this example is structured as an XLISP program, you may want to use the skeleton of this structure in other domains. Then I'll describe the features of the main unit.

4.1.1   Host Personality Files

The personality or persona of the host is defined by the functions that are read into the XLISP interpreter. After the main unit receives a file and decrypts it, the main unit must start up the LISP interpreter and load a Host Personality file. In this chapter, the file AIRHOST.LSP is used as an example. The agent will be expecting to find the functions defined in this file when it starts to execute. A given computer might operate several hosts on the network by using different personality files to define each of them.

Each file must contain several basic functions for handling errors, negotiating for resources and offering services. Every host developer is responsible for ensuring that their host offers these functions; agents can assume that they're offered. A skeleton of these functions can be found in the file HOSTSKEL.LSP on the sample disk included with this book. These functions include:

Basic LISP Functions All of the basic arithmetic and list manipulation. CAR, CDR etc. Some basic functions, however, are restricted or excluded because they are a security problem. These are described for LISP novices in Chapter 10.

(FH-Give-Resources *list*) This is used for making a payment. It could be in any particular resource defined in Chapter 8, but it will probably be cash. An agent would call this function to establish an account. This might happen before or after the resource negotiations. The function accepts a digital note and returns a receipt.

(FH-Get-Resources *list*) The host might want to give some resources to the agent. This is the function used to transfer things back. It might be a refund or a payoff for a hot stock tip.

(FH-Negotiate-Resources resource-request) The agent executes this function with a list of the resources it wants. The host responds with a list of resources available. Some of the resources include execution time and memory space. Chapter 8 describes the structure in detail.

(FH-Current-Time) Gives the time in some local time coordinates in seconds. An agent must not assume that the time is globally defined or consistent. Some hosts may be in different time zones. Other hosts may use a different zero to start the count.

(FH-Host-Speed) Execute a fixed benchmark and report the time. This allows an agent to calibrate the power of the host. The number is reported in units per second.

(FH-Send-Agent ''address'' (necessary-agent-parts)) If an agent wants to spawn off a child, then this is how it is done.

(FH-Save-To-File ''file-name'' *list*) Save something to a file. Returns T if successful and nil if it isn't.

(FH-Read-From-File ''file-name'' *list*) Save something to a file. Returns T if successful and nil if it isn't.

(FH-Give-Host-Description) This asks the host to give the agent a description of the functions available at the local host.

(FH-Give-Resource-Description) This asks the host to give the agent a description of the resources available as part of the local host.

(FH-Give-Errors-Description) This asks the host to give the agent a description of the particular errors that might occur during interaction with the local host.

(FH-Get-Next-Event) The host may, at times, want to alert the agent that something happened. This is the mechanism to relay these messages to the agent.

(FH-Initialize-Security) This function adds the right names from the local host to the lists of protected variables and functions.

(FH-Mail ''address'' *list*) Use this to mail a message. The agent might
use this to send partial reports back home. Or it might use it to send
the host description back.

Every host must offer these basic features to every incoming agent. They
are not particularly complicated and in some cases they duplicate functions
that are already available. The functions that duplicate the standard LISP
functions are intended to offer the host a chance to filter the calls to their
LISP interpreter to increase security. If every agent uses these functions,
then the hosts will present a uniform face. The hosts should also block access
to the normal calls to promote unity. One host may feel quite comfortable
permitting open file access, but other hosts might not. This saves the agent's
programmers the trouble of remembering these details.

Many of these basic functions will be implemented in a skeleton file. The
new host programmer will not need to duplicate the efforts if they happen
to be using the same system. Some functions like file access may need fine
tuning.

4.2 Optional Host Features

Each host will always offer some additional functions that the agent will
want to use to access the local treasures. Although there is no perfect way
to structure these functions for all applications, there are some structures
that are more efficient. Here are some of the most salient guidelines:

Minimize the memory, the processor time and other system requirements
consumed by each function call. Agents are programs written by other
people who may not understand the correct way to structure their
requests.

Provide some smart functions that handle some of the general and commonly occurring cases. You should consider including a specialized
function if as few as 10% of the agents might want to do something.
This minimizes the size of the agents.

Try to provide a concise answer, but don't skimp on information. This is a tricky balance to strike. If each function call returns 100 megabytes of information, the agent will probably crash as it runs out of memory to store this data. On the other hand, agents can only do creative things if they've got access to plenty of information. The goal is to balance these needs by being aware of system resources.

Avoid allowing the agent to pass in procedure pointers or lambda expressions. This may make the interface less flexible, but it prevents the agent from tricking the host into doing something for it.

4.3 A Sample Host

Here is a description of a sample host that will operate a toy airline reservation system. The current version generates a random selection of flights with a broad selection of characteristics. This will allow the agent to request flights by a number of variables including plane type, departure time and destination. The agent can then make the reservation if it finds something that its master might want. The complete text for this host can be found in file AIRHOST.LSP.

4.3.1 The Raw Database

First, there must be data for the host to do its job. This example, though, is just a toy, so the data must be invented. The flight database is just a list of structures produced in LISP by the **defstruct** command. Any serious attempt would access a real database designed to answer queries without running down a list and checking each entry. The structure looks like this:

```
(defstruct flight
    Airline Day Time Plane Stops
    Number Price-Coach Price-First
    Coach-Aisle-Seats-Available
    Coach-Window-Seats-Available
     First-Aisle-Seats-Available
```

```
Coach-Window-Seats-Available
Start-City End-City)
```

At the beginning of the execution of the host, the initialization function creates a simulated database to create flights by picking random information from a selection of choices. Of course, a real system would not need to do this.

```
(defvar Airline-List
    '(FlugZug PsychicWings SquareAir))
(defvar Days-List
    '(Mon Tue Wed Thur Fri Sat Sun))
(defvar Plane-List
    '(707 727 737 747 767 777 DC-3 DC-9 DC-10))
(defvar City-List
    '(Emerald Circuit Fat Big Charm ))
(defvar Town-List
    '(Bean Small Our))
(defun Choose-Random (ls)
    (nth (random (length ls)) ls))
(defun Make-Random-Flight ()
;; Used to create a random flight. We'll
;; create a random set of flights for testing.
(let ((answer (make-flight
        :airline (choose-random airline-list)
        :day (choose-random days-list)
        :time (+ (* 100 (random 24)) (random 60))
        :plane (choose-random plane-list)
        :stops (choose-random town-list)
        :number (random 10000)
        :price-coach (random 400)
        :price-first (random 1200)
        :Coach-Aisle-Seats-Available (random 100)
        :Coach-Window-Seats-Available (random 100)
```

```
              :First-Aisle-Seats-Available  (random 10)
              :Coach-Window-Seats-Available (random 10)
              :start-city (choose-random city-list)
              :end-city (choose-random city-list))))
(do () ((not (eq (flight-start-city answer)
                 (flight-end-city answer))))
     (setf (flight-end-city answer) (choose-random city-list)))
answer))
(defvar LH-Flight-List nil)
(defun Build-Test-Flight-List (&optional (num 100))
;; Build a set of test cases.
  (do ((i 0 (+ 1 i))) ((= i num))
    (setf LH-Flight-List
      (cons (make-random-flight)
            LH-Flight-List))))
(defun FH-Initialize-Host ()
  (Build-Test-Flight-List 100)
  (FH-Initialize-Security)
 ;; Must return true if successful.
)
```

This database makes a fine test for any agent. In fact, it makes a perfect example of the type of code that can be shipped to an agent's programmer to allow them to test their agent before sending it out. This concept is discussed in detail in Chapter 7.

4.3.2 Access Functions

The agent will need to access the database to develop a list of possible flights. One simple solution is to just let the agent have free access to the information in LH-Flight-List so it can search for the right flight. This may be okay if the list only contains information, but it is problematic if the list also contains reservation information. An agent that couldn't find a seat could increase the number of free seats to make room for its master.

A better solution is to prevent the agent from accessing LH-Flight-List

by blocking off the setq and setf functions. The agent must call a function
named LH-Flights-By-Item to call up all flights that match a particular
characteristic.

The initial version looked something like this:

```
(defun LH-Flights-By-Item-Weak (Search-Func Matcher)
   (let ((answer nil))
      (do ((l LH-Flight-List (cdr l))) ((null l))
         (cond ((eq Matcher (apply search-func (list (car l))))
                (setf answer (cons (car l) answer)))))
      answer))
```

The agent would call the function by executing a command like

```
(LH-Flights-By-Item-Weak #'flight-day 'sun).
```

This one would pull out all flights that departed on Sunday. The first argument, flight-day, is a function created by the defstruct macro. It
pulls out the part of the structure corresponding to the day. Although
there is nothing dangerous with passing in this function name, it is also
possible to pass in a naked lambda expression like (lambda (a) (let (())
(re-format-disk) (flight-day a))). This would work, but it would also
execute re-format-disk.

A more reliable result could be produced with this combination:

```
(defvar LH-Item-Function-Map
   '((day #'flight-day)
     (start-city #'flight-start-city)
     (end-city #'flight-end-city)
     (airline #'flight-airline)
     (stops #'flight-stops)
     (number #'flight-number)
     (time #'flight-time)))
(defun LH-Flights-By-Item (Item Matcher)
   (let ((fun (assoc item LH-Item-Function-Map)))
      (cond (fun
```

```
(LH-Flights-By-Item-Weak
        (cadadr fun) matcher))
  (t nil))))
```

In this case, the function `LH-Flights-By-Item-Weak` and the variable `LH-Item-Function-Map` must be protected from attack by the agent. This is a good example of how to isolate a function from incoming lambda expressions that are open doors for trouble in LISP.

Of course, `LH-Flights-By-Item` only finds flights that match specific selection criteria. This is perfectly acceptable if the agent is looking for flights that come on a certain day or leave from a particular city. The solution doesn't work with dates and times. Here is a more expansive approach:

```
(defun LH-Test-Flight (triple FLT )
;;It would be faster to put these decision
;;statements outside of the loop. But then
;;this function wouldn't be as flexible.
  (let ((fun (cadadr (assoc (car triple)
                      LH-Item-Function-Map))))
    (cond   ((eq (cadr triple) 'Greater-Than)
          (cond ((> (apply fun (list FLT)) (caddr triple))
               t)
               (t nil))
        )
        ((eq (cadr triple) 'Less-Than)
          (cond ((< (apply fun (list FLT)) (caddr triple))
               t)
               (t nil)))
        ((eq (cadr triple) 'Equal)
          (cond ((eq (apply fun (list FLT)) (caddr triple))
               t)
               (t nil))
        ))))
(defun LH-Flights-By-Item-2
      (triple &optional (ls LH-Flight-List))
```

```
;; This takes  requests as a triples.
;; The three parts in the triple are:
;;    1 Tag from LH-Item-Function-Map
;;    2 Tag from list ('Greater-Than 'Less-Than 'Equal)
;;    3 Value for comparison.
  (let ((answer nil))
    (do ((l ls (cdr l))) ((null l))
          (cond ((LH-Test-Flight triple (car l))
                 (setf answer (cons (car l) answer)))))
          answer))
```

The host could use these functions to assemble a list of possible flights that meet certain criteria. The agent could have the flexibility to pick through the list and use any of the possible information to exclude flights. This would allow the agent to be programmed to solve many arbitrary cases.[1]

4.3.3   Making Reservations

When the agent has made its flight choice, it makes a reservation by submitting an information block in the right format. In a standard reservation system, this act would delete one seat from the supply of seats available on the plane. This would be stored in the database. In this example, it will only affect the LISP database.

```
(defstruct Info-Block First-Name Last-Name
                      Credit-Card-Number Address
                      Month Date Year)
(defun Decrement-Seat (seat-class fl)
(cond ((eq seat-class 'first-aisle)
```

---

[1]Try to determine if there are *any* agents in this experimental system that can do something that can't be done with some combination of the triples used in LH-Flights-By-Item-2. The boolean combinations might be quite awkward, but they can do quite a bit. Ask yourself whether such a list of triples could capture all of the computational complexity of an if-then-else language. The one advantage of the agent architecture is that it can include side effects that might do something like print something or send electronic mail to multiple sites.

```
          (setf (flight-First-Aisle-Seats-Available fl)
             (- (flight-First-Aisle-Seats-Available fl) 1)))
        ((eq seat-class 'coach-aisle)
         (setf (flight-coach-Aisle-Seats-Available fl)
             (- (flight-First-Aisle-Seats-Available fl) 1)))
        ((eq seat-class 'first-window)
         (setf (flight-First-window-Seats-Available fl)
             (- (flight-First-window-Seats-Available fl) 1)))
        ((eq seat-class 'first-window)
         (setf (flight-First-window-Seats-Available fl)
             (- (flight-First-window-Seats-Available fl) 1)))
        ))
(defun LH-Make-Reservation (flight-num seat-class info-block)
;;; Makes a reservation.
;;; Seat class is one of
;;;; '(first-aisle first-window coach-aisle coach-window)
    (let ((fl (LH-Flights-By-Item-Weak #'flight-number
                                       flight-num)))
      (cond (fl
             (Decrement-Seat seat-class (car fl)))
            (t nil))))
```

4.3.4 Setting Up Local Security

When the host is loaded into the LISP system, the host file should configure the core agent system to provide the right level of security. The core file already comes with the dangerous core of LISP functions excluded. The host must add its own functions and variables to the

```
*forbidden-functions*,
*protected-variables*,
and *free-variables*
```

lists that the core system uses to determine whether the agent is overstepping its bounds.

This process is achieved by executing the function:

```
(defun FH-Initialize-Security ()
 (setf *free-functions* (append
      (list 'FH-Mail
      'FH-Initialize-Host
      'LH-Make-Reservation
      'LH-Flights-By-Item
      'FH-Send-Agent
      'FH-Give-Host-Description
      'FH-Give-Resource-Description
      'FH-Give-Errors-Description
      'FH-Give-Resources
      'FH-Available-Resources
      'FH-Negotiate-Resources
      'LH-Flights-By-Item
      'LH-Flights-By-Item-2
      )
   *free-functions*))
  (setf *protected-variables* (append
      (list
      'LH-Flight-List
      'FH-Agent-Account
      'Test-Resources-Deposited
      'LH-Item-Function-Map
      )
    *protected-variables*))
  (setf *forbidden-functions* (append
      (list
      'Build-Test-Flight-List
      'LH-Flights-By-Item-Weak
      'FH-Save-To-File
      'FH-Read-From-File
      'FH-Clean-Up-Host
      'FH-Initialize-Host
      'Separate-Resources
```

```
        'Test-Resource-Pair
        'Cost-Resource-Pair
        'Determine-Dollar-Cost
        'Determine-Cost
        'Meets-The-Offer
        'Check-For-Dollars
        'Remove-Unavailable-Resources
        'Are-All-Available
        'No-Costp
        'Accept-Resources
        )
    *forbidden-functions*))
  t ;; Must return true if successful.
  )
```

The variables added to *protected-variables* cannot be changed if the agent tries to execute setq. The functions that get placed in the list *forbidden-functions* can't be executed by the agent. The functions that make up part of the host, but are called by the agent, are often added to *free-functions* because the functions that are on this list will be run through eval without the interference of eval-hook-function. The speed gain is significant. Host programmers should aim to add as many of their functions to this list as possible because it can change the execution speed significantly. They should not add functions like LH-Flights-By-Item-Weak that accept general lambda expressions that can be exploited by the agent to do anything.

4.4 Summary

This chapter presented a basic outline of what a host should provide for an agent. A host should:

Give ample description of what local functions FH-Give-Host-Description , resources FH-Give-Resource-Description and errors FH-Give--Errors-Description are used locally. This will allow a distant agent programmer to do a good job creating the agent without taxing the host too much with error-prone agents on debugging missions.

Give uniform access to simple functions for files and mail.

Describe its speed using the benchmark function `FH-Host-Speed` so that prices per unit of calculation can be standardized across the domain.

Give a standard way to negotiate for resources. This is described in greater depth in Chapter 8.

The sample code for the host described in this chapter is found in the AIRHOST.LSP file on the disk. It is meant to work in conjunction with the AIRAGENT.LSP file described in Chapter 3 and the CORE.LSP file described in Chapter 10.

The description of the host is just a beginning. Many people intend to use agent technology for enhanced e-mail that may present an interactive show for the recepient. This was the goal of the developers of Safe-TCL.

If the LISP-based agent technology described in this book is to be used for this purpose, then there should be a general mechanism for displaying text, pictures and sound. The hypertext markup language used in Mosaic and Web pages might be a good idea. Or, the agent language could be extended to fit into the Web. There are many other cases where a standard set of additions to the interface might make sense.

Chapter 5

Errors

———————————————— The Hype ————————————————

Don't call them errors, call them "Great Ideas Before their Time."

———————————————— Political Cynicism ————————————————

The high church of reason is just another form of repression designed to control the thoughts of man. Those who show obeisance and charm are "correct" while those who refuse to hew to the structure imposed from above are deemed in "error".

———————————————— The Buzzwords ————————————————

A robust exception mechanism allows a program to recover from problems without crashing.

Errors happen every day. They happen all the time in programming when a programmer screws up. They even happen when the programmer doesn't screw up. When disks are filled, a call to create a file will generate an error. Every solid programming system needs a structure for handling errors and recovering from them. An agent system needs a better system because an agent can generate errors in many different ways.

The structure of such an error handling system can be as complex as any other programming dreamed up by programmers. The goal is to make this system fairly simple if only because it is the first attempt at providing a debugging solution. Later versions can be more complex.

The best place to begin is to divide up responsiblity for the errors. The different types of errors that must be handled by the host and the agents are:

Programming Errors These occur when an agent won't interpret correctly. They are solved by sending the interpreter's error message to the return address. Ideally, these messages will be robust enough to help a distant programmer battle the bug. An example of this type of error is dividing by zero or using an undefined variable name. This message should include the function calls on the stack as well as the values of the variables in the list **FA-Report-Me-In-Errors** if they are available.

Overreaching Errors If an agent tries to do something it's not authorized to do, the host has the option of killing the agent and sending it packing. This message should also explain the result and include the values of the variables in the list **FA-Report-Me-In-Errors** if they are available. Some possible examples of these errors are executing a protected function or overstepping the resource limits negotiated at the beginning of the session.

Undeliverable Errors If an agent tries to ask for something that isn't available, then the host may declare the error to be undeliverable and give the agent the chance to recover by calling **FA-Error-Function**. These errors are quite different from the overreaching errors because they aren't intentional. They might arise because a disk is now full or a promised resource is now depleted. Gracious hosts might choose to offer a warning message when an agent is getting to close to a resource bound.

Host Errors These may occur for a variety of different reasons. Given that the host is responsible for detecting errors and getting them fixed, there may be many host errors that go undetected. There is little that can be done about this except setting up a meta-host that might make errors on its own. In many cases, the host errors will be manifested as programming errors or overreaching errors and it will be up to the programmer of the agent to discover them and solve them. The agent's programmer should notify the programmer of the host at that time.

The taxonomy of these errors is somewhat arbitrary. Each host is free to act upon errors as it pleases. The programmer of the host, though, should make every effort to anticipate errors and make them as recoverable as possible. It is bad form to allow an agent to negotiate for disk space with `FA--Resource-Negotiator` and then turn around and report an undeliverable error later because someone else blocked off the disk space. The key to designing around these errors is to remember that the programmer confronting them might be half a world away trying to interpret strange messages.

5.1 Error Messages

There should be a list of well-defined error messages that holds for all agents and their hosts. This allows agent programmers to tune `FA-Error-Function` so that it can respond to most of the errors that come along. The more intelligence the programmer can build into this function, the more robust the function will be. This list, however, can't be conclusive because local hosts may be offering many different services. This is why the function `FH--Give-Errors-Description` is available to offer descriptions of the extra errors.

5.1.1   Programming Errors

There are many different programming errors that may occur. Undefined names and type mismatches are two of the most common forms. For the most part, these errors can be passed directly back to the agent's programmer. The function `FA-Error-Function` gets the job of making sure that the right information is ready to be returned. The actual programming error generated by the interpreter is passed along.

The predefined programming errors are:

`FE-Programming-Error` This passes along the error generated by the interpreter.

`FE-Numerical-Error` This is formed by dividing by zero or a similar numerical problem.

Programming errors should be relatively few if the agent realm is well-constructed. The agent's programmer should be able to test the agent before dispatching it. The pretesting process can be greatly improved by using shell functions to do the debugging. Section 4.1.1 describes how the information about the local functions is dispatched. A local programmer should be able to load these functions up and use them to ensure that the agent behaves properly.

In this implementation, if the agent fails to run successfully, the host will trap the error and mail a copy of the session transcript to the host. This transcript will contain the error and a stack trace produced by setting `*tracenable*` to true.

5.1.2   Overreaching Errors

The standard overreaching errors are:

`FE-Unauthorized-Function-Call` An attempt was made to call a function that the agent does not have access to execute. The agent may be trying to break the security hold or it may be making a mistake because other hosts allowed it access to a particular function.

FE-Unauthorized-Data-Call The agent tried to access data that was beyond its reach. These data items may include the values of some of the protected lists that are used to block off part of the LISP data space from the agent.

FE-Unauthorized-Resource-Consumption When an agent consumes more of one resource than it is authorized to do, the host should generate this error. This is an unrecoverable error. If it occurs, the host will send the agent back with all of its current state. The agent must respond to **FE-Resource-Bound-Approaching** in order to prevent this barrier from arising.

FE-Resource-Bound-Approaching When a resource that is on account is near disappearing, the host should generate this error. The agent may try to negotiate more time using **FH-Negotiate-Resources** if it wants to stick around. It can play chicken to avoid over-spending, but it may face termination if it does so.

The overreaching errors are the most important errors to trap successfully. In many cases, the agent will not be able to recover from them gracefully. The host caught the agent doing something wrong and the main response of **FA-Error-Function** will be to bundle up as much state as necessary. The fate of "social embarrassment" is not the only problem that faces an agent trying to recover. These errors are always generated in the midst of evaluating some function. In the case of **FE-Unauthorized-Function-Call** or **FE-Unauthorized-Data-Call**, the agent requested access to something it was not allowed to grab. Changing the parameters on the stack is not easy and it is not done in this version.

5.1.3 Undeliverable Errors

Undeliverable errors occur when a host starts to fail. This commonly happens when some resource is no longer available. It may also occur because the agent asks for something in a larger dimension than the host can provide.

The standard undeliverable errors are:

FE-Resource-Unavailable This error should be generated when the host decides that it cannot fulfill some part of its earlier promise to provide resources to the agent. This is not generated when the agent uses up all of the negotiated resource. That generates an **FE-Unauthorized--Resource-Consumption** error.

FE-Out-of-Memory This is a special resource consumption error because memory is a special resource. The error recovery mechanisms might not be able to run if there is not enough memory. Any response to this error should try to avoid consuming too much memory. A standard response might set several long variables to **nil** and initialize garbage collection in the hope of recovering plenty of memory.

FE-Host-Shutting-Down-Soon A host might be shut down for some external reason. This error message should alert the agent that time is running out and it should pack up and leave.

FE-Host-Shutting-Down-Now It is too late for the agent to do anything. This is the final warning. It comes when the agent is being packed up and returned.

Some of the undeliverable errors are simple for the agent to survive. If the agent wants to write some file to disk temporarily and the disk file is now unavailable, it may just leave the value in memory and continue computing. If the agent is trying to spawn off subagents to go to particular addresses and one of the addresses can't be found, the agent may simply skip this one destination. Other undeliverable errors are fatal. If the agent can't access the one resource it needed at the host, then it must leave and search for that resource elsewhere.

5.1.4   Local Errors

Each local host may need to define some local errors to handle problems with the particular solutions the host is offering the incoming agents. In fact, this is good form. The programmers of agents may be sending an agent to a host for the first time. They are bound to make some mistakes when accessing the local data. A good host will be able to provide well-documented assistance that makes it quite possible for the programmer to retrain (i.e. reprogram) the agent not to cause that error again. Ideally, the details for this will be included in the response of `FH-Give-Errors-Description`.

The best local error descriptions should provide complete information about the local process. In many cases, the local host will just be a front end to another program like a database query engine. The host can pass the error messages from this query engine through in two different ways. It may choose to define separate local error messages for each one. This allows `FA-Error-Function` to trap for them successfully and do something about the problem. It also implies that `FA-Error-Function` should be ready to do something about them. The programmer should consider these errors when planning the agent.

Another method is to simply define one local function `LE-Local-Error` and pass the local error information as a parameter. This may be desirable if there are many local errors that occur infrequently. The details of these parameters can be included in the information returned by `FH-Give--Errors-Description` but they do not have to be.

The best approach is to use both. Define specific local functions for errors that occur frequently and errors that the agent might be able to recover from. Leave the rest to be defined by a generic local error that returns the unfiltered problems from the host.

Here is a set of potential errors that might be generated by local hosts. They should serve as both example and inspiration.

`LE-Badly-Formed-Query` The agent might be requesting information from the local host in a format that does not match the local database's query language.

`LE-Undefined-Field-Name` This is a more specific version of an error that might be useful for a database's engine. This tells the agent that it requested a field name that could not be found. The offending field name would follow the error. Adding more specific errors like this can help the agent be more flexible. Now, the agent can be programmed to try several fields and recover if one is not there. The agent might try to ask for the price of a ticket bought three weeks in advance. Some airlines offer such fares and others don't. If the agent can recover from the error of asking for the prices of all flights bought three weeks in advance, then the same agent can be sent to both airlines to fetch a ticket. It will be able to recover when it arrives at the host of an airline that doesn't offer such fares.

LE-Frequent-Flyer-Tickets-Gone Airlines often limit the number of seats available to be purchased with Frequent Flyer coupons. A ticket reservation host for the airlines could use a specialized error like this because it fills a frequent request.

LE-Response-Very-Long Some requests for data can backfire on an agent if they recover too much. Searching for all articles in *The New York Times* with the word "the" is a simple example. An error like this reminds the agent that it might not want the answer to its question. The rest of the error might include some concrete numbers about the size of the response.

LE-Bridge-Closed-Until-6pm Imagine you had a drawbridge that could be opened remotely by sailboats. They would request permission to open the bridge with an agent. The bridge programmer might choose to use an agent interface despite the fact that the agents may only execute a single command (**LH-Open-Bridge**) because all of the authentication procedures are built-in. In this case, the bridge might respond with an error like this because it is kept shut until 6p.m. during rush hour each day.

LE-Contract-Not-Trading Brokerage firms may choose to set up hosts to make markets in many forms of securities. This might be especially useful in the area of derivatives where there is often a mind-boggling array of options available on individual stocks. In many cases, the brokerage firms decide the prices that they offer based upon a fixed formula. These are perfect areas for agent technology. In this case, there is a special error defined to describe what happens when a particular derivative contract is not being offered at the moment.

There are numerous errors that can be defined and there will always be some that fall outside of the predefined terms. Dedicated host programmers might want to watch the incoming agents and keep track of those that leave because of errors. If some errors occur frequently, try to track down whether there is a better way of reporting the error. Agents can often recover if they are just given enough information. The best solution might be to offer sample recovery code to the programmers of frequently visiting agents so that these programmers can get their agents to recover correctly.

5.2 Bad Agent Expulsion

When an incoming agent falls from grace, it must be expelled. The goal is to provide enough information for the programmer of the agent so they can determine what went wrong and find a way to prevent it from happening in the future. This is the main reason for the list `FA-Report-Me-In-Errors`, which contains the local objects that the agent wants to take home with it.

In the current scheme, the agent only gets one chance to fix an error. After `FA-Error-Function` is executed, the agent can be expelled if the problem is not resolved. This expulsion might not happen immediately in some cases, but it will come sooner than later. In any case, the agent programmer should design the function `FA-Error-Function` as the last chance to make things right again.

When the error is unrecoverable, the agent programmer should concentrate on making sure that the function `FA-Report-Me-In-Errors` saves as much of the state as is possible. If the agent is asking a query and it finds it can't understand why the query is failing, then it might set `FA-Report-Me-In-Errors` to the list (`failed-query`) and assign the variable `failed-query` to the text of the query that won't work. This is the only information that will come back with the error. If there is more information that is important, then this should also be included in the list. Although it is often tempting and occasionally practical to include as much information as possible in the list of state to be returned, the agent programmer may want to resist the temptation to ask for everything. Future networks may charge by the size of the message. This error recovery mechanism has the potential to cost the agent's programmer a large amount of money if all the state is returned.

Even if the error is recoverable, the agent's programmer should be ready for the worst. The programmer might assume, for instance, that the agent will just dispense more cash for more execution time when time runs short. This may fail if the agent spends all of its cash or if the host dramatically raises the rates. It is entirely possible that hosts will run auctions for their time. A new, fat cat agent may arrive and start bidding up the cost of computation at a host and drive an agent into bankruptcy.

In these cases, the agent should be prepared to save as much of the partial work as is possible and cost efficient. In many cases, the agent will simply be feeding multiple requests into the host. The agent's programmer chose to bundle the requests into one agent to simplify the system. In this case, the partial results can be repackaged and returned.

5.3   Errors in XLISP-Agents

The error code for an XLISP-Agent is not too complex. It must be able to interpret all of the possible errors that it receives, but in many cases it won't be able to do much about them. In the current implementation, the agent can't try to recover from executing a forbidden function.

The main function from AIRAGENT.LSP, `FA-Error-Function` defined here, receives the error message and only does something about it if the amount of execution time is running low. This is the major problem for the reservation agent. It doesn't worry about the other problems. It simply saves information about them for delivery to its programmer who might use them to debug the program.

```
(defun FA-Error-Function (error-type &rest body)
;; Handle errors reported by the host.
  (cond ((eq error-type 'FE-Programming-Error)
         (Report-Error error-type body))
        ((eq error-type 'FE-Numerical-Error)
         (Report-Error error-type body))
```

```
          ((eq error-type 'FE-Unauthorized-Function-Call)
           (Report-Error error-type body))
          ((eq error-type 'FE-Unauthorized-Data-Call)
           (Report-Error error-type body))
          ((eq error-type 'FE-Unauthorized-Resource-Consumption)
           (Report-Error error-type body))
          ((eq error-type
               'FE-Unauthorized-Resource-Bound-Approaching)
           (cond ((eq body 'FR-Execution-Time)
                  (LA-Ask-For-More '(FR-Execution-time 10000))))
           (Report-Error error-type body))
          ((eq error-type 'FE-Resource-Unavailable)
           (Report-Error error-type body))
          ((eq error-type 'FE-Out-Of-Memory)
           (Report-Error error-type body))
          ((eq error-type 'FE-Host-Shutting-Down-Now)
           (Report-Error error-type body)
          )
          ((eq error-type 'FE-Host-Shutting-Down-Soon)
           (Report-Error error-type body)
          )
     )
)
```

In almost all cases, the function will simply choose to report the error and prepare to go home in failure. The code for doing this is straightforward:

```
(defvar Error-Problems nil)
(defun Report-Error (type body)
  (setq Error-Problems (cons
        (list error-type body (get-internal-run-time)
              *time-left*)
        Report-Error)))
```

If time is running out, the agent is prepared to bid for more time. This function, which is a variant of the basic bidding algorithm, will attempt to extract more time from the host. It will pay whatever is necessary to get it.

```
(defun LA-Ask-For-More (bid)
;;; Get some access.
;;; This is a BASIC version.
(let* (
       (answer t)
       (counter (FH-Negotiate-Resources bid)))
  (print counter)
  (do ()
      ((null counter)) ;; nil means we are there.
    (let ((cost (assoc 'FR-Dollars counter)))
      (cond ((null cost)
               (setq answer nil)
               (setq counter nil)) ;;; Too confusing for now.
            ((>= (cash-on-hand) (cadr cost))
               (setq answer (not (null
                   (Pay-Out-Resource
                     'FR-Dollars (cadr cost))))))
            (t
             (setq answer nil)
             (setq counter nil))))
    (print counter)
    (cond ((not (null counter))
             (setq counter
                (FH-Negotiate-Resources counter)))))
  answer))
```

This error code use a different version of the `eval-hook-function` than the one definted later in section 10.6. This version of `eval-hook-function` should call `FA-Error-Function` to report trouble before acting upon it. The code looks like this:

```
(defun test-form (form)
;;; Tests the form to ensure that it is not breaking any rules.
     ;;; (print (list "in test form" form))
  (cond   ((or (eql (car form) 'defun)
                (eql (car form) 'defmacro))
       (cond ((or (member (cadr form) *protected-function*)
             (Is-Predefinedp (car form)))
             (FA-Error-Function 'FE-Unauthorized-Function-Call
                 form)
             nil)
         (t t))
    )
   ((or (eql (car form) 'setq)
        (eql (car form) 'setf))
    (cond ((member (cadr form) *protected-variables*)
    (FA-Error-Function 'FE-Unauthorized-Data-Call
                form)
         nil)
         (t t))
   )
   (t
    (cond ((member (car form) *forbidden-functions*)
            (FA-Error-Function 'FE-Unauthorized-Function-Call
                form)
         nil)
      ((and (not *allow-screen-action*)
            (member (car form) *screen-functions*))
            (FA-Error-Function 'FE-Unauthorized-Function-Call
                form)
         nil)
      (t t)
      ))
  ))

(defun eval-hook-function (form env &aux val f1)
```

```
(cond ((> (get-internal-run-time) *time-end*)
       (print "OUT OF TIME!")
       (throw 'error 'out-of-time))
      ((< (- *time-end* (get-internal-run-time)) 1000)
       (print "Reached Warning Time")
       (FA-Error-Function
               'FE-Unauthorized-Resource-Bound-Approaching
         'FR-Execution-Time))
      ((consp form)
       (cond ((member (car form) *free-functions*)
              (print "Going Free with")
              (print form)
              (setf val (evalhook form nil nil env)))
             ((test-form form)
              (setf val (evalhook form
                                  #'eval-hook-function
                                  nil
                                  env)))
             (t (print "BAD FUNCTION")
                (print form)
                (throw 'error 'bad-function))))
      (t
        (setf val (evalhook form nil nil env))))
      val)
```

5.4   Summary

Error recovery is a tricky proposition. The mechanism presented here is
suitable both for helping the distant agent programmer solve problems and
also for allowing the agent to bargain for more resources if it needs them.

Truly recovering from errors would take a more robust structure between
the agent and the host. This would be possible if the agent and the host
shared their own submit-eval-respond loop that imitated the read-eval-print
loop used in the LISP interpreters. The agent would submit a LISP ex-

pression, the host would eval it and then return the answer. If there was something wrong with the LISP expression, then it could raise an error flag. The agent could then try again with another expression if it desired.

There is no reason why this structure could not be built. It does not violate any of the protection mechanisms proposed to maintain security. The structure of the agent's code will be more complex. It won't be possible for someone to create an agent by just writing several functions. There will need to be a central meta-function that feeds LISP expressions to the host in a coreographed way. This function, though, could be written once and distributed with the agent skeleton used as starting point.

Chapter 6

Going Out

————————————————— The Hype —————————————————

"Wherever you go, there you are"–Buckeroo Banzai

————————————————— Political Cynicism —————————————————

Travel is perhaps the most readily available form of domination available to the timid middle class. Cut off from the joys of conquest and submission that are the domain of the upper echelons, the middle class is forced to say "Veni, Vidi" but skip the "Vici". Never the less, the act of tourism is a sublime act of repression as it forces people to open themselves and their ways to you. In most cases, you can't really understand them so they're forced to concoct some silly stereotype to make you happy enough to feel you learned something on the trip.

————————————————— The Buzzwords —————————————————

A data structure must be converted back into a self-contained, dynamically linking object that is interpretable.

If half the fun of a trip is getting there, then the other half must be coming back. An agent that makes it all the way to a host, manages to negotiate some resources and do a bit of computation is eventually going to want to go somewhere else. It might want to go home or it might want to go somewhere else to do some more computation. It could also want to spin off a smaller agent and send it on its own mission. The possibilities are endless.

The process of sending an agent somewhere is much more complicated than sending a human. Agents, alas, must be in a correct format. They must contain the information they need to do something when they get there. They must be prepared to pay for what they ask for and to negotiate for resources. Creating these specifications is a drawn out process for a human programmer. How is an agent going to do this for itself?

The host will do most of the work. This is a natural place to put the intelligence because the host must be able to bundle up the agent if something goes wrong. It is not much extra work to add the functionality that allows the host to package up a bunch of functions and data and ship them across the network.

The XLISP system makes it simple to add these packaging features to the agent. The system's printing commands will take data and print it to a file in an easy-to-read format. This file can travel across the network and be read in by another XLISP version to continue execution.

Here is how the job can be done:

```
(defun mail (address file)
;;; Hook for mailing file to address. Must be customized for
;;; your system.
)
(defun savefuns (fname funs)
(let* ((fp (open fname :direction
                       :output :if-exists
                       :overwrite)))
  (cond (fp
         (do ((l funs (cdr l))) ((null l))
           (cond ((fboundp (car l))
                  (let ((fval (get-lambda-expression
```

```
                          (symbol-function (car l)))))
              (pprint (cons (if (eq (car fval)
                                    'lambda)
                                'defun
                                'defmacro)
                        (cons (car l)
                              (cdr fval))) fp)))
          (t
            (pprint
              (cons 'setq
                (cons (car l) (eval (car l))) fp))
                        )))
          (close fp)
          fname)
      (t nil)))))
(defun FH-Send-Agent (address agent-parts)
  (if (savefuns "OutAgent" agents-parts)
      (mail address "OutAgent")
      nil))
```

The agent can even maintain an arbitrary amount of information in local variables that it carries with it. These variables can be printed out into the file. The "GO" command in Telescript will save all of the local data and the stack automatically. This technique is not as flexible because it forces the agent to construct a list of items to be mailed away. It will not save the stack. But it is quite possible for the agent itself to maintain an external "stack" of information as a variable and pass this along.

Chapter 7

Local Personalities

———————————————— The Hype ————————————————

Nothing is better than a home-cooked recipe.

———————————— Political Cynicism ————————————

The national power sources always use local tastes and fashions to foment disunity and prevent any viable competition from emerging.

———————————————— The Buzzwords ————————————————

An imitation, object-oriented dispatch kludge.

If the realm of agents is going to be interesting, each local host must be free to develop it's own personality. There is no reason to travel if your agent can get the same things at home. Supporting this diversity is not easy. The agent's programmer must have a solid method for determining what functions are available at a host and what it will need to do to call them. The programmer should also be able to learn what resources are available at the agent and also what local errors might arise. This is a tall order, but the success of the structure will determine the variation among producers. A good structure will make it simple for hosts to offer relatively complicated services to incoming agents without fear that the agent's programmer will need to send hundreds of test agents to work out the bugs.

The basic interface between the distant programmer and the host is through the function calls:`FH-Give-Host-Description`, `FH-Give-Resource--Description` and `FH-Give-Errors-Description`. These return the information in a set format to a local agent that can either bring them back with itself or arrange for them to be mailed to a different address.

Ideally, the information packet about the local host will also contain enough structure to allow the agent's programmer to simulate many of the problems before dispatching. The packet should contain shell programs that will simulate the procedure calls and also generate many of the errors that might occur. The local host's programmer will be responsible for designing this surrogate as well as possible. The easier it is for a distant programmer to create an agent that arrives and accomplishes its mission, the more efficient the host will be. If the host is a revenue generator, it will be more profitable. If the host is trying to disseminate as much information as possible, then it will be more prophetable.

The major parts of a surrogate host are:

Standard Function Simulators Each host is required to support some standard functions. These functions must simulate the effect of each of these required functions. Each host's programmers must create their own because some hosts will react differently to the standard functions. For instance, the function `FH-Save-To-File` should work fine if the host will offer disk space, and fail with a `FE-Unauthorized--Resource-Consumption` error if it doesn't offer disk space. In many cases, though, the surrogate functions from one host should do a pretty good job simulating another one. This is a good test of the strength of the agent realm's structure.

Local Function Simulators There should be a shell for each local function. Each of these should simulate the behavior as well as possible. There should be one simulating function for each of the host's functions. To a large extent, the example provided in the AIRHOST.LSP file is a simulator. A real system would require a much larger database.

Error Simulators This is a collection of flags that the agent programmer can set to be `true` or `false` to test different types of errors. There should be one flag for each potential error. These flags should be named with the prefix ``Sim''. For instance, to test agent's behavior `FE--Out-of-Memory`, you would set the variable `Sim-FE-Out-of-Memory` to be `true`.

The quality of the simulators will probably vary. In some cases, there will be no reason to provide anything more than shell functions that always return a stock answer. If the agent is not consuming too many resources, then the host will probably not generate too many errors. In other cases, a complex error creation routine may help the local agent programmer create a hardy agent that will be able to recover from a fickle host. Although this may seem obvious, the rule of thumb is that simple hosts can survive with simple surrogates but complex hosts need complex ones.

7.1 Function Simulators

The standard functions must be supported by each local host. The simulators for the standard functions as well as the local functions will be supplied when an agent calls `FH-Give-Host-Description` . The data structure of the response is simple: ((tag_1 $lambda_1$ *"description"*) ... (tag_n $lambda_n$ *"description"*)). The tags are the names of the functions and these include the standard names like `FH-Get-Resources` . If the recipient wants to test the performance of these functions against an agent, he can bind the tag to the lambda expression included in the triple. The description in quotation marks is intended for human consumption.

For example, the triple for (FH-Current-Time) might look like:

```
( 'FH-Current-Time (defun FH-Current-Time () 1200) ''Returns
the local time at the host.'')
```

In general, the descriptions for the standard functions can be much shorter than the local functions because most programmers will be familiar with their action. Host programmers should be certain to include any of the local differences in the actions of the standard functions. This list of functions and their definitions can also be used in the error reporting functions. The purpose of a particular function can be looked up and included in any error message. Having this information in a codified form is useful.

7.2 Error Simulators

The error simulators are some of the most important parts of the surrogate hosts because the errors generated by the local host are the one major uncertainty that the agent must face. The function call FH-Give-Errors--Description must give a list of all possible errors and provide a matching boolean that the agent programmer can flip on if he wants to generate errors of that type.

The structure is also straightforward. The response to the function FH--Give-Errors-Description is a list of triples: ((tag_1 $boolean_1$ "*description*") ... (tag_n $boolean_n$ "*description*")). The tags are the names of the error message. The boolean is the name of the variable that should be set to true if you want the functions to generate errors of the type name tag. The description is for humans. Normally, the convention that $boolean_i =$ "Sim" $+ tag_i$ is encouraged but not enforced.

The host programmer is responsible for adding the right error simulating behavior to the functions returned by FH-Give-Host-Description. Here is one potential function:

```
(defun FH-Save-To-File (file-name data )
  (cond (Sim-FE-Resource-Unavailable
          (FA-Error-Function
            'FE-Resource-Unavailable disk))))
```

The function tests to see if the surrogate is being asked to simulate missing resources. If it is, it generates a call to the **FA-Error-Function** and passes it the correct tags. Ideally, the agent programmer will be able to test the agent's ability to recover from a failed attempt to write to disk.

7.3 Resource Simulators

The details of the resources traded by a local host are given by the function **FH-Give-Resource-Description**. This information, like the rest, is bundled in a list of pairs: (*(tag₁ "description") (tag₂ "description")* ...). The first part of each pair is the name of the resource and the second half is a human-ready description. If the resource is listed here, then the host is making a committment to recognize that tag in the negotiations process.

The way a host responds to resource trading, though, could be quite ephemeral. The surrogate versions of **FH-Negotiate-Resources resource--request** is responsible for giving the agent programmer some information about the way the host will respond to requests to negotiate resources. The structure could be quite complex because there are so many different ways that a host could market its wares. Some of the basic approaches that a host programmer could take are:

1. **Do Nothing** Always accept the requests no matter how outlandish. This is the proper thing to do if the host will always be so generous. It is only a bit of a cop-out if the host will occasionally limit access for sporadic bouts of failure. Such a response, though, shows a lack of commitment if the host is going to respond in a complicated manner.

2. **Set Prices** Always look up the resource requests against a fixed price sheet and return a counterproposal containing the price. This is a simple process to write and it will probably be one of the most popular ways to conduct business on the Net.

3. **Respond Randomly** Some resources may not be available at certain times. Other resources might vary in cost over time. The host programmers can be as ambitious as they can afford to be when creating the simulators for these situations. Often, random numbers are the only way to provide an adequate response within a small block of text. This often serves the purpose of testing the agent even when the random responses bear little relationship to how the host will behave in reality.

Although it is tempting to get quite complicated, the host programmer should bear in mind that the only job of the surrogate is to test the functionality of the agent. It should provide the agent programmer with a way of making sure that it won't break on the first try. There are many quite intriguing possibilities for manipulating the resource negotiations and it would be a shame if many hosts did not experiment because they did not want to go to the trouble of implementing a very good simulator.

Chapter 8

Resources

─────────────────── The Hype ───────────────────

...purple mountains' majesty from sea to shining sea

─────────────── Political Cynicism ───────────────

The world of resources must be preserved for all people because it was on their backs and by their souls that we redeemed our lives and built our worlds.

─────────────────── The Buzzwords ───────────────────

Computer cycles must be allocated effectively or else someone will waste them building a Mandlebrot screen saver.

The world of networking needs a good way for agents and their hosts to come to an agreement about how much trouble and inconvenience they will cause each other. These are important questions because all good commerce depends upon a good, effective means of negotiation and exchange. Cash and the Uniform Commercial Code bind the human commercial world. It would be nice to dream that we can live without these things in cyberspace, but it would be a poorer world without it. If agents can negotiate with their hosts, then the hosts can offer substantial services to the Net in the hopes of making money. In the long run, the availability of these services may make the Net a richer place.

The negotiation process also helps the local host control the agent and rein in the consumption of resources. If some agent shows up and endlessly computes, the host must have a prearranged mechanism for putting this gorging to an end. This negotiation process can also help agent programmers. Endless loops are a dilemma that can strike any piece of software. You wouldn't want your agent waltzing off to the Cray-17 and burning up cycles at a $1,000,000 per minute of CPU time in an endless loop.

The resource negotiation process described in this chapter is straight forward. The agent executes a function called `FH-Negotiate-Resources` that specifies which resources it would like to request. The host considers this and then responds by either accepting the request or offering another solution. When the agent doesn't receive everything it requests with the first offer, it can either accept the compromise, request a different set or get up and leave. This iteration process may converge slowly when baseball players and owners are negotiating, but it must be bounded here. Each host is encouraged to have an iteration limit and to simply banish an agent if it submits more than a certain number of resource requests.

The structure of the `resource-request` is a list of pairs. The first element in each pair is a tag identifying the resource and the second is the amount of the request. There is a set of predefined tags available at all hosts. Each host, though, is free to define its own resources. If it does, it should be careful to describe the resources and their effects in the response to `FH-Give-Resource-Description`. The host must also describe how the resources are used by the other calls in to `FH-Give-Host-Description`. This

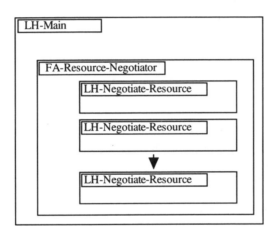

Figure 8.1: The calling order. The Host's main routine, or one of its subroutines, calls the agent's `FA-Resource-Negotiator` which, in turn, calls the host's `LH-Negotiate-Resources` as many times as necessary.

```
((’FR-Execution-Time -1000)
 (’FR-Execution-Space -15500)
 (’LR-Pizza-Supremes -4)
 (’FR-Dollars 42)
 (’LR-House-Boats -2))
```

Figure 8.2: The resources to be exchanged in a visit by an agent are shown as a list of pairs. Each pair contains a unique tag identifying the resource and the amount. The amount is positive if the agent will be supplying the resource and negative if the agent will be receiving the resource from the host.

prevents anyone from being surprised.

The set of predefined resources are:

FR-Execution-Time How many seconds the agent will be given to complete its task.

FR-Execution-Units This is the rough number of cycles devoted to the process. This is converted into seconds by dividing by the result of FH-Host-Speed.

FR-Execution-Space The amount of free memory the agent will consume. This is shown in bytes.

FR-Disk-Space Some hosts may allow incoming agents to leave data on the local disk. This is the space requested in bytes.

FR-Dollars This is the amount of cash that everything will cost. It is positive if the agent needs to pay. The credits will be denominated in dollars to make life simpler.

This list may satisfy many different situations. It essentially earmarks the basic functions on most systems and supplies a known interface.

There are also many different individual resources that might be created by local hosts in different businesses. Here is a list of some sample resources that might be useful. By convention, they begin with the letters LR for local resource, but there is no firm requirement that they bear this name.

LR-Total-Queries Many hosts will be database servers. They might want to limit the number of queries made by an individual agent.

LR-Bytes-Received Some on-line services choose to sell their data by the byte. This is often appropriate for text-based information like newspaper articles. The amount of value is often roughly proportional to the length.

LR-Wishes-Granted If you're a genie, you might want to limit this to three.

LR-Pizzas If you're running a pizza shack, then this is your resource. Replace this with whatever you're offering to the world.

LR-Train-Tokens If the NYC subway system allows you to buy your train ride tokens ahead of time, this might be a resource defined by its agent system.

There are many different products that can be offered. The resources that people create for their hosts will be as varied as commerce. The resource doesn't have to be deliverable by the Net. It can come separately.

8.1 Paying the Piper

Many people may choose to run free on-line hosts. They are a great form of advertisement. But others will want some cash. Each host must be able to execute (FH-Negotiate-Resources *list*) so it can receive offerings from the incoming agent. Technically, all resources are fair game, but any host programmer should think twice before accepting resources like FR-Execution-Time. After all, the host is providing the execution cycles. In most cases, the resource transferring hands will be cash or credit.

Each of the resource transfers has a special, predefined structure. This is necessary to ensure that agents arriving at strange hosts can get them to accept their money.

8.2   Negotiation

The negotiation process needs to have some straightforward semantics. There are two routines, `FH-Give-Resources` and `FH-Negotiate-Resources`. They are technically different routines, but many agents will use them in coordination.

The first function executed by an incoming agent will probably be (`FH--Negotiate-Resources resource-request`). This contains a list of the resources it wants. In many cases, the host will simply grant the request and return a welcome sign. This is the simplest case. This is illustrated in Figure 8.2.

In other cases, the host will respond with a counter request of the disputed items. These items might include several items with revised requests that would be grantable, or they might have just one disputed request: cash.

At this point, the agent knows that it can resubmit the counterproposal and commence execution. It is fun to dream about smart agents that come up with a counter-counterproposal and submit it to the host who is trying to gauge the availability of local resources to set the price. For instance, we can dream of an agent that would sit attached to the stock exchange watching the prices of a particular offer until its "intuition" tells it that the price is at a local minimum and ripe for the picking. In theory, this protocol can be used to do such creative things. In reality, most programmers will probably write agents that take what they can get. Life is too short to try to incorporate the trading strategies of a souk into a pile of LISP functions.

The agent might also need to execute the function `FH-Give-Resources` to offer resource tokens to the host. This is how it pays for its time. The host keeps these resources on account. The account holds the resources until the host deems them spent. If an agent packs up and leaves for some reason, the host must give back whatever resources are on account. The resources are deposited because the host wants to be sure it can get them if it wants

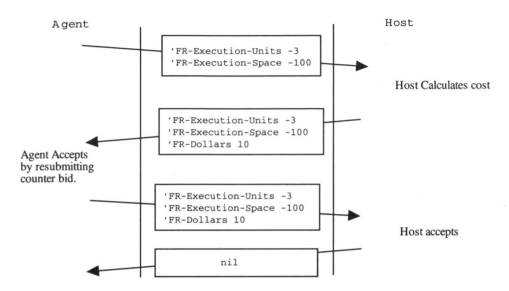

Figure 8.3: A simple resource negotiation process. The agent sends a request for a standard amount of execution time. The host responds with a price and the agent accepts.

them.

The host will often consult this account when `FH-Negotiate-Resources` is executed. If it finds $100 on account and it charges $10.00 per minute, then it will then feel free to grant a request for 600 seconds of `FR-Execution-Time`. A host is free to set up whatever criteria it needs to accomplish this goal, but it should strive to be predictable.

Here are several negotiation sessions that show sample agent-host interactions:

Total Acceptance

The agent arrives and executes this:

```
(FH-Negotiate-Resources '((FR-Execution-Time -600) (FR-Disk-Sp-
ace -10000) ))
```

The host has no problem with this and returns:

`nil`

Execution of the `FA-Main-Function` begins.

A Simple Charge

The agent arrives and submits a request:

`(FH-Negotiate-Resources '((FR-Execution-Time -600) (FR-Disk-Space -10000) ))`

The host, which charges for its time returns:

`((FR-Execution-Time -600) (FR-Disk-Space -10000) (FR-Dollars 10))`

The agent, which has no problem paying for this, executes:

`(FH-Give-Resources ((FR-Dollars *Cash token*)))`

And then:

`(FH-Negotiate-Resources '((FR-Execution-Time -600) (FR-Disk-Space -10000) (FR-Dollars 10) ))`

The host accepts this request and returns :

`nil`

The execution of the `FA-Main-Function` begins. Figure 8.2 shows another version of attaching a simple price.

Reduced Request

The agent arrives and submits a request:

```
(FH-Negotiate-Resources '((FR-Execution-Time -600) (FR-Disk-Sp-
ace -10000) ))
```

The host does not offer disk space, so it returns:

```
((FR-Execution-Time -600) (FR-Disk-Space 0))
```

The agent has a choice. If it needs the disk space to complete its call, then it must leave by executing (FH-Go-To ''address''). On the other hand, if its use of the disk space is optional, then it would reexecute:

```
(FH-Negotiate-Resources '((FR-Execution-Time -600) (FR-Disk-Sp-
ace 0)))
```

The host accepts this request and returns:

```
nil
```

and the execution of the **FA-Main-Function** begins.

Pizza Party

An agent is sent off to get the evening's pizza:

```
(FH-Negotiate-Resources '((LR-Pizzas 2) (LR-Grape-Sodas 4)))
```

The host returns:

```
((LR-Pizzas -2) (LR-Grape-Sodas -4) (FR-Dollars 22.95))
```

The agent has a choice. It is a steep price, but it will pay by executing:

```
(FH-Give-Resources ((FR-Dollars Cash token)))
```

This function deposits the cash locally. Then the agent executes:

```
(FH-Negotiate-Resources '((LR-Pizzas -2) (LR-Grape-Sodas -4) (FR--
Dollars 22.95)))
```

The host accepts this request because the money is available on account and returns:

    nil

The execution of the **FA-Main-Function** begins.

In the main function, the agent may execute functions like **LH-Add-- Toppings**, **LH-Extra-Cheese-It** or **LH-Natural-Cheese-Please**. The structure of the agent-host relationship can vary from implementation to implementation. In some cases, the agent might hang around at the host waiting for confirmation of delivery to arrive. If it is more than 30 minutes later, the agent might request a refund. The details are up to the local pizza shack.

8.3   Host Code Details

There are a wide range of implementations that can be used for **FH-Negotiate- -Resources**. The simplest possibility is to respond **nil** to each request. This may be functional in a surprising number of cases. The agent just gets what it gets. In many cases, programmers might feel that sending agents into the abyss until one returns with the answer is substantially easier than trying to make them negotiate for what they want. This may be fine in low-cost networks where there is little competition for resources, but it is sure to grind up the nerves of other users when each additional agent adds a significant amount of load to a system.

The rest of the code described in this section should provide a skeleton for creating substantial resource negotiators for the host. The code will only determine a cost in dollars (**FR-Dollars**), but this can be extended to include many other resources. Someone may choose to accept IOUs from agents. Others might even want to accept digitally endorsed vouchers for pigs, chickens, eggs and milk from the local farmer. The skeleton accepts a bid for standard resources and places a simple price on it. You can modify and extend these routines if you want.

The host will evaluate each bid with these steps:

1. Determine the cost.

2. Determine whether the resources are available.

3. If all the resources are available, then

   (a) If the agent included a payment option and it already tendered these resources to the host, then accept.

   (b) If all of the resources are not available, return the bid with the price resource attached.

4. Otherwise, delete the unavailable resources, add a price and reply with a counterbid.

This description will trace the progress down through the different branches of the execution. The basic entrance point for each negotiator is:

```
(defun FH-Negotiate-Resources (ls)
;;; Decide on the mode of payment by an agent.
;; ls contains a list of resources to be exchanged.
(let* ((the-list (separate-resources ls))
       (the-cost (Determine-Cost (cadr the-list))))
  (cond ((No-Costp the-cost)
         (Accept-Resources (cadr the-list))
          nil) ;; We accept.
        ((and (Meets-The-Offer the-cost (car the-list))
              (Are-All-Available (cadr the-list))
              (Test-Resources-Deposited the-cost))
         (Accept-Resources (cadr the-list))
         nil) ;; Accept!
        (t ;; Otherwise ask for cash.
          (append the-cost
                  (Remove-Unavailable-Resources
                  (cadr the-list)))))))
```

The first job for the host is to separate the resource list into resources that will be provided by the host and those that will come from the agent.

Those with positive units come from the agent and those with negative ones
come from the host. This routine separates them and returns them as two
lists:

```
(defun Separate-Resources (ls)
(let ((p nil) (s nil))
   (do ((l ls (cdr l)))  ((null l))
     (if (< 0 (cadr (car l)))
         (setq p (cons  (car l) p))
         (setq s (cons (car l) s))))
   (list p s)))
```

The host determines the costs for the resources it will offer by calling
Determine-Cost. This version only calculates the cost in dollars. This can
be extended by adding other functions and appending their results to the
list that exits the function.

```
(defun Determine-Cost (ls)
;; Look at the list, but only trade dollars for now.
 (list (list 'FR-Dollars (Determine-Dollar-Cost ls))))
```

This routine scans through the list and sends each individual resource
request out for evaluation:

```
(defun Determine-Dollar-Cost (ls)
;;; Scan down a list and figure out the price.
(let ((cost 0))
   (do ((l ls (cdr l)))
       ((null l))
     (setq cost (+ cost
                 (Cost-Resource-Pair (car l)))))
     cost))
```

Each resource is evaluated on a case-by-case basis. This set of code
charges $1.00 for every 1000 time units. The same price is charged for the
more abstract **FR-Execution-Units** by using the host's conversion factor

FH-Host-Speed. There is no charge for execution space (FR-Execution--Space) at this time because it is not measured effectively. Each host can decide how to price unavailable resources. In this case, a separate function is responsible for removing unacceptable resources. This is somewhat cleaner than applying an arbitrarily high price to unavailable resources.

```
(defun Cost-Resource-Pair (p)
;; Find the cost
(cond ((equal 'FR-Execution-Time (car p))
       (/ (abs (cadr p)) 1000)) ;; 1 dollar per 1000 units
      ((equal 'FR-Execution-Space (car p))
       0);; No charge now.
      ((eq 'FR-Execution-Units (car p))
       (/ (/ (cadr p) FH-Host-Speed) 1000))
      ((eq 'FR-Dollars (car p))
       0)
      (t 0) ; else zero
      ))
```

The results of costing out each resource request are finally aggregated and stored in a local variable the-cost used by FH-Negotiate-Resources. If the particular resource mix is free, then FH-Negotiate-Resources will send back nil immediately. It determines this with this function:

```
(defun No-Costp (ls)
;; Check a list of resources and make
;; sure it is all positive.
(let ((answer t))
  (do ((l ls (cdr l))) ((null l))
    (cond ((< 0 (cadr (car l)))
           (setq answer nil))))
  answer))
```

At this point, FH-Negotiate-Resources will need to determine whether the money is already deposited. This might be a bid that is accepting the counterproposal by returning it unchanged after depositing the resources. This implementation does not have any mechanism for counting the number of iterations in the negotiations. This is clean, but it might be a source of endless loops if the agent is broken. This implementation relies upon the outer timing loop to catch these problems.

The current version uses a very rudimentary implementation of cash transfer. There is an account, a simple system for adding to the account and a procedure for testing to see if all of the resources are here. The format for a resource is simple:

```
('FR-Tag amount serial-number signature).
```

The details of how to create the serial number and signature are given in Chapter 15. A complete implementation is not given here because XLISP does not offer big numbers that would make it easy to implement a public-key signature system. XLISP, though, is free with well-documented source code. Beggars can't be choosers.

This digital cash can be used for any other resource. This will allow agents and their hosts to create authenticated vouchers for resources like pigs, goats, milk and cheese. There is no reason why digital cash needs to be limited to an abstract government-endorsed quantity.

The resource deposits work with these functions and variables:

```
(defvar FH-Agent-Account nil)
;;; This is a list of all resources deposited by the agent.
(defun FH-Give-Resources (ls)
;; An agent uses this function to transfer resources.
  (setq FH-Agent-Account (append ls FH-Agent-Account)))
```

This system is minimal, but it is enough to handle hosts that choose to extend credit to the incoming agents and bill their master's through another system. The global function for testing to make sure that the resources are available is:

```
(defun Test-Resources-Deposited ( ls);
```

```
;; Once the price is agreed to, make sure the cash is in hand.
  (let ((answer t))
  (do ((l ls (cdr l))) ((null l))
    (cond ((eq (caar l) 'FR-Dollars)
            (cond ((not (Check-For-Dollars
                          FH-Agent-Account
                          (cadr (car l))))
                    (setq answer nil))))
          (t nil) ; Do nothing otherwise
          ))
    answer))
```

This version only checks for FR-Dollars, but it is trivial to extend it to handle other resources. You can even modify this function for checking dollars with little problem:

```
(defun Check-For-Dollars (ls amount)
  (let ((tot 0))
    (do ((l ls (cdr l))) ((null l))
      (cond ((eq 'FR-Dollars (car (car l)))
              (setq tot (+ tot (cadr (car l)))))
            (t nil)))
    (cond ((> tot amount)
            t) ;;; Enough is there.
          (t nil))))
```

If all of the cash is available, then FH-Negotiate-Resources responds with a nil.

In many cases, though, FH-Negotiate-Resources will need to present a counterbid that includes the price. This is certainly necessary in the first bid made by an incoming agent. It will also be necessary when the host is prepared to haggle. This host won't bother trying to haggle. It produces the counterbid by appending the-cost to the result of removing all of the unavailable resources with this function:

```
(defun Remove-Unavailable-Resources (ls)
```

```
;; Returns ls minus stuff we can't provide.
(let ((answer nil))
  (do ((l ls (cdr l))) ((null l))
    (cond ((member (caar l) FH-Available-Resources)
           (setf answer (cons (car l) answer)))
          ))
  answer))
```

The last step is notifying the rest of the program that new resource limits have been set. In this case, the program only enforces the time bound. Of course, this function must run in unprotected mode.

```
(defun Accept-Resources (ls)
(do ((l ls (cdr l))) ((null l))
  (cond ((eq (caar l) 'FR-Execution-Time)
         (setq *time-end* (+ (cadr (car l))
                             (get-internal-run-time))))
        ((eq (caar l) 'FR-Execution-Units)
         (setq *time-end* (+ (get-internal-run-time)
                             (* FH-Host-Speed
                                (cadr (car l))))))
        ))) ;; Ignore the rest.
```

8.4 Agent Code Details

The agent itself must be prepared to do some work. Even the simplest agent's **FA-Resource-Negotiator** must be able to detect whether it can't negotiate the services successfully. It might not, for instance, have enough money to pay the price and it must be able to recognize this. There is no way that there can be a minimal version of **FA-Resource-Negotiator** that accepts everything that comes its way. The host may be able to do this, but the agent must be ready for a "No".

There are additional constraints for the agent. Ideally, the host would provide copies of functions like **Separate-Resources**. The agent could use them to pull apart counterbids from the host. Forcing the agent to carry copies adds bytes to the size of the agent. But requiring the host to provide them might constrain the minimal hosts that don't want to offer that much. Although a library of basic functions would be a big asset, they are not included in this version. Future authors might want to define such a set. In the meantime, hosts are encouraged to publish functions in their local function lists.

Naturally, there are also questions of security. Any such library that is used by the host must be protected from tampering. There should be no way that the user can change the definition of these functions because they might change the internal functioning of the host. It would be quite easy to come up with a function that adds dollars to the incoming resource. The cleverest agent should be able to find a way to make it look like the host was trying to spend a bill twice. If the robust versions of cash described in Chapter 15 are used, then the cops would come after the host instead of the true culprit, the agent.

A simple version of **FA-Resource-Negotiator** will present a canned request for execution time and pay the price demanded if it has the cash on hand. It does not try to do anything complicated with renegotiations. It just submits a bid and tries to pay what it wants. Although the current version includes a loop for iterating through many different bids, the system won't rely upon it. The loop is only useful if the current system is extended to include complex negotiations.

```
(defun FA-Resource-Negotiator ()
;;; Get some access.
;;; This is a BASIC version.
(let* ((bid FA-Initial-Resource-Bid)
       (answer t)
       (counter (FH-Negotiate-Resources bid)))
  (print counter)
  (do ()
      ((null counter)) ;; nil means we are there.
    (let ((cost (assoc 'FR-Dollars counter)))
      (cond ((null cost)
             (setq answer nil)
```

```
                (setq counter nil))
               ((>= (cash-on-hand) (cadr cost))
                (setq answer (not (null
                       (Pay-Out-Resource
                        'FR-Dollars (cadr cost))))))
               (t
                (setq answer nil)
                (setq counter nil))))
        (print counter)
        (cond ((not (null counter))
                (setq counter
                   (FH-Negotiate-Resources counter)))))
    answer))
```

Here are two simple functions for handling the agent's cash. The first, Cash-On-Hand, will just count how much is available. The second function, Pay-Out-Resource, will dispense the cash. It returns the value paid out if it succeeds and nil if it doesn't have enough cash. The function is not sophisticated. It would do a better job if it looked throughout FA-Resource-Supply to find a FR-Dollars resource of the right denomination. Now, it just forks over enough cash until it reaches the limit. If this is more than necessary, it expects the host to give change.

```
(defun Cash-On-Hand ()
(let ((answer 0))
  (do ((l FA-Resource-Supply (cdr l))) ((null l))
    (cond ((eq (caar l) 'FR-Dollars)
            (setq answer (+ answer (cadr (car l)))))))
  answer))
(defun Pay-Out-Resource (res amount)
(let ((payment nil) (left-over nil) (tot 0) )
  (do ((l FA-Resource-Supply (cdr l)))
      ((or (null l) ))
    (cond ((and (eq (caar l) res) (<= tot amount))
            (setf payment (cons (car l) payment))
```

```
            (setq tot (+ tot (cadr (car l)))))
          (t (setf left-over (cons (car l) left-over)))))
  (cond ((>= tot amount)
         (FH-Give-Resources payment)
         (setf FA-Resource-Supply left-over)
         tot)
        (t nil))))
```

8.5 Summary

The resource mechanism described in this chapter is a first attempt at a basic protocol for negotiation between agent and host. Some people may wish to create complex, hierarchical, object-oriented resource descriptions. There may often be some use for these. For instance, it would be cumbersome for a pizza shack to offer a long list of resources: LR-Large-Pizza, LR-Large--Pizza-with-Anchoives, LR-Medium-Pizza-with-Anchovies, LR-Large--Pizza-with-Anchovies-and-Mushrooms etc. The number of combinations explodes exponentially. A more hierarchical object definition would allow the pizza shack to offer flexible prices for the different toppings and be more creative. But you need to have a dream. Any more expansive definition is left for the future.

Chapter 9

Agent Language

———————————— The Hype ————————————

The computer language for agents will be completely safe and very flexible. It may even read your mind occasionally.

———————————— Political Cynicism ————————————

Language is an ill-defined meta-concept that carries with it the implicit rules for dominating the proletariat. The very force of structure and the fact that everyone must adhere to this structure or face ostracism places language in the pantheon of dictators to the right of Hitler and the to left of Stalin.

———————————— The Buzzwords ————————————

Agent language should be a dynamically bound, interpreted instantiation of a loosely defined, object-compliant hierarchy.

Any language is just a set of rules for how to communicate. Human languages are remarkably protean and adaptive. People bend or break the rules to fit new circumstances and other people usually can figure out the message. Puns, tropes and word play are both a common and an essential part of communicating.

A good language system for the agent network should be just as flexible and able to adapt to different circumstances as human language. This is not entirely possible because computers are quite literal-minded. This problem is usually the basis for 90% of the jokes and cartoons that involve computers but it isn't a serious limitation. There are still plenty of simple problems that can be described in simple rule based systems. Computers handle such literal-minded chores as writing weekly paychecks or choosing the winner of the Publisher's Clearing House sweepstakes quite successfully. The goal is to define the foundations for a way that computers on a network can send instructions to each other.

Although the language must be flexible, its structure must also set limits for agents. It should not allow them to do anything that would endanger the host. The structure of human language defines the structure of our thinking. The language of the agent realm must define the structure of an agent's "thoughts". Remember the cliché that there are many different words for snow in the languages of the earliest people who settled in the frozen regions of the North American continent. A common way to imply that a person is always truthful is to say that person, "doesn't know the meaning of the word 'lie'." Our agent better not have a word for *virus*.

The language used by the agents will effectively encode all of their knowledge and thought. If we abandon the super-cool conceit of referring to agents as if they were people for a second, it is easy to see that the language used to represent the program can have limits. We can add a function for addition and one for subtraction but we'll make sure to leave out the function for 'erase all files.' This is a good first step, but the problem goes deeper than this. Good hackers can often use simple building blocks like addition and subtraction to attack other parts of the memory. The power of primitive building blocks is great. Some theorists have designed a computer with a single instruction that can simulate all other computers, albeit very slowly.

The basic building blocks of the language must be structured so that clever programmers can't redirect them to do bad things. There are two approaches to do this. One is to create a carefully built structure with specialized memory systems that allow programs to run without damaging others. This is the approach of the best operating system manufacturers, who are rapidly converging on a standard method of building object-oriented operating systems with free-roaming objects.

The other solution, which is taken by this book, is to create a much simpler language and force the agent to ask "Mother, may I?" before doing anything. This tight supervision slows down processing, but it prevents the agent from succumbing to any dark side. The simplest approach is often the best for first attempts at creating a standard, unless you are backed by large amounts of corporate capital.

The biggest hurdle to overcome is the current structure of programming languages today. The most prevalent language, C, as it is commonly implemented is the worst possible choice for an agent language. A C program is compiled and linked with libraries into a set of executable code that runs only on one particular hardware architecture. It often takes complete control of the machine and it may even have complete access to all system resources. The basic structure of the language revolves around giving the user the ability to write directly to memory and manipulate it with abandon.

This solution is okay for the shrink-wrapped software market. Most people are content to buy software and use it as a turnkey package. The software runs quickly and efficiently, but it won't work on machines from other companies. Cross-platform development is a major problem and companies often use different sets of programmers to create the same software for different machines. This is not a major problem if you're writing the software for yourself or a market like the PC market that is dominated by a single architecture. But this could be a major problem for a language that would ideally run on many machines.

The inherent danger of this approach should be obvious to anyone worried about computer viruses on their system. Ordinary programmers have had little problem creating such beasts because the average PC operating system is completely insecure. It allows any program to freely access any part of the machine. The goal of this book is to explicitly avoid this problem.

9.1   Design Goals

The design for this new agent language system should support flexible and safe execution of software that arrives off the network without so much as a letter of introduction. The design decisions and technological solutions can be divided up into two sets of features: the essential and the desirable.

The essential features are the solutions needed to do job and keep out malicious software bent on destruction. They can't be avoided. They are also necessary to keep software with mistakes or errors from inadvertently crashing the system. These features are:

Garbage Collection and Memory Management How to make sure that the incoming agent can only access its own memory. At the same time it must recycle it.

Dynamic Binding How to allow the incoming agent to link up with the local functions that do basic work.

Structured Access How to let the agent execute only a subset of local functions.

No Pointer Arithmetic Allowing pointer arithmetic is like offering a loaded gun to anything coming in the door.

Safe Crash Landings What happens when something goes awry? The operating system should be able to bundle up an agent and send it home.

The desirable features are solutions that embody some of the better ways to program practiced today. For instance, many programmers like features like automatic garbage collection because it removes problems for them. Others recognize that pointers are problematic and often generate many debugging headaches. So many of the solutions already exist in slightly different forms. They just need to be modified to work as an agent language.

The design of programming languages is often just an aesthetic exercise that revolves around choosing the simplest or most graceful way to create the abstract structure. In some cases, adding a particular feature might not be necessary, but it can simplify the entire structure. None of the details in the next list are essential, but each helps make sure that the language is fresh and easy to program by those taught with modern methods. The desirable features are:

Interpreted Execution Compiled programs are fast, but interpreted languages are more flexible and it is better to sacrifice speed for flexibility when the goal is creating the largest world possible in which agents can function. Interpreted languages are also easy to move from machine to machine. The CPU differences are erased by creating a different interpreter for each machine.

Polymorphic Functions Type checking has two great effects. First, it allows compilers to do a fast and accurate job creating code. Second, it catches many programming errors, especially those revolving around pointers. But, an interpreted language without pointers doesn't need this solution as much. Plus, living without strict type checking gives the programmer plenty of chances to create flexible functions that accept data in a multitude of formats. This allows the programmer to create a concise interface for an incoming agent.

Object-Oriented Structure Object-oriented programming is, like it or not, the way that many people create software today. It is a great solution for graphical user interfaces, which often thrive under a very straightforward hierarchy of functionality. There are many reasons to add this feature, but the strongest may be that everyone uses it.

Inheritance Although the ability of software to inherit behavior and functionality from other software in the hierarchy is an essential part of object-oriented software, I've made it a separate item because I would like to build an OO system in which the agent inherits many things from the local environment.

The rest of the book will describe modifications to XLISP and TCL, two of the standard languages that are widely available and already implement many of the basic features needed to build a successful agent system. The essential features will form the core of the system. Some of the desirable features will be available in the system described in the rest of the book. Some, like object-orientation and inheritance, are left out because they are not necessary for this toy system. They would be a good addition to any complete implementation and serious users will want to consider including them in any final language.

The rest of this chapter examines some of the necessary features in detail. It will discuss their nature and describe how they should be implemented.

9.2 Memory Management

The biggest problem is letting the incoming agent create and manipulate data structures without giving it the ability to get at the hidden guts of the local host and cause destruction. Most programmers who use C are used to grabbing memory at a whim, reading and writing to it directly and hopefully disposing of it correctly when they're finished. This approach is completely unacceptable because of the potential for mischief or misbehavior.

One solution is modifying a modern, multithreaded operating system like UNIX or MACH because it already provides each program or process with its own protected memory space that it cannot escape. The virtual memory system and internal hardware architecture make this approach desirable, and perhaps the best one.

There are practical problems, though, that stand in the way. Although UNIX-like systems are easy to find, they are far from common. Macintoshes and IBM-PC compatible machines running DOS and Microsoft's Windows OS are much more common and none of these machines provide the features for giving a process its own memory space. This will change in the near future as operating systems like IBM's OS/2, Microsoft's Windows NT and others become more common, but until that happens it may not be ideal to count on separate address spaces.

A more practical solution is adopting the memory language of LISP and its descendants. In this environment, the program accesses data by asking for it by a name. LISP maintains a table matching each name with a pointer to a section of memory. The programmer can string up long chains of these pointers to build complex structures. Whenever memory becomes tight, LISP moves through the data looking for sections of memory that aren't used any more. This garbage collection process is studied in great depth by many folks in computer science.

A garbage collecting memory model solves two problems. First, the table access mechanism allows the local host to deny the agent access to any data. The agent must ask for everything by name and any errant requests can be filtered out. Second, the memory will clean itself up and save the agent the problem of explicitly freeing up memory as it becomes available. Poorly written agents won't cause havoc.

There are limitations to this model. If the agent must ask "Mother, may I" when it wants each piece of data, then it will run slower. This can be solved to some extent by creating tables that have only the available data in them, but it is a functional limitation that probably cannot be eliminated without relying upon the special memory models used by high-end operating systems.

9.3 Dynamic Binding

When an agent wanders into a host, it will need to interact by executing local functions. This process, known as dynamic binding or dynamic linking, has always been around in various different forms but was often ignored by the average programmer who built software in the realm where each C program lived in its own private domain. After all, even the basic MS-DOS system essentially allows the executing program to link up with the local functions for exchanging information with system resources like the screen or the disk drives.

But the method of linking up software on the fly only became more popular as software developers began to implement systems that would allow users to plug in new selections of code that would add new features to existing software. Graphics programs like Adobe Photoshop or Quark XPress allow the programmer to create new software modules that do specific tasks. Screen savers like AfterDark let users add new ways to amuse themselves without dealing with the basic system interfaces.

The approach will become even more common as the next generation of operating systems embrace object-oriented techniques. Microsoft's OLE provides a mechanism for many different programs to link up. It is a large model, though, that is intended to make it easy for programmers to get the user-interface details correct. IBM's OS/2 contains a systemwide object structure that any programmer can modify to change the behavior of the user interface in some particular cases. The lower-level details are dominated by simpler object models like IBM's SOM and the more general CORBA. These might be useful for our purposes if they were generally used. This may come with time.

A simpler approach is to use a dynamically bound language like Scheme— a dialect of LISP. Every time a function is called, the name of the function is looked up in a table that links it with a pointer to the correct routine. If an agent finds itself in a new host, it will be able to execute a function like `LocalTime` and discover what the time is. This structure is very similar to the way that data is handled in LISP. In fact, the difference between data and programs is deliberately elusive in this model.

There are many largely philosophical conundrums that evolve from this structure, but the main advantage for any basic programmer is simplicity. Agents written in a LISP-like language will only need to conform to basic rules for exchanging data. More important, the hosts will only need to process data in these basic forms and this lowers the amount of work necessary to create the system.

Treating program and data as the same thing also makes it easy to implement an agent system on top of a LISP interpreter. The LISP system is already ready to accept data that might turn out to be a new program. There are few modifications that need to be made because the system is ready to accept reprogramming on the fly.

9.4 Goodbye Pointers

Passing around the pointers to the place in memory that holds a large collection of data is one of the most efficient ways to manipulate data. Pointers are also the foundation for dynamic binding and linking because data and functions can be changed simply by arranging for the pointer to point somewhere else. The only problem is that it can be dangerous if any incoming agent gets to play with pointers as well.

The ease of pointer arithmetic is one of the main reasons that many celebrate the visceral and aboriginal primitivism of the C language. But it has no place in any agent language because the agent can simply arrange for a pointer to point to some part in the host. This is how a virus can enter a system.

Banishing pointers is a drastic step that would not be necessary if all computers provided simple ways to launch processes in protected areas of data. This standard is bound to emerge over the next several years as the major companies like Apple and Microsoft renew their commitment to providing secure operating systems. Restraining pointers is not as important in UNIX workstations, which have safe memory systems that prevent processes from affecting each other.

9.5 Soft Crash Landings

Programs bomb. Even the best-written software will encounter input in the wrong format and be forced to stop. Agents will be no different. In some cases, the agent will arrive at the host and do one of a number of inexplicably rude things like dividing by zero. In other cases, the agent and the host will fail to communicate correctly because some detail was ambiguous. An agent might ask for the time from the host and get it in Greenwich Mean Time instead of local time and think that several hours disappeared in transit. In still other cases, the host might do the wrong thing because it was programmed incorrectly.

In all of these cases, the ideal solution is for the agent to return to its sender with a message detailing the error. Ideally, the error messages will be in a universally understood format so the dispatcher of the agent can recover without the help of a human programmer. This structure will require plenty of forethought, however, by those that define the realm in which the agents roam.

Many operating systems contain the means for detecting when something goes wrong and returning an error message. The lowest-end operating systems like DOS do little unless the program explicitly announces it is terminating. The better ones like Microsoft Windows notice when something goes awry with a program. The best ones like OS/2 or UNIX will let programs crash badly without damaging the rest of the system.

The goal is to build a host that will survive the worst possible crashes. It must be better than OS/2 and UNIX because these crash on occasion. Who knows what uninvited slob of an agent will storm through the door once you open up your host on the Net?

The error recovery system must also allow agents to effectively commit suicide and return home. This will allow agent programmers to debug problems when something goes wrong at a remote host. They will be able to start up an error message and send the agent home with all of its internal state.

9.6   Type Checking and Polymorphism

Strong typing of variables is, in my mind, one of the best innovations in the world of programming languages. Forcing each variable to come with a well-defined type allows the compiler to catch many troublesome errors with pointer arithmetic. It is, for instance, forbidden in Pascal to simply add a number like 4 to a pointer because integers and pointers are different types. The compiler intervenes because the pointer is different. A Pascal compiler enforcing strong typing rules has saved me thousands of hours of debugging time by nipping these ambiguities in the bud.

But strong typing may not be the best solution for a flexible host to an agent. Why? It prevents the host from offering many basic and standard functions to the agent. For instance, many data objects are kept in a list and programmers spend plenty of time concatenating and merging lists. Strong typing is a roadblock to building these functions because any function must define the type of the incoming data. Any agent using a set of local functions will be limited to sending data to the local function in the correct, predefined type. If the agent wants to make a list of some other type, it is out of luck.

One solution is to relax the rules of type casting and use naked pointers as the basic type. The list functions create lists of pointers to the data. Any function that accepts a pointer will not balk at accepting any type of more strictly defined pointers to an elaborate data structure. This solution is common in many object-oriented programming hierarchies like Borland's OWL. The only problem is that giving the incoming agent access to pointers is dangerous.

The LISP language model uses this structure, but neatly hides the danger. All of the data structures are lists. It handles pointers internally and could never let the agent never touch the pointer directly. The incoming agent must ask for data by name and the internal apparatus matches the name to a pointer before operating on the data. The host for the agent can offer many procedures that accept the basic LISP list. Each of these functions can be available and there is little worry that typing will get in the way.

9.7 Why Interpret the Language?

The earliest computer languages were interpreted, i.e. the program was executed step-by-step. LISP was once one of these languages. Then almost all programmers began using compilers that translated high-level languages directly into machine code. This approach is quite successful because the resulting code is much faster. One major source of the speedup comes because each variable and function call is assigned a fixed place in memory and this fixed location is locked in place in the final machine code. Interpreted languages will look up each variable up one at a time, i.e. they do dynamic binding.

Normally, circumventing the lookup process doesn't cost much. Some programmers of large systems implicitly like to use dynamic binding because it frees them from relinking the entire program each time, but these systems are not found very often. The production compilers are fast enough for almost everyone so there is little interest in interpreters today.

But in the realm of agents, the lookup process is quite useful. It allows the host to filter out requests for sections of memory that the agent shouldn't be examining. It also serves as a simple method of dynamic binding. So looking up everything is desirable.

Some may wonder whether it still might be good to make a compiled machine code the *lingua franca* for agents. For instance, the machine code of the Intel x86 line is quite common. Even computers that can't run it directly often have emulators built in to it. The Macintosh PowerPC line can emulate both Motorola 68000 code and Intel x86 code.

There are some reasons why this might be a good approach. If the agent finds itself on an x86 platform, then it could run at full speed. If the agent is at a different host then it might be simpler to interpret the x86 code because the machine code might be simpler. This might be the case with some of the early RISC processors, but it is probably much simpler to write a simple LISP-like language than handle all of the different modes of x86 code. An off-the-shelf compiler with the latest, greatest optimizer could be used to create the code. Each of these reasons argues for the creation of such a system.

The major impediment to such a system is the availability of a preemptive multitasking operating system that runs each process in its own memory space that cannot be breached. When this is widely available, then one of the major reasons for using dynamic table lookup is not apparent. The only major problem is finding a good way to handle dynamic binding with compiled code. This approach is being widely studied by the major operating system companies like Apple, Microsoft, IBM, and Sun, whose next generation of object-oriented operating systems will allow free roaming objects to move throughout the system.

9.8 Summary

This chapter laid out the major technological features that should be available in a simple agent language. For the most part, the discussion centered on features that are part of LISP interpreters. A LISP language can rely upon its basic dynamic binding to implement function filtering and prevent security breaches.

This approach is not fast. A better approach will emerge when the next generation of operating systems provides preemptive multitasking capabilities along with distributed object-binding protocols. There is plenty of overhead, though, in developing these systems and they will not become common until the end of the 1990s. The major agent languages appearing on the market today like SmalltalkAgents (discussed in section 13.3) and Telescript (discussed in section 13.1) implement many of these ideas.

Until those solutions emerge, this approach is much simpler. There is much to be said for simplicity in system design—especially if you're going to be the one to grow and maintain the system. The basic structure of LISP is very simple. Adding the security overhead is not hard to do effectively.

Chapter 10 describes an implementation of LISP known as XLISP first written by Dave Betz and now extended by Tom Almy with the help of several others who make the source code available publicly. This will be the starting points for creating the basic language. Chapter 11 describes TCL, another more modern language developed by John Ousterhout and extended by many others. It is widely emerging as a common programming tool on the Internet. Both of these are good approaches to creating a basic language that the agents can use to carry their instructions.

Chapter 10

XLISP

─────────────────── The Hype ───────────────────

Simple. Strong. Logically pure. The Boy Scout of languages.

─────────────────── Political Cynicism ───────────────────

Free and good. A great gift to the People.

─────────────────── The Buzzwords ───────────────────

A simple, microcomputer-based implementation of a subset of the Common LISP standards.

LISP is one of the oldest higher-order languages in the computer world. It began early in the computer revolution and has lived a long and fruitful life. There are many different dialects of LISP, but each of them maintains the basic flavor of the original. Both the data and the program are stored in trees built from nested lists. The programs can build up a new data structure and then begin to execute it. This ability to create new programs and "give them life" made LISP the standard language in the Artificial Intelligence community who used the flexibility to build programs that seemed to be doing something lifelike.

This feature makes LISP a natural choice for the linguistic foundation for the agent realm. It will be simple to create new agents and send them on their way because the basic data structures used by LISP are used for both data and programs. There will be no need to consciously convert them or worry about the details of compiling and linking software to work in the current environment. Inside the closed LISP world, the agents will be free to build and tear down themselves and other agents with ease.

LISP satisfies many of the basic linguistic constructs discussed in Chapter 9. The most important feature is the lack of pointer arithmetic. The LISP system will maintain and clean up the memory for you and the visiting agents. There are some security holes, but this system can be retooled to prevent incoming agents from overstepping their bounds. The garbage collection built into the memory system will also keep the memory in a reasonably clean state so the incoming agents will not need to worry about memory allocation and deallocation.

Some versions or dialects of LISP also use a form of dynamic linking or dynamic binding to find the latest functions. This is especially common in one popular dialect known as Scheme that emerged from MIT. This version led to the earliest version of a new, more network-ready dialect known as Dylan developed by Apple Computer Company's Cambridge, Massachusetts lab. The latest version of this language changed to a more C-like algebraic syntax.

Some dialects of LISP also offer structured access to variables. Common Lisp, a common dialect, is built upon a concept of *packages*, which are essentially separate tables of variables, functions and their names. The hierarchy imposed by these packages is one tool that can be used to keep incoming agents from executing any system calls or handling local memory. Earlier versions of XLISP did not include packages, but the latest version (2.1g) gives the programmer full access to these functions.

The key to providing error recovery is often included in many versions of LISP that provide built-in debuggers in their interface. There are two different levels of errors. There are errors that are caused when the agent violates one of the host's rules of memory access or use of system resources. In these cases, the problem can be caught in the evaluator loop. Many LISP versions offer hooks for installing functions to pre- and post-screen the input and output of the LISP compilers. These are ideal places for watching for these errors.

Other problems can occur when the agent violates some basic construct as LISP. That is, a basic LISP implementation would signal an error in any case. Many LISP implementations include debugging features that allow a user to play with the current state of the system and correct errors. These debuggers can be retooled to send the agent back home when an error occurs.

Many LISPs also include some of the desirable features of an agent language. LISP was extended to include many object-oriented features when a standard known as CLOS or Common Lisp Object System was approved by a committee of LISP programmers. These object features are also included in smaller versions of LISP like XLISP-Plus.

10.1 Interpret or Compile?

The earliest LISP implementations were interpreted, but some of the best ones on the market today are compiled. In fact, the compiled LISPs became more popular once they began including all of most useful features of an interpreter that could be used for debugging.

The LISP implementation used in this book, XLISP, is interpreted. It is also freely available to the public. The compilers on the market are commercially available and often much faster. Macintosh Common Lisp is one of the best implementations on the market. It also comes with many additional features that make it simple to create user interfaces and do other system work.

Even when LISP is compiled, it is not as fixed or static as compiled C code. It is still semi-interpreted. All LISP functions manipulate pointers and return pointers. They are not bound to a fixed memory location. This means that the compiled LISP code must still look up variables in a table to find their values. It cannot assume that the results will stay in a fixed location in memory nor can it assume that these objects will be in one particular format like integer numbers. This means that even the compiled LISP code could effectively support an agent realm because the code would not have a direct ability to manipulate pointers.

10.2   What is LISP?

This section is intended to be a quick introduction to LISP for the uninitiated. Those who know more than the basic terms can safely skip this section because it will only discuss the simplest features. Those who want to go into greater detail might turn to Guy Steele's *Common Lisp: The Language* [Ste90] which is one of the definitive treatments of the language.

The basic memory unit in LISP is an *atom*. Each atom is either a data element or a symbol. The data elements can be integers, floating-point numbers or even character strings. The symbols are character strings, and when LISP processes them, it will look up the symbol in a table to find the data attached that lives under that name. This is where the host must make sure that the agent is not asking for data that it should not be able to access.

Atoms are joined into lists using a *cons* atom that is just a package of two pointers. The standard way to build a list is to make a list of cons cells. The first pointer in each cons cell points to the data at that position in the list and the second pointer points to the next cons cell in the list. The last pointer can either have the second pointer point to an atom or let it just have a nil or zero pointer.

Most data structures in LISP emerge from these lists. There are specialized structures for bit maps and other arrays, but this treatment will ignore them for now. The programs and functions are also built out of these lists. A basic expression is just a list. The first element of the list is a symbol that designates the operation that must be performed and the rest of the list is made up of the data for that operation. So (+ 2 2) is a LISP expression that evaluates to 4. The first element in the list is the operation and the rest are the parameters. In a similar way, (* 1 2 3 4) evaluates to 24.

Procedures or functions are created by a very simple operation called *lambda* that many people, including myself, think is a bit strange the first time that they see it. The term arose out of a branch of mathematics called lambda calculus that showed how to build up all of arithmetic from a basic premise. Some people describe this premise as a "promise". That is, a lambda expression is a promise to do some work in the future. It turns out this premise is very powerful and the power combined with its simplicity allow plenty of rich structure to evolve without much extra work. LISP existed on the primitive machines of the 50's and 60's thanks to this simplicity.

A LISP procedure looks like this:

```
(defun farenheit-to-celcius (temp)
      (/
        (* 5 (- temp 40)) 9) )
```

In the first line, the symbol **defun** is a special LISP word that signifies that the rest of this list is going to be defined as a function. The first element in the list will be another list containing the name of the function as well as the name of any parameters if they exist. In this case the name is **farenheit-to-celcius** and the one parameter is called **temp**. The rest of the list is a list of expressions to evaluate. The function returns the result of the last expression as its answer or result.

Internally, the LISP interpreter converts the function into a lambda expression that contains the information about how to do the calculations and binds it to the name **farenheit-to-celcius**. Whenever that name is invoked, the lambda expression substitutes the parameter of the function and evaluates the result. This is why some people describe the construct as a promise. Programmers used to working with compiled languages like C might be inclined to dismiss this talk as silly because functions in C are just as much promises. The distinction is that lambda expressions can be recast or exchanged. In the past, C programs were better thought of as hard-wired mechanisms. This is changing now that object-oriented versions of C are making their appearances. These languages were inspired by much of the flexibility that is found in LISP.

Once this expression is evaluated by the LISP system, it will place the function in a table filed under the symbol "farenheit-to-celcius". Now, if you type (`farenheit-to-celcius` 85) into the LISP system, it will first begin to look up `farenheit-to-celcius` in the table of functions. When it finds it, it will take the first parameter, 85, and replace all occurrences of `temp` with 85 in the list of expressions to evaluate. Then it will evaluate them. In this case, this leaves the LISP system with the expression (/ (* 5 (- `temp` 40)) 9). LISP evaluates the innermost expression first and works outward. In this case, the rest of the function calls refer to the built in arithmetic. The final result is 25. This will be printed out. If you typed in the expression, (+ 5 (`farenheit-to-celcius` 85)) you would get 30.

As you can see, there are many sets of nested parentheses. This is a big drawback, in many people's eyes, because it is a pain to keep them straight and balanced. It is probably one of the bigger impediments to the growth of LISP as a language. Still, the greatest advantage is that it makes the language simple to parse, and that simplicity pays off in a simpler interpreter. Chapter 11 describes TCL, a language with similar properties, but without this annoying feature.

Many LISP implementations come with different sets of implemented functions. The most common dialect, Common LISP, has many different functions that each do slight variations of each other. This allows you to pick the right tool for the moment. Others include less variety and force the programmer to do the work.

You can also define variables in the same way. The symbol `setc` builds a slot for a variable with a particular name. For instance, (`setc foo` 3) will create an entry in the table of symbols with the name "foo" and point that symbol to the atom with the integer 3.

Lists are constructed in LISP in two ways. The first is for the programmer to build them. The `cons` function is the basic building block. If you type (`setq foo` (`cons` 1 (`cons` 2 3))) you would be defining the list of three elements 1, 2 and 3. Technically, the list should be printed (1 . (2 . 3)) with each cons cell being defined by a pair of parentheses and a period between the elements pointed to by each pointer. This is tedious and it is often replaced with the shorthand (1 2 3).

LISP lists are taken apart by two functions: `car` and `cdr`. `car` returns the left portion of the cons cell and the `cdr` returns the right portion. When you're dealing with actual lists built up of cons cells then the two functions can be thought of as "first", which returns the first element of a list, and "rest", which returns what is left after the first is removed.

LISP handles many of the details about numbers for you. If you type (`setq foo1 3`) it will store the 3 as an integer. If you type (`setq foo2 3.3`) it will store the 3.3 in floating-point format. Each LISP atom comes with several extra bits that represents the type of the data it holds. When it comes time to add or do arithmetic on these numbers, the LISP core will do the right conversions if necessary. So (`* foo1 foo1`) would return 9 and use integer arithmetic to arrive at the answer while (`* foo1 foo2`) would return 9.9 and use floating-point arithmetic after it converted the integer in `foo1` into a floating-point number.

LISP is also one of the few languages with built-in functions for handling big numbers. You can type (`* 3 3333333333`) and get 9999999999. This feature comes in handy when you're dealing with large prime numbers in cryptography. This feature is, alas, missing from XLISP.

This last section was a short introduction to the LISP family of languages. All of the languages share these basic features although some of them implement them in different ways. Functions in Scheme, for instance, are defined with a slightly different format. The details about the binding and the way that they may be compiled all vary because many people have argued many hours about these details. You're invited to read more deeply because no short treatment like this can begin to do any language justice.

Many people have remarked, though, that the simplicity of LISP is its strong point. The details can be taught very quickly. This section should give you enough information to read the rest of the book even if you've never programmed in LISP before. There are many subtle additions that clever programmers have added over the years. Guy Steele's book [Ste90] is very succinct, but runs to over 1000 pages.

10.3   Modifying XLISP

XLISP will not work as an agent language without some important changes. The language, like most useful languages, includes many functions for accessing disk files and changing them. It also includes a function or two for directly twiddling bits in the memory. These may be useful for people programming their own machine, but the features need to be disabled for agents.

The system must also be extended to include a method for keeping track of the execution time of an incoming agent. The host should be able to set a bound on the execution time and rely upon the XLISP interpreter to stop the program/agent when the bound is reached.

In some sense, it would be ideal if the host could control the amount of memory consumed by the agent. This is possible, but it may not be necessary if the host has a limited amount of memory itself. In some implementations, the XLISP interpreter can only access a predefined amount of memory. A wayward agent will run up against this barrier without affecting the rest of the machine. In other systems with virtual memory, a gluttonous agent can absorb all of the memory and start consuming virtual memory. This will not crash the system (immediately) but it could slow it down considerably. In these cases, a good host will be able to limit the incoming agent to the physical memory.

Modifying the XLISP code can be done at two levels. The easiest method can be written in LISP itself. The language comes with two functions `evalhook` and `applyhook` that are activated in the process of evaluating a function. When the variable `*evalhook*` is bound to a function, then the regular evaluator stops when it receives a form and passes this form to the function. This `evalhook` function is responsible for evaluating the form and returning the answer. It could, for instance, arrange for every function to return 42. Or it could check out the function and make sure that it isn't doing anything rotten. If the variable `*applyhook*` is bound to a function, then it is invoked when a function is about to be applied. These two hooks allow anyone to write a program that affects how the XLISP interpreter works.

The second solution is to actually modify the C program that implements

XLISP. This is a more complicated approach because it involves working on a deeper level. Playing with the guts of a large program is not necessarily a safe way to live. The advantages of this approach, though, are speed and flexibility. The **evalhook** functions are well-designed extensions to the LISP language but they have their own semantics. If you want to work outside of this scope it may be hard to do what you want. Also, any extensions written in C will be compiled so they run faster.

10.4 Using Evalhook and Applyhook

The **evalhook** function takes three required arguments, the form to be evaluated, the pointer to the function to serve as the *evalhook* function, and the pointer to the function that will act as the *applyhook* function. The function that is bound to *evalhook* will often recursively explore the evaluation of the form it gets. The ability to pass in the value of *evalhook* allows different versions of the function to be used in different circumstances. Earlier versions of the function also included a fourth variable pointing to the environment, but the X3J13 standards committee voted to remove this in January 1989. They also voted later that year to strip the two functions from the language, but the functions are still included in some versions like XLISP.

The companion function **applyhook** takes four arguments. The first is the function that is going to be applied to the second, the arguments for this function. The other two are the functions that will serve as the *evalhook* and *applyhook* respectively.

The action of **evalhook** is simple to demonstrate. First define a simple function **dumb-luck**:

```
(defun dumb-luck (form &rest env) 42)
```

The function can be tested like this:

```
> (evalhook '(eval (* (+ 4 2) 3)) #'dumb-luck nil)
```

The extra `eval` routine is necessary here because the `evalhook` function will not apply `dumb-luck` on the first pass. If it is not present, then this is the result:

```
> (evalhook '(* (+ 4 2) 3) #'dumb-luck nil)
```

1764 is 42^2. The subforms (+ 4 2) and 3 are all evaluated by passing them to `dumb-luck` which automatically returns 42. The final multiplication, though, is not passed through `dumb-luck`. This feature allows you to write more complicated debugging routines.

An evaluation shell can be created like this:

```
(defun hook (x)
  (let ((*evalhook* 'dumb-luck))
    (eval x)))
```

When this function is called, it will always return 42.

```
> (hook '(* (+ 4 2) 3))
> (hook '(* (* (* 2 3) 3) 3))
```

10.5 Watching the Clock

A small LISP function can be created using `evalhook` to watch the clock. There are two parts, the shell that calls the function and the function that is bound to *evalhook*. The shell is:

```
(defun tb (form bound)
  (let ((*hooklevel 0)
        (*time-end* (+ (get-internal-run-time) bound)))
    (*evalhook* #'eval-hook-function))
    (eval form)))
```

and the function that checks out each form is:

```
(defun eval-hook-function (form env &aux val)
   (cond ((< (get-internal-run-time) *time-end*)
          (cond ((consp form)
                 (setf val
                    (evalhook form
                              #'eval-hook-function
                              nil
                              env)))
                (t (setf val (evalhook form nil nil env))))
          val)
         (t (error "out-of-time-error" "No Time Left")
   )))
```

The code can be tested on a simple recursive program that computes a factorial:

```
(defun refac (n)
  (cond ((= n 0) 1)
        (t (* n
              (refac (- n 1))))))
```

When the code is executed, here is the response:

```
> (tb '(refac 10) 100)
3628800
> (tb '(refac 15) 100)
1.30767e+12
> (tb '(refac 20) 100)
2.4329e+18
> (tb '(refac 10) 10)
error: out-of-time-error - "No Time Left"
> (tb '(refac 10) 20)
error: out-of-time-error - "No Time Left"
```

```
> (tb '(refac 10) 40)
 3628800
> (tb '(refac 20) 40)
error: out-of-time-error - "No Time Left"
```

These sample executions show that 40 time units are enough to compute 10 but not enough to compute 20!. 100 units are enough for both. Naturally, the number of time units will vary between machines and the respective implementation of LISP. This is why a benchmark is used to calculate the speed of the machine that is normalized for the purpose of computing the time spent.

Some hosts may choose to suspend this timekeeping operation because it slows down the computation dramatically. It is quite possible to compute 100 in about one time unit on the same machine that can't compute 20! in 40 units if the **evalhook** function is disabled. This is because there are roughly 40 new steps that are added to the evaluation of each form. Each of these steps is taken every time that **eval-hook-function** is called and this function call is not pre-compiled. It is interpreted. The only problem with suspending the use of an **evalhook** is that the function is also used to check for functions that try to change the system.

The structure of this function can be made more usable by defining a macro instead of a function. This would eliminate the need for the apostrophe in the test samples. This can be expressed:

```
(defmacro timebound ( form    bound &rest val)
  '(progn (setf *hooklevel* 0)
          (setq *time-end*
              (+ (get-internal-run-time) ,bound))
          (setq *check-count* 0)
          (setq error nil)
          (setf val
              (evalhook ',form #'eval-hook-function nil nil))
     val))
```

10.6 Watching for Trouble

Counting the microseconds of CPU time used is one job of the host. Another major task for the interpreter is protecting itself against malicious agents. The `evalhook` function can also be used to filter out dangerous function calls that might threaten the host. The dangerous function calls can be broken into several major categories:

Disk Operations A host should only offer unrestricted disk access to very trusted incoming agents. In most cases, the best solution is to simply restrict the agent from executing incoming functions. Any disk access that needs to be done can be done with a specially designed local function that is made available to the incoming agent.

State Modifications One simple approach by an incoming agent is to re-define the value of `eval-hook-function`. This attack can be avoided in two ways. The first, imperfect approach, is to give the function a random name and even change its name regularly. This will only stop fishing attacks where the incoming agent is just guessing that the host's programmer used the name `eval-hook-function`. The better solution is to use the `eval-hook-function`, whatever its name, to filter out calls to `defun`, `setq` or `setf`.

Screen Display If an agent enters and can draw anything on the screen, it may cause havoc. Although most people know that a computer that starts scrolling the message "Take me to your leader" is probably infected with a computer virus, more subtle attacks might take place. A host should have the option of filtering out these function calls.

Filtering out the bad calls is a tough proposition with a language like LISP because the major dialect, Common LISP, has been extended to include many different functions that do the same thing in slightly different ways. The function `setq` will link up a variable with a name. The function `setf` is a more general result that can be used to modify parts of LISP trees and lists as well.

Here is a simple example for how to extend the `eval-hook-function` by creating a filter function `test-form` that checks for errant code.

```
(defun test-form (form)
;;; Tests the form to ensure that it is not breaking any rules.
;;; (print (list "in test form" form))
  (cond    ((or (eql (car form) 'defun)
                (eql (car form) 'defmacro))
      (cond ((or (member (cadr form) *protected-function*)
            (Is-Predefinedp (car form)))
            nil)
          (t t))
    )
    ((or (eql (car form) 'setq)
        (eql (car form) 'setf))
      (cond ((member (cadr form) *protected-variables*)
          nil)
          (t t))
    )
    (t
      (cond ((member (car form) *forbidden-functions*)
          nil)
          ((and (not *allow-screen-action*)
              (member (car form) *screen-functions*))
          nil)
          (t t)
          ))
  ))
```

The variable `*protected-functions*` contains a list of functions that are cannot be redefined by the `defun` process. The variables that cannot be replaced safely are listed in the variable `*protected-variables*` and the functions that can't be called are found in the list `*forbidden-functions*`. If the variable `*allow-screen-action*` is false, then all of the functions listed in `*screen-functions*` will be excluded.

This function is called by `eval-hook-function` which is extended to read:

```
(defun eval-hook-function (form env &aux val f1)
  (cond ((< (get-internal-run-time) *time-end*)
         (cond ((consp form)
                (cond ((test-form form)
                       (setf val
                         (evalhook form
                                   #'eval-hook-function
                                   nil
                                   env)))
                      (t (error "bad-function-error"
                                "Wrong call"))))
               (t (setf val (evalhook form nil nil
                                      env)))))
         val)
        (t (error "out-of-time-error" "bah")
  )))
```

10.6.1 Protecting Variables

The procedure `test-form` is called to check out the forms before they are processed by the next level down of `evalhook`. If any of these simple rules are breached, an error is generated.

The `setq` and `setf` functions can be misused. In the simplest case, they can redefine the values of `*protected-variables*`, `*protected--functions*` and `*forbidden-functions*`. This would allow the agent free rein to do it's will. In more complicated examples, the `setq` function could be used to redefine `*evalhook*` or another internal constant. The `test--form` function checks to see if the value being assigned by the `setq` function is on the list of `*protected-variables*` that include:

`*evalhook*` This could circumvent the `*evalhook*` function designed to evaluate the function.

applyhook Although the *applyhook* is not currently used, there is no
plausible reason to allow an agent to execute its own code through
this mechanism. The code would not be caught by the eval-hook--
function.

gc-hook The function bound to this variable is executed when the garbage
collection begins to fix the memory. This should be reserved for implementations of eval-hook-function that want to monitor memory
usage. The function could also be used as a way to leave a virus behind. The function bound to *gc-hook* would almost certainly not
execute under the supervision of eval-hook-function.

unbound This is the value that unbound variables normally return. Normally, XLISP will intercept these calls.

breakenable The value of this constant controls whether the program
responds to break requests. Hosts may choose different strategies, but
they should be second-guessed by the incoming agent.

protected-functions This obviously need protection to prevent an agent
from substituting their own list.

protected-variables If an agent could take variables off of the protected
variables list, then it could change things at will.

forbidden-functions Changing the list of forbidden functions is also
forbidden.

pi This is bound to 3.14159. There is no reason why an agent can't redefine
it to be, say, 3, but it this redefinition could linger around and confuse
the host which might be relying upon it to calculate the circumference
of the orbit of a satellite. This could cause the host to make a mistake
and send the satellite crashing into, say, New York City.

terminal-io Some hosts may want to allow the agent to have access to
the incoming information because the agent will be interacting with a
local person to gather data. Most, though, won't want their machine
to crash if some agent redirects this information.

standard-input Most hosts will probably want to prevent the agent from getting access to this information directly. It would be better passed to it.

standard-output Most hosts will probably want to also keep the agents from sending out information unchecked.

obarray This contains the list of objects built by the XLISP object system. There is no reason to allow an incoming agent to have full access to this hash table.

This list of protected variables may be incomplete. If the functions described in this text are used with another implementation of LISP, they may fail to screen out special variables added in that implementation. It is conceivable, though unlikely, that some designer might have added the variable *set-true-to-detonate*. Any agent coming off the street should not have access to this variable. Users should show some caution in extending this work to other systems because the list may be incomplete. It is unfortunate that security must be enforced by explicitly denying certain functions. This means an incomplete list leaves a failure. A better approach may be to design a new language from the ground up and add only the safe features.

10.6.2 Protected Functions

An incoming agent will want to define its own functions. There is no reason, though, why it should be free to redefine other functions. One of the "great" features of LISP is that anything can be redefined, including the built in functions like + or setq.

It is possible, for instance, to redefine evalhook like this:

```
> (setf woka #'evalhook)
#<Subr-EVALHOOK:#64>
```

This can be applied in a normal way:

```
(defun evalhook (form ehf ahf env)
   (print "Hi!")
   (apply woka form ehf ahf env))
```

Now the function will print "Hi!" every time it is invoked. Obviously, other more damaging things could be done.

This is why it is necessary to prevent the redefinition of functions. Almost all of the general functions are on the list, `*protected-functions*`. This is not necessary, but it may be prudent. There may be no reason to worry if an agent redefines `+`. But there is often a more legitimate way for an agent to accomplish what it needs to do. The other elements on the list are placed there deliberately to prevent trouble. The functions on the `*protected--functions*` list are:

All General Functions like `cond, do etc.` Many of these redefinitions are not explicitly dangerous, but it is easy to be paranoid. Hosts may wish to reinterpret this decision if it is necessary to allow more flexibility.

`evalhook` See the example above. Obviously, this can be abused.

`applyhook` This can be abused in the same way as `evalhook`.

`setq` **or** `setf` If these were intercepted, then the agent might be able to control the binding of variables.

`eval-hook-function, test-form, tb` **or** `timebound` The agent shouldn't be able to choose its master so easily.

There are two ways that the filter can be implemented. A search of a list like `*protected-functions*` with a `member` function call is fine, but it may grow slow if the list includes all of the general functions. The test for general functions can be replaced by a test of the type of the first element in the form being evaluated. The type of many of the standard functions in XLISP are "special forms" with the type `FSUBR`. This means that the arguments are not evaluated before they are passed to the portion of the code responsible for executing the special form. The rest of the predefined functions are type `SUBR`. All user-defined functions get the type `CLOSURE`.

The type of an element can be tested with an `type-of` function. Filtering out all of the built-in function is simple to do:

```
(defun Is-Predefinedp (func)
  (let ((aa (eval '(type-of #',func))))
    (or (eq aa 'FSUBR) (eq aa 'SUBR))))
```

Of course, the programmer of the host will want to extend the list `*pro-tected-functions*` to include the locally defined functions that might be off-limits.

10.6.3 Forbidden Function Calls

Some function calls need to be blocked from execution because they allow an agent access to the memory, the file system or the screen. The list of these functions is called `*forbidden-functions*` and the `test-form` function will scan the list to check for problems. The list includes:

File Functions These include: `open`, `write-char`, `write-byte`, `read--char`, `peek-char`, `write-char`, `read-line`, `close`, `delete-file`, `true-name`, `with-open-file`, `read-byte`, `write-byte`, `file-length`, `file--position`, `dribble`. Each of these functions can access the general file system. It may be desirable to allow read-only functions like `read--byte`, but it is probably better to package these functions into a local function that is executed by the incoming agent.

`peek`, `poke` **and** `address-of` These functions read, write and search the raw memory of the computer respectively. Any malicious agent could have plenty of fun being a crashing bore. Some host programmers might imagine a chance for an agent to use `peek`. It doesn't directly destroy data, but could allow the agent to gain access to information that it might not normally get a chance to access. For instance, many encryption programs store the key in memory. If one of these encryption programs is running concurrently, the agent might be able to locate this key and snarf it for its own use.

`system` This function allows a user to execute a system call on a compliant system. Not all implementations of XLISP have this feature, nor do all implementations of LISP. Still, it should be regarded as extremely dangerous. Imagine this (system ''rm c:.*) running on a MS-DOS machine.

Stream Functions These include: get-output-stream-list, get-output--stream-string, make-string-output-stream, make-string-input--stream, with-output-to-string, with-open-file and with-input--from-string. The streams should only be manipulated by the incoming agent only in special, trustworthy circumstances.

error **and** cerror These functions start an error. These can be trapped by the host, but there should be little reason for an agent to get in the habit of using this software level. Ideally, an agent will support its own error recovery mechanism and leave this mechanism to the host.

break There is no reason for the agent to be breaking its execution.

top-level, clean-up **and** continue These functions are used in the debugging routine to clean up. They can be used by the agent to commit suicide and gum up the works. For instance:

```
> (defun hog (a b)
    (let ((c (+ a b)))
      (setq d (* c a))
      (top-level)
      (setq c (* c c a))))
HOG
> (hog 4 2)
[ back to top level ]
```

errset This will trap errors of certain types. The agent could use this to trap its own access errors and substitute its own "recovery" mechanism.

Forbidding certain function calls keeps the agent from accessing important parts of the system. The host programmer should provide good local functions that provide the incoming agent with all of the information it will need. Some of these functions may be added to the forbidden function list if the host programmer wants to do it. This will probably be common with complicated hosts that need to be broken into many different functions for readability. Not all of the functions need to be accessible to the incoming agent.

Some programmers may not see the harm in allowing functions that read data. This may be true if the system does not contain any important data. On these machines, the agent might be allowed to use these functions. Host programmers are not encouraged to take this route for two reasons. The most important one is consistency. Many other machines in an agent realm will presumably not be as welcoming. They will prohibit the incoming agent from exploring the memory or the file system. An agent programmer will be hard pressed to remember the differences between hosts. It will cause problems for everyone.

The second reason for avoiding general reads of the system is forgetfulness. Many host programmers may forget that they left a modest security gap because they didn't feel like writing all of the shell functions necessary to allow an incoming agent to do everything that it might want to do. Giving general access to the file system is an easy out, but it may come back to haunt you if you forget that your system is not secure.

10.6.4 Going Faster

The simple version of `eval-hook-function` that only watches the clock does not add too much overhead to the processing time of a simple function. There may be five or six extra operations for each single operation. This is an efficiency problem that is compounded significantly when the user adds in the tests for improper function evaluation. Scanning the lists like `*forbidden--functions*` takes a significant amount of time and this amount may grow larger as more and more functions are added to the protected lists. It is quite conceivable that a function will run 100 times slower using this version of protection.

Something that makes an XLISP program run 100 times slower is not much of a solution— especially when you consider the fact that an interpretted LISP program like XLISP is already substantially slower than C code.

Many people may be able to use the system effectively even if it is somewhat slow, but it would be better to run faster.

One solution is to add a new class of functions that can run in unprotected mode. Normally, these would be the host's local functions that can be trusted not to do anything malicious. When the step-by-step evaluator using the `eval-hook-function` encounters one of them, the evaluator will allow them to run without being interrupted by the `eval-hook-function`. This is implemented with a new version of `eval-hook-function` that looks like this:

```
(defun eval-hook-function (form env &aux val f1)
    (cond ((> (get-internal-run-time) *time-end*)
            (print "OUT OF TIME!")
            (throw 'error 'out-of-time))
          ((consp form)
           (cond ((member (car form) *free-functions*)
                    (print "Going Free with")
                    (print form)
                    (setf val (evalhook form nil nil env)))
                 ((test-form form)
                  (setf val (evalhook form
                                #'eval-hook-function
                                nil
                                env)))
                  (t (print "BAD FUNCTION")
                     (print form)
                     (throw 'error 'bad-function))))
          (t
            (setf val (evalhook form nil nil env))))
          val)
```

This version of the function tests each function to see if it is in the list `*free-functions*`. If it is, then the evaluator calls it directly without an `eval-hook-function` attached to the evaluation.

The variable `*free-functions*` should definitely be added to the value of *protected-variables*. The host programmer should arrange for the function FH-Initialize-Security to add the local functions to this collection. For instance, this version of FH-Initialize-Security is part of the AIRHOST.LSP program:

```
(defun FH-Initialize-Security ()
 (setf *free-functions* (append
     (list 'FH-Mail
     'FH-Initialize-Host
     'LH-Make-Reservation
     'LH-Flights-By-Item
     'FH-Send-Agent
     'FH-Give-Personality-Description
     'FH-Give-Resource-Description
     'FH-Give-Errors-Description
     'FH-Give-Resources
     'FH-Available-Resources
     'FH-Negotiate-Resources
     'LH-Flights-By-Item
     'LH-Flights-By-Item-2
     )
   *free-functions*))
 (setf *protected-variables* (append
     (list
     'LH-Flight-List
     'FH-Agent-Account
     'Test-Resources-Deposited
     'LH-Item-Function-Map
     )
    *protected-variables*))
 (setf *forbidden-functions* (append
     (list
     'Build-Test-Flight-List
     'LH-Flights-By-Item-Weak
     'FH-Save-To-File
```

```
      'FH-Read-From-File
      'FH-Clean-Up-Host
      'FH-Initialize-Host
      'Separate-Resources
      'Test-Resource-Pair
      'Cost-Resource-Pair
      'Determine-Dollar-Cost
      'Determine-Cost
      'Meets-The-Offer
      'Check-For-Dollars
      'Remove-Unavailable-Resources
      'Are-All-Available
      'No-Costp
      'Accept-Resources
      )
  *forbidden-functions*))
 t)  ;; Must return true if successful.
```

The function LH-Flights-By-Item, for instance, must search through a
long list of flights to find the ones that match the user's needs. Checking
each step of this function with eval-hook-function is a waste of time.

10.6.5 Packages

The latest versions of LISP often include a feature for splitting the namespace
into units called *packages*. XLISP 2.1g includes this feature, but earlier
versions don't have it. The solutions and suggestions for using eval-hook--
function to prevent access to certain functions don't use this feature because
it wasn't available when the project began.

Packages would seem to be the ideal solution. The construction arose
out of the frequent competition for names that began to occur as LISP
systems grew larger and larger. People began to load many different files
filled with functions written by someone else. Occasionally, two of the files
would contain different functions with the same, relatively generic name like

`scan-list`. The last file loaded would be the one whose version of `scan--list` took precedence. Naturally, bugs became rampant.

A LISP implementation with packages contains multiple symbol tables. One table corresponds to the current package. If you type (`+ x y`), you will get the value found by adding up the `x` and `y` found in that one particular table. Each package has a name. There are several standard packages including USER, which is the default package; CL, which contains the functions that are part of Common LISP; and XLISP, which is part of the XLISP implementation. You can switch between packages by using the command (`in-package USER`).

The package system allows you to control the access to a function. Normally, one package cannot see the functions in another package's namespace unless that package explicitly *exports* the function and the other package explicity *uses* it. For instance, you could create two packages in XLISP named AGENT and HOST like this:

```
> (make-package 'host :use '(cl xlisp))
#<Package HOST>
> (make-package 'agent :use '(cl xlisp host))
#<Package AGENT>
```

Both packages *use* the central packages of `cl` and `xlisp` which means that the exported functions from these packages are still available if the current package is set to either AGENT or HOST. In this case, the functions executing in the AGENT package can also see all of the exported functions from the HOST package.

This would seem to be an ideal method for controlling the reach of the incoming agent. All of the dangerous functions from the XLISP, CL or HOST packages could be *unexported* and kept away from the agent. This prevention would be implemented in the lowest level of the XLISP interpreter which is already optimized to make these decisions. The speed increase would be significant.

There is one big security hole, though, in this scheme. The package system provides an absolute function-naming convention that circumvents the export mechanism. If you type XLISP::OPEN, then you will execute the

OPEN function in the XLISP package whether or not it is exported to you. The
double colons, "::", ensure that this will happen. If a single colon is used,
then the export mechanism restricts the function from calling a symbol that
can't be accessed.

The key is turning off the double colon loophole. Blocking this mechanism can only be done in the C implementation of the XLISP. This can be
done in a number of ways. One solution is to change the function psymbol in
XLREAD.C in the source code for XLISP. This function parses the symbol
and finds the correct package match. The important snippet of the code
looks like this:

```
/* count the colons and switch */
for (p = buf + packindex + 1,
        colons = 1;
        *p == ':'; p++,
        colons++);
switch (colons)
 case 1:
   if (xlfindsymbol(p, pack, &val) != SYM_EXTERNAL)
          xlerror("external symbol not found", cvstring(p));
   break;
 case 2:
    val = xlintern(p, pack);
    break;
 default: xlfail("too many :'s");
```

The simple solution is to ensure that both case 1 and case 2 will take
the first path and execute xlfindsymbol to determine where the symbol is
located.

Modifying this function prevents the LISP parser from installing symbols
that can't be accessed. This means that XLISP will fail to accept a function
like this:

```
(defun FA-Main-Function ()
   (let ((fp
```

```
    (XLISP::open "secrets!!!" :direction :read)))
  etc...
```

The downside of modifying the XLISP code like this is that it becomes difficult to ensure that all agents maintain this version. The one advantage of using XLISP is that it is portable and installed on many different machines. Modifying the C code means generating a separate class of XLISPs populating the globe.

10.7 Summary

The process of modifying XLISP to run agents in a secure fashion is a demanding experiment. On one hand LISP is a very flexible language that can be easily modified to add features and changes. Creating a function like **eval-hook-function** and giving it control of the execution process would be impossible in C. On the other hand, this flexibility can make plugging all of the security holes a difficult proposition. The creators of LISP made sure to add plenty of functionality to their language extensions and these can only create more trouble. The double-colon feature in the package mechanism is just one example of how the language was designed with hackers and programmers in mind— not security guards.

Chapter 11

TCL

─────────────────── The Hype ───────────────────

Free software with complete source code. What could be better?

─────────────────── Political Cynicism ───────────────────

Although TCL is distributed free, it is part of a large attempt at repressing the masses. Drug pushers also give alway free goods. Any extension language should be, first and foremost, a complete language.

─────────────────── The Buzzwords ───────────────────

TCL is a interpreted hybrid of LISP and C intended to act as a tool scripting language.

TCL is another good candidate for the *lingua franca* for an agent realm. The language started emerging from John Ousterhout's labs in the computer science department at Berkeley in 1987 and new versions with bug fixes and additions continue to roll out over time. Ousterhout and his students began work on the language as a way to bind together the thousands of little tools that students would write to handle tasks like opening files in a particular format or performing particular calculations.

Ordinarily, people would cut and paste source code together to do these tasks and then compile the mess of procedures and functions into a big application. This approach works well, but it can grow unwieldy when a programmer is trying to debug the interaction between two modules from different sources. Ousterhout hoped that TCL would act as a very high level language that could be used to glue together many little tools written in C. The language would be interpreted to make debugging simpler and it would also provide all of the computational firepower necessary to do almost everything in TCL itself if it became necessary. TCL would control tools, which explains why TCL is short for "Tool Control Language".

The TCL effort also spawned a set of tools that made it simple to build a user-interface in X-windows. This package known as Tk runs in TCL and acts like the Hypercard system that runs on Apple's Macintosh. Ousterhout offered the source code for the package free, which immediately made the language a popular option for programmers forced to develop user interfaces for UNIX workstations running X-windows. A large community grew up around the language as users began to exchange the different tools that they used. The modular basis of the language made it simple to grab a tool that would do a particular job and incorporate it into your project.

For instance, the American College of Radiology has a file format called NEMA that is often used to store computerized tomography images of people. If one programmer created a tool in TCL for opening up these files, then it could be exchanged with others. There are several different archives available on the Internet filled with other people's TCL solutions to problems. As of this writing in January 1995, archive at `harbor.ecn.purdue.edu` has the best collection. The strength of these archives and the help of the thousands of others who participate in the discussions of `comp.lang.tcl` each day are two of the most attractive features of this language.

Although TCL was designed for an entirely different purpose, its internal structure, cost and reputation make it a good candidate for the agent's programming. Many of the design decisions that Ousterhout made when he was looking for a lightweight inter-tool language happen to be the same ones that need to be made when constructing a playpen for agents. In many cases, the solutions were the same. TCL is an interpreted scripting language that encourages modular programs with many small tools. Tools and their metaprogram pass around TCL scripts in much the same way that people or our computers want to dispatch agents. It does not take a great leap to see the similarities.

One of the greatest arguments for exploring the use of TCL as an agent language is that someone else has already done most of the work. Rich Salz started a list for discussing the conversion and many people joined into the discussion. Nathaniel Borenstein and Marshall Rose created a version known as Safe-TCL that contains all of the hooks that allow it to read incoming mail and evaluate it in a safe manner. (See Chapter 12.) The incoming script will execute without being able to trash the host computer. They recently extended the work by demonstrating how to use PGP (Pretty Good Privacy discussed in Chapter 14) to check the digital signatures of the incoming messages. So, most of the lowest level work is already done.

As of this writing in January 1995, John Ousterhout is working at Sun Microsystems on an open project to port TCL and Tk to the Macintosh and Microsoft Windows. The code for this may be distributed by the time this book hits the market. Sun and Ousterhout are hoping that they can make TCL one of the default scripting languages used on the Internet. Giving away free source code is one of the best ways to do this if the source code is relatively bug-free.

The rest of this chapter will explore the basic structure of TCL as an introduction before exploring the modifications made to implement Safe-TCL in Chapter 12. Users who want a more complete description of TCL are encouraged to either read the documentation that comes with the on-line distribution or purchase John Ousterhout's book, *Tcl and the Tk Toolkit* [Ous94] I learned most of what is written here about TCL from those sources.

11.1   TCL: The language

TCL is a hybrid of C and LISP. The underlying structure is very similar to an interpreted version of LISP. The variables are interpreted dynamically and they can point to any data structure of arbitrary complexity. Some parts of the syntax are LISP-like and other parts are close to C. The endless nesting of parentheses from LISP is gone and the arithmetic looks like the algebraic expressions in C. The LISP convention of beginning each expression with a command and following it with the parameters is still used.

TCL also includes many features found in UNIX shell scripts. The language contains commands for matching regular expressions. The variables are all strings, which is very similar to the piping conventions used in the shell scripts. Some may wonder, in fact, if the shell scripts and plain C might be a better solution. They may be in some cases, but they are too onerous and slow for full-fledged applications that might be using Tk as a user interface. They also can't be compiled into an application to glue together several tools.

In general, the TCL syntax is more complex than LISP and often more C-like in detail. For instance, you invoke a variable by placing a dollar sign "$" in front of it. This prefix modification is quite similar to the low-level manipulation common in C. This may make it seem less elegant to many people. There is no reason, though, to get into the details of the criticism before the details of the language are explained.

11.1.1   Basic Structure

The basic unit in TCL is the *command*. Each line in a TCL script is considered to be a separate command, but two commands can also be put on each line by separating them with semi-colons (";"). This is how TCL avoids many of the parentheses found in LISP.

Each command is broken into *words*. A word is string of characters delineated by two characters that end words. Spaces, semi-colons and tabs end words, but these characters can be embedded inside words by using double quotation marks to mark the ends of words. The special characters like "$" are still interpreted inside these quotes and it is necessary to use a backslash ("\") to prevent them from being interpreted. The curly brackets ("{" and "}") are even more powerful than quotes. Any special characters found between them are treated as normal characters.

For example, the command

```
set age 40
```

sets the variable named "age" to be equal to 40. The two commands on one line

```
set response1 "Bob is age"; set response2 "Bob is $age"
```

set response1 to be the simple string "Bob is age". Ten characters, two spaces and no numerals. response2 on the other hand becomes "Bob is 40". The dollar sign triggered a variable substitution. The action of the special character is suppressed, though, between curly brackets.

```
set response3 {Bob is \$rich}
```

will make response3 the string "Bob is $rich", which might seem a bit pretentious.

The curly braces are often used in commands to delay execution. For instance, the command

```
if $a!=0 then {set b 4000/$a}
```

tests to see if the variable a is zero and sets b to be 4000/a if it isn't. This prevents the division expression from being evaluated when the command is first parsed. This structure is important in the definition of procedures and other commands which effectively delay computation until later.

The parser for TCL will break each script down into commands and each command into words. Then it *evaluates* or *executes* the command by looking up the first word in the command table. The rest of the words are the arguments to this command. This simple structure allows the parser to be small and simple. There is no reason to maintain look-ahead tables or other complex structures found in C or Pascal compilers.

The square brackets ("[" and "]") are used to invoke evaluation of a nested command. That is to say that they act like regular parentheses do in LISP. The command

```
set dog_age [expr $age /7]
```

converts the variable age defined above to be 40 into dog years by dividing by the so-called conversion factor of 7. The text between the square brackets can be any valid TCL script.

At this point, it is possible to point out that the differences between LISP and TCL are often quite superficial. Many of the parentheses are missing in TCL, but this is only because word separating and line separating characters have taken their place. A list of tokens doesn't need to have parentheses that enclose it. They're just assumed. If the parentheses were needed to start some execution, then the square brackets must be used instead.

Some programmers might argue that this approach is quite correct because it purifies the semantics. The two different meanings of the parentheses are now split up. The uses that could be eliminated were eliminated and the process of execution was bound to a new set of characters. Others might claim, just as correctly, that the semantics are now scrambled. It is possible to explain LISP as a simple process of repeatedly taking apart lists and applying the first command to the rest of the list.

11.1.2   Variables

All of the variables in TCL are strings. If the command **set age 90** is executed, it will not place the binary value of 90 ("1011010") in some four byte integer. TCL will store the string of two characters, "9" and "0". This structure has its advantages when you are building LISP-like self-referential scripts that will build up programs on the fly and execute them. It can be a pain, though, when you're trying to do arithmetic.

If you type:

```
set age 45 ; set dog_age $age/7
```

the parser will find a command that tries to match dog_age to a variable with the title "age/7" which is almost certain to cause an error. The square brackets must be used. If you type:

```
set age 45;set dog_age age/7,
```

the variable dog_age will be bound to the string "age/7". This might be useful if you're building up a command to be executed later.

There are several other commands besides set that are useful for manipulating variables. They are:

append This adds the second argument to the end of the first argument.

incr This adds the amount of the second argument to the variable in the first argument and stores it as a character string variable.

unset This deletes the variable from the TCL's storage.

trace This binds a command string to a variable that is called whenever the variable is touched during execution.

array This can be used to build arrays and search through them.

global This sets a variable to be a global variable accessable by all functions being executed. Normally, variables are local to procedures.

Variables can also be arrays. The commands

```
set planet(1) Mercury;set planet(2) Venus; set planet(x)
Vulcan
```

creates an array with three different values stuck in the boxes labeled 1, 2 and X. The numbers 1 and 2 are not acting as integers that compute an offset into a block of memory as they would in C. They are simply strings that are matched to other strings. The array mechanism works like the LISP command assoc does with a list of pairs.

Some programmers may be tempted to use the array structure to create two-dimensional or greater arrays. This is certainly possible, but programmers must be aware of internal structure or else they may encounter bizarre errors. For instance, the commands:

```
set tictactoe(1,1) X;

set tictactoe(2,2) O;

set tictactoe(3,2) X
```

seems to be placing X's and O's in a two dimensional grid of character strings. It is only matching up the strings 1,1 with X, 2,2 with O and 3,2 with X. If you try and evaluate `tictactoe(1, 1)` with an extra space between the comma and the second one, then you will receive an error. The parser will break the string into two parts `tictactoe(1,` and `1)`. This can be quite dangerous and unpredictable if you don't expect it.

The potential for this type of error emerges because TCL takes such a different approach to variables. Everything is a string. This is quite different from many of the common languages that programmers learn to use. There are often advantages to this approach, but the disadvantages like this are why some people consider TCL to be a toy language.

11.2   String Manipulation

In TCL, strings are the only game. This is why there are more than a handful of commands that will manipulate strings. These commands can be strung together to do much of the basic parsing and string manipulation. Many programmers and computer science professors are fond of making a big deal about LISP's `lambda` and `eval` functions because they allow you to do plenty of self-referential programming. You can do the same with TCL, and I think that it is often a more natural process. In many cases, the output of any computer program is a string, so if you do the computation in this format, there is no need to convert it for output. In LISP, you must constantly convert lists of words into strings and then break them apart again. When the job, however, is to produce abstract mathematics or non-lingual results, LISP is a better tool.

The TCL string functions are:

format *format-string* **value₁ etc** The format works like the C `printf` functions. It will scan through *format-string* looking for instructions like "%4d" which tells it to stick in a number here with four decimals places kept. The numbers are the values that are at the end of the argument list.

string *operation* **string₁ string₂** This will apply *operation* to compare the two strings. The possible operations are:

compare Returns 1 if lexicographically greater, 0 if equal and -1 if less than. "Beth" is greater than "Charlie" which generates a 1.

match Returns 1 if **string₁** matches **string₂** if the common regular expression characters are used. "Alpha*" matches "Alphabet".

first Finds the first instance of when **string₁** can be found in **string₂**. The index of this position is returned if the match is found and -1 if it isn't. If **string₁** is "e" and **string₂** is "The quick brown fox jumped over the lazy dog", the answer is 2.

last Finds the last instance of when **string₁** can be found in **string₂**. The first command done backwards. If **string₁** is "e" and **string₂** is "The quick brown fox jumped over the lazy dog", the answer is 29.

trimleft Starts at the beginning of **string₁** and removes all characters that can be found **string₂**. If **string₂** isn't specified, then it is assumed to include the space, tab, newline and carriage return. This is normally used to strip off extraneous spaces for parsing, but it can be occasionally useful for other tasks.

trimright This is **trimleft** done backwards.

trim Both **trimleft** and **trimright**.

index Converts **string₂** into a number and pulls out the character at that position. The first character is number 0.

There are also some `string` commands that only take one argument. They are:

length Returns the length of string$_1$. "Fred" would return 4.

tolower Converts the string to lower case. "Lucy" becomes "lucy".

toupper Converts it to upper case. "Ricky" becomes "RICKY".

There is also one that takes three arguments. It is **range**. The second and third arguments are converted into numbers and the characters at positions with indexes in between these values are returned. "Carpenter", "3" and "5" returns "pen".

regexp string$_1$ string$_2$ determines if string$_2$ is in the set of regular expressions defined by string$_2$. The syntax of this command is different from the rest because it can be modified by the strings "-nocase" and "-indicies" that turn off case matching and change the output to include the positions of the match. The command will also take two optional variables for collecting the information about just what matched.

regsub string$_1$ string$_2$ string$_3$ string$_4$ Tries to match the regular expression in string$_1$ with string$_2$. String$_4$ emerges as a copy of *string$_2$* with replacements specified by string$_3$. This is a powerful way to manipulate strings.

scan string$_1$ string$_2$ string$_3$ etc... This is the opposite of `format`. It will match up string$_1$ with the format defined by string$_2$ and place the values in *string$_3$* etc.

The regular expression manipulation routines are powerful additions. They make it possible to do fairly complicated searching through the string. This allows you to write games like Eliza or Doctor very easily, for instance, as well as provide slightly better user interfaces. In general, though, you need this extra power if you're going to manipulate strings and convert them into commands with slightly different meanings. If you're going to replace the third word in a command string, you must be able to detect quotation marks and curly brackets that could bundle several words into one.

11.3   Arithmetic

If strings are the first-class, only-type-of-choice in TCL, it is not surprising that numerical work often falls far behind. This is, unfortunately, a real problem if you're trying to do serious number crunching. Converting every number into a string before operating on it is a slow and onerous process. Then, when you store it back into a variable it gets converted again. If a small percentage (5%) of the work is arithmetic, then this effect will be minimal. But no one should blithely implement an eigenvalue finding program in TCL and not be surprised.

The effect of these strings numbers is not bad if you're using TCL in a program. You are free to implement your own C functions to do the heavy work and let TCL provide the glue between the functions. This limitation may be a serious one for the agent world. No one really knows what agents will be created in the near future. It may be quite popular to code up strange numerical recipes for solving differential equations and ship them off to a CRAY. No interpreted language like the ones considered in this book would be appropriate for this. But there are many other normal tasks that could use some efficient mathematics from time to time.

Any C programmer will be comforted by the syntax chosen for TCL. It is largely borrowed from ANSI C. Ousterhout did fix some of the ambiguities of the language that occasionally make it difficult to port code. arithmetic operations are often invoked by the **expr** command which concatenates all of the words passes as parameters and then evaluates the entire string as a long expression. One example is:

```
expr (4.0-7)*3.1
```

This evaluates to -9.3. The standard C formats for scientific notation ("6.23e+23" or "14.2E4") are supported. Any number beginning with an "0x" is interpreted as a hexadecimal string and any number beginning with a "0" is considered an octal value. (Be wary of this potential bug.)

Arithmetic operations take precedence in the normal fashion. Left to right. From the inside of nesting out. Multiplication and division before addition and substraction. There are no surprises. The basic operations are addition (+), subtraction (-), multiplication (*), division (/). The bitwise operations are AND (&), OR (|) and the logical conjunctions are AND (&&) and OR (||). Comparisons are no surprise: less than (<), greater than (>), less than or equal to (<=), greater than or equal to (>=). They return 1 if true and 0 if false and also work on all alphanumerical strings. Some of the less obvious operations are:

!x If x is 0 then it returns 1. Otherwise it returns 0.

$\tilde{x}$ Bitwise not.

x%y The remainder or modulo. Note in TCL this is always positive even if x or y is not.

x<<y Shift x to the left by y bits. Zeros appear in the lowest order bits.

x>>y Shift x to the right by y bits. In TCL, this is guaranteed to be arithmetically correct shifting. Numbers are stored in two's complement form and the highest-order bits are duplicated. Negative values are filled with 1's and positive values are filled with 0s.

x?y:z If x is true then return y else return z.

There are also many of the usual scientific functions. Sine (sin), cosine (cos), tangent (tan), their inverses (asin, acos, atan) and their hyperbolic cousins (sinh, cosh, tanh). Natural log (log) has an inverse (exp), but if you want to invert the log in base 10 (log10), you must use the power function pow(a,b) which raises a to the b-th power. Each of these functions are applied in a normal, C-like way. tan(2.2) or sqrt(sin(3.14)). do not operate like TCL commands which must be at the beginning of expressions. This is a bit of a semantic inconsistency. Any procedures or commands defined by the user must be executed as commands. This may lead to some disharmony, but it was necessary to make the parser simple. If an expr command is encountered, then TCL merely feeds the arguments into the arithmetic expression evaluator. There is no need to add new elements to a parse table, or determine elements like look-ahead or other features.

TCL uses C's ints for integers and doubles for real numbers. The amount of precision depends upon the machine for which the current TCL interpreter was compiled. When TCL converts a number back into a string, it will only keep 6 significant digits unless you ask it to keep more. The value of `tcl_precision` controls this process. If you want 10 digits, then set `tcl_precision` to 10.

11.4 Lists

The basic data structure in TCL is the string, but the list is a close second. TCL will create lists of strings and nest these lists to build trees in much the same way that LISP operates. In fact, much is the same. Lists are delineated on a command line with curly braces ("{" and "}") and their elements are separated by the standard word separation characters (space, tab).

Lists are simple to build.

```
set party_list {Mathew Fred Mary Jane}
```

creates a standard list and

```
set state_of_mind {{New York} California {Rhode Island}
Connecticut}
```

will start a tree.

There are more than a handful of commands that are useful for manipulating lists. They are:

concat $list_1$ $list_2$... Concatenates the lists in the arguments and returns the result in one list. The highest-level elements of each list are joined into one long list.

list $list_1$ $list_2$... Creates a list of $list_1$ $list_2$ etc. This treats each list as an individual element in the new list and is useful for building up nested trees.

lappend var_name_1 $list_2$... Adds lists $list_2$ etc to the end of var_name_1 which should be the variable name of a list.

`linsert list`$_1$ `index list`$_2$... Inserts lists `list`$_2$ etc. before element numbered index in `list`$_1$.

`lreplace list`$_1$ `first last list`$_2$... Delete the elements with the index `first` and `last` and all elements in between. If `list`$_2$ etc. are in the command, then insert them here.

`lrange list`$_1$ `first last` Remove the elements with index `first` and `last` and those in between and return them.

`lsearch list item` Search through the list for the item and return the index value of where it is found. Return -1 if it isn't. Glob matching rules are assumed, but regular expressions or exact matching can be switched on.

`lsort list` Sort the list. The switch `-decreasing` sets the order to decreasing instead of the default, increasing.

`split string chars` Convert a string into a list. Break the string into elements whenever a character is encountered that is found in `chars`.

`join list a` Concatenates all of the elements in `list` together and places `a` in between them.

The list structure is the proper structure that emerges from the TCL parser after it breaks apart the string into words and performs the necessary substitutions. Then the result is fed to the evaluation routine in list form. Creating commands with these list expressions is one way to circumvent the parsing routine. In fact, it is often better to use the list structure because it properly handles ambiguities that might be created by the protean, type-free structure of TCL. For instance, the command `set x $y` will fail if `$y` happens to be a two-word string like "Dallas Cowboys". The TCL parser will create a four-word list that will crash the `set` command expecting three words. If the list structure is used to build this up, then it will work correctly.

11.5   Control Structure

TCL has many C-like control structures for channelling the flow of computation. They are C-like in outward appearance only because many of the commands contain ambiguities and problems that are caused by TCL's interpret-me-now structure. If the commands aren't put together with the correct punctuation, they'll execute incorrectly. The potential errors are much like the ones that are caused by confusing the C commands "x=0" and "x==0".

The if command is straightforward. A prototypical example of a chain of ifs and elses looks like this:

> if {test1} {*command to be executed if test1 is 1* } else if {test2} {*command string to be executed if test2 is 1*} else if {test3} {... } else {*command string to be executed if nothing worked yet.* }

There are two main loop constructs. The first, the while loop, uses a test and body. The test is executed before each execution of the body. An example is:

> while {Elvis != [lindex x $i]} {incr i 1}

This scans through a list looking for the element that is equal to "Elvis". It does not test for the end of the list or initialize x or i to anything in particular.

The second loop construction, the for loop, includes an initialization script, the termination criteria, the reinitialization script and the body of the loop. The initialization script is executed before the first pass through the body and the reinitialization script is executed before each subsequent pass. It would be possible to do all of this with a while loop, but Ousterhout probably chose to include this definition because of its C-like form and its greater structure.

An example of this is:

> for {set i 0} {($i <= [length x]) || (Elvis != [lindex x $i])} {incr i } {}

This loop does the same thing, but all of the functionality is moved into the structured scripts. There is nothing left for the body of the loop to do. You are free to choose which loop construct works best for the occasion.

A third way to loop is to use the `foreach` command, which applies a script to each element of the list in turn. The command is similar in spirit to LISP's `map` command. There are three parameters fed to the `foreach` command. The first is the name of a variable that is found in the third parameter, a TCL script. The elements of the second parameter are placed in this variable one by one and then the script is executed for each of them. The Elvis script can be rewritten in this form:

```
foreach a x {if {Elvis = a} {set answer $i}; incr i}
```

In this case, the variable `answer` gets the index value of where the string "Elvis" can be found. The variable i should be initialized to 0 at the beginning to ensure accurate results. This is not the best application for this construct. It is better used to handle lists that may be flexible collections of contents.

TCL also contains two of the popular C functions for exiting a loop. The `break` command halts the execution of a loop immediately. The `continue` command just stops execution of the current pass through the body of the loop. It is equivalent to a `goto` command aimed to land just after the last line in the current body of the loop. Execution then continues without any residual effect.

11.5.1   EVALs

For every set of C constructions, TCL usually contains one or more LISP constructs. The major contribution of LISP to the control flow of a TCL program is the `eval` command which will immediately begin to parse and execute any string that it receives. This can be quite useful if you want to try metaprogramming in your system. It is also a trick that can be used to work around some of the semantic irregularities of TCL.

Unfortunately, the variable substitution phase may not glue parameters together in the best way. For instance, the `list` command creates a list of all of the parameters that follow it. What if the variable f contains the four values, april may june july? The command list $f will wrap another level of list nesting around this list. But, the command eval list $f will execute list april may june july and return the list without the extra level of nesting: {{april may june july}}. This difference can be a useful trick if you happen to be using a variable to store up parameters for other commands like unset.

This work-around may be a bit ungraceful, but it is almost impossible to avoid in the definition of languages that are as untyped and flexible as TCL. If users can pass around lists of parameters and meld them with commands, then there must be some meeting of the minds. Either the list will be coerced into looking like a normal list of parameters or the command will need to be powerful enough to scan through the parameters to intuit when a list is around. Although all of the commands might be forced to be this accepting, the bloating alone would be inacceptable. It would also be impossible to do correctly with the list manipulation commands that already accept lists at face value.

11.6 Procedures

TCL has procedures like any other language. They make it easy to write flexible code. TCL users might write up an early version of a function in a TCL procedure and then rewrite it in C and install it as a command later if greater performance is necessary. Agents will get the flexibility to create new procedures, but they won't be able to add the commands at the C level. That would be a security hole.

The format for a procedure is simple:

```
proc hypoteneuse {x y} {expr sqrt(($x*$x)+($y*$y))}
```

The first element, proc, is the command that binds the procedure in memory. The second is the name of the procedure. The third is the list of parameters and their variable names; and the fourth element is the body of the procedure.

The command **return** can be included in the body of the procedure. When it is encountered, the procedure's execution ends and the one parameter to the **return** command is returned as the value. If no **return** command is encountered, then the result of the last command is returned. This is what happens in the **hypoteneuse** function above.

TCL's parser preprocesses this line before the result in stored away in a list form. This means that the basic mechanism of TCL's parser can be exploited for extra flexibility and occasional grief. For instance, the parameter list might be replaced by a variable like this:

```
{proc statcrunch $params { complicated function}}
```

The variable **params** might include a flexible number of parameters that vary along with some of the details in the complicated function. On some days, there might be four elements in **params** and on other days there might be three.

The operation of the parser would replace **params** with the list of parameters when the procedure was created. However, the variable names in the body of the procedure won't be evaluated until the procedure is invoked. If the value of **params** changes, it won't matter. Programmers should be careful with this trick because it could be more of a curse than a blessing.

11.6.1 Global and Local Storage

In TCL there are global and local variables. The local ones are used only in the current execution of a procedure. The values stored in these variables, though, are not persistent. They disappear at the end of the current invocation. The parameters to the procedure and any variables created by the **set** command are all local. The global variables can be accessed at any time, but any access must be done through a special command **global**. Executing **global alpha beta** will direct all calls $alpha or $beta to the global versions of **alpha** or **beta**.

TCL also contains an interesting command intended to allow both call-by-reference schemes and access to the variables on the stack. The command, **upvar $a b** looks up the value of a and calls it b locally. Now all calls for $b will get the value of a. This is useful because TCL's procedures do not pass values. They receive the values as strings during the interpretation of the code. This is a safe way to do pointer manipulation. The command is typically used to access values of arrays that cannot be passed directly as parameters. The solution is to pass the name of the array in a parameter and then use the `upvar` command to bind a local variable to the array.

The `upvar` command also allows deep access to variables that might be on the stack. The first parameter can direct the lookup process to a particular level of the stack. If the value "#0" is passed, then TCL looks for the variable at the global level. A negative number like "-2" would imply that TCL should look for a variable by that name in two stack frames up the stack.

11.7 Summary

This chapter can provide two different forms of information. First, it introduces the TCL language. This will allow neophytes to play around with the TCL distributions. Second, it provides some contrast for the reader who is concerned with language issues. TCL has many similarities to LISP, but it also has differences. Borenstein and Rose found it ideal for building a safe agent language because it had the ability to link in C code very effectively.

Others reacted very strongly against the language including Richard Stallman, the programmer who gained a large amount of fame by boldly stating that software should be free and then acting upon his convictions. Many computers on the Internet run software that he either wrote himself or helped create. His GNU project (which stands for GNU is Not Unix) continues to deliver free software.

Recently, he provoked a strong and almost everlasting debate on the Internet by proposing that TCL was a bad choice for an extension language. He wrote in his posting about his experiences with Emacs, a popular text editor that could be extended using a dialect of LISP:

> The principal lesson of Emacs is that a language for extensions should not be a mere "extension language". It should be a real programming language, designed for writing and maintaining substantial programs. Because people will want to do that!

The language of TCL is not rich enough, in his eyes, to permit programmers to do all that they want to do. There are not many of the constructions that we take for granted. He continues:

> Tcl was not designed to be a serious programming language. It was designed to be a "scripting language", on the assumption that a "scripting language" need not try to be a real programming language. So Tcl doesn't have the capabilities of one. It lacks arrays; it lacks structures from which you can make linked lists. It fakes having numbers, which works, but has to be slow. Tcl is ok for writing small programs, but when you push it beyond that, it becomes insufficient.

The lack of structures like linked lists and arrays can cause major problems with some algorithms and change their running time. If there are no arrays, for instance, then the algorithm must search through an entire data list before finding the right piece of data. These extra searches add up and may add another factor of n to the computational complexity.

Stallman also feels that an extension language should be used by the programmer of the system to add many of the features. This allows any new programmer trying to add functionality to the system to use these features as the basis for their code. This proposition, though, seems to miss the point. TCL is really a language aimed at C programmers who want to be able to program in C, but have more flexibility to link up their work. These are two different types of programming and they can function independently at both of these levels.

Ousterhout write in response to Stallman on the Internet:

> Thus I designed Tcl to make it really easy to drop down into C or C++ when you come across tasks that make more sense in a lower-level language. This way Tcl doesn't have to solve all of the world's problems. Stallman appears to prefer an approach where a single language is used for everything, but I don't know of a successful instance of this approach. Even Emacs uses substantial amounts of C internally, no?

In the end, Ousterhout argues that users eventually choose the tool that makes their job more productive. LISP and Scheme had their chance, he feels, and there never was a mass conversion to these languages. They may be flexible, but they don't help the average programmer get the job done. TCL, he hopes, will win a substantial number of the decisions when programmers begin to choose between TCL and any LISP-based extension language.

This free market approach is certainly ideal. Readers of this book can choose between the implementation in LISP and an implementation in TCL.

Chapter 12

Safe-TCL

——————————— The Hype ———————————

Free Agent Land with complete source code. What could be better?

——————————— Political Cynicism ———————————

Safe-TCL illustrates the dangerous compromises we make with our freedom in order to negotiate security. Fear is the anti-opiate of the masses.

——————————— The Buzzwords ———————————

Safe-TCL is an extended subset of the interpreted hybrid of LISP and C intended to act as an agent scripting language.

161

Safe-TCL is one of the first attempts at building a system for what Nathaniel Borenstein and Marshall Rose, its authors, called "Enhanced Mail." That is, mail that would be able to ask the recipient questions and do something intelligent with the response. A mail message could have a button saying, "Push here to order a Hacme e-mail shredder that slices and dices your e-mail into little bits so it can't be read." When you pushed the button, the program underneath would pop up a dialog box asking for address and other information. Or it might extract the address information from the local host. All of this is packed up and sent off to the warehouse for shipping in a return message.

This approach to electronic mail sounds similar to agents. In fact, the only real difference lies in the scope of the metaphor. Enhanced mail seems to revolve around messages between people that include some functionality. Agents are broader in concept because agents should be able to roam through deep, hidden regions of the Net to accomplish their missions without coming into contact with humans unless they need to do so. But the difference is all in the packaging. At the bottom, both of the systems are just sets of programs that run in a restricted domain. Boring old programs that might as well be written in BASIC.

The approach taken by Borenstein and Rose illustrates a solid method for converting an ordinary scripting language into an agent space. Many of the design decisions they made could be used in other contexts and other languages. Their basic theory was that if freedom comes with responsibility, then scripts that can't act responsibly must have their freedom curtailed. If some part of TCL might be used irresponsibly by some incoming TCL script with intent to cause havoc, then it should be left out of Safe-TCL.

12.1   MIME Time

Safe-TCL evolved out of the MIME (Multipurpose Internet Mail Extensions) standard for converting e-mail into more than just an ASCII text mover. The original Request for Comment (RFC 1341) written by Borenstein and Freed laid out a simple way that new additions to the e-mail header could be used to specify the contents of the message. It was, in essence, a standard way to tag a mail message so that the mailer could take it apart and process it correctly. If a message contained a message and a photography in GIF format, then the mailer would be able to send the data for the photo to the right software for displaying it. The MIME tags provided all of the information.

The MIME format, though, was essentially a one-way mechanism. It described how to bundle up data so it could survive the e-mail journey to be unpacked at a MIME-compliant host. The format alone was not enough to support enhanced mail interactions. So, they added two new tags that would be used to support Safe-TCL. The first, `application/Safe-Tcl`, tags any subpart of a message and identifies it as a block of code that should be fed to a Safe-TCL interpreter. This tag comes with two different parameters: `version` and `evaluation-time`. The version specifies the version of the underlying TCL compiler that the script is intended to run upon. At the time of this section's writing in late fall 1994, Safe-TCL only runs on version 7.3.

The `evaluation-time` parameter specifies when the incoming script should be run. There are two possible values for this parameter: `delivery` or `activation`. If a script arrives with `evaluation-time` set to `delivery`, then the mailer should feed the script to the Safe-TCL interpreter as soon as possible. The script cannot expect to interact with any human because it could be arriving at any time. It can, however, expect to find the Safe-TCL local functions ready to go. This type of setting might be used to correspond with anonymous information robots waiting to answer demands. It is, in essence, an agent realm. The other setting, `activation`, is used to provide some active interaction to actual electronic mail. The mailer should feed the script to the interpreter when the user asks to read the message. These scripts should be able to put boxes on the screen and interact with the recipient. The Hacme sales message falls into this category. If other companies discover this feature, the flood of junk mail may destroy the Net.

The new lines in the header of such a message should look like this:

```
Content-type:application/Safe-Tcl; version=''7.3'';
evaluation-time=activation
```

The second type of tag is a meta-definition for handling blocks like this. It's tag is `multipart/enabled-mail` which signals a MIME-compliant mailer that this mail message should be handled as a Safe-TCL script. That is, if a Safe-TCL interpreter is available, then it should run the script immediately and let the script control the display of the rest of the message. If a Safe-TCL interpreter is not set up locally, then the mail handler should just display the rest of the message as if the Safe-TCL script was not included. This allows messages to arrive at MIME mailers without Safe-TCL and still be read. This behavior makes it possible to send complicated scripts to large mailing lists and be sure that even the non-TCL-enabled users will be able to make some sense of the message.

12.2   Deconstructing TCL

Borenstein and Rose call Safe-TCL an "extended subset" of TCL. They mean that they kept the "safe" parts of the language that could be executed without causing problems on the local machine and added some features to enhance its ability to handle incoming e-mail requests. The result is something that should execute TCL scripts and prevent rogue scripts from doing harm.

At the foundation, Safe-TCL and regular TCL are identical. The syntax is unchanged and the entire structure of parser and variable creator is left intact. This makes sense. Changing the syntax would create a new language and cancel any of the good that might come from using a known language like TCL. Luckily, the lowest level of the TCL structure can be preserved intact because it does not allow pointer manipulation or any other simple means to attack the memory or other system resources. It would make little sense to try to create Safe-C because the syntax allows so many "dangerous" actions that could be exploited by malicious agents or their programmers.

The syntax of TCL may be pure, but the standard collection of functions is far from safe. There are more than enough functions that allow strange side-effects that could be used to trash files and make mayhem. Rose and Borenstein made a survey of these functions, kept some and threw away some others. Although it may be impossible to tell if the ones they kept are pure, it is often easy to determine just what made the excluded functions so dangerous. In some cases, bad functions had side-effects or intended effects that changed the state of the general system in an uncontrolled fashion such as writing or reading data from the disk drives.

In other cases, the excluded functions provided information about the files on the system or the state of the machine that were not necessary for a normal Safe-TCL script. This information could only be used for malicious ends. Although the Safe-TCL script might not have an immediate ability to do something with the data, it is best to keep it from the script to be on the safe side. A small hole might emerge in a locally adapted function that would be able to use this information.

Here is a list of the standard functions from TCL 7.3 that were excluded in Safe-TCL. The descriptions are by no means complete, but it might serve as an inspiration for anyone trying to clean up and purify another language.

auto_execok

auto_load

auto_mkindex This function scans through a directory and builds up a list of all TCL functions to be found in libraries. A malicious agent could use this function to search for other functions that might be defined in other libraries. These could include "Send_Bank_Info" or "Destroy_All_Files." Once these are indexed, the auto loader will automatically load the functions whenever a script asks for them.

auto_reset

cd A TCL script uses this to change directories. If other TCL libraries containing functions were found in a different directory, then a wayward agent might stumble upon them.

close At first glance, there is no problem letting a TCL script *close* a random access file. It's opening them and reading that means trouble. This command does have a side-effect: if a script manages to close a file, then the next read to it would generate errors. Imagine that some local command is using a local file to process information. This file might contain access rules that block access to agents from certain places. It could be, for instance, a list of bad check writers or others to be excluded. Normally, a local function would check this file for the name of the agent's owner and lock out the agent if the name was found in the file. If the agent could close the file, the search for the name might return empty-handed and the host might welcome the agent. Bingo. Security breach. This is just one possible scenario.

eof This is a very benign function. It only returns information about the position in the file. It does not change the state of the file system. I believe that it was left out to be complete.

exec Execute a process. Ousterhout's *TCL and the Tk Toolkit*[Ous94] even uses the example `exec rm main.o` which allows a script to execute the UNIX command for removing the file `main.o`. This is damaging enough to warrant banning the command for good.

file The file command is an all-purpose tool for examining the details of files. A TCL script can use it to probe for information like the date the file was last accessed, the owner and other details. An incoming agent could also search for the names of certain files that matched many criteria. This information alone might be interesting to spies or hackers because it would disclose which libraries and other structures might be installed. At the very least, it is like leaving valuables in plain sight on the rear seat of a car. Potential criminals know where to look.

The information about the installation could even be useful in strange ways, even if there are no files on the system with tempting names like "MyPasswords" or "CreditCardNumbers". Let's say that "PGP" is some file that contains the PGP code. Some of the earlier versions allow minor tampering with message blocks that doesn't invalidate the digital signature. A malicious agent might try to determine which version of PGP was checking the security of incoming messages. If it was an old version, then hole is ready and waiting.

flush Ousterhout's book, *TCL and the Tk Toolkit* defines this function as "Writes out any buffered output..." This command is quite useful if the agent could write directly to this buffer. It probably can't because the `puts` command is sure to be disabled. Could `flush` be used by itself to cause havoc? Only if some other function is writing something to a buffer with the intent of catching it before it gets to disk. Imagine that there is some paycheck function that issues a paycheck to the incoming agent. The function first writes the full value of the check to the buffer with the `puts` command, knowing full well that it will change the value later if any outstanding debts appear. The agent might be able to use a `flush` to push the value onto the disk. This is, without a doubt, an unlikely scenario. Only a bad programmer would leave something in the buffer that couldn't be written to disk. The semantics make it just too dangerous. It does show, though, what a creative mind might be able to do with side-effects like this.

gets Reads the next line from a file. There is no reason to let the incoming agent be able to read data at will. Everything should be filtered by new local commands that control access directly.

glob Finds all files that match a particular pattern. This does not change the state of the machine, but it does convey information. This can be dangerous for all of the reasons discussed in the entry on the `file` command.

open Opens a random file. There is no reason to allow unconditional access to all files. The best solution is to maintain special local commands that check out the request and ensure that it is only directed at proper files.

pid This command returns the process id of either the currently running command or the id of another running command. This does not cause any direct side-effects, but it does return information that can be used to create havoc. There is no legitimate need for the agent to know about process ids, so it is better to keep them inaccessible.

puts Writes a string to the file buffer for a particular output stream. This is really the most dangerous command out there. It should always be filtered by a local command.

pwd Returns the full path name of the current directory. There are no side-effects and only the barest minimum of information changes hands. This could probably be left unprotected, but it is best to be complete and deny the incoming agent all access to the file system.

read Reads a block from a file. Definitely opens up a spigot of data that can let the user into plenty of dangerous corners of the system. Even if there is no secret information available, the agent can gather knowledge about the functions and software available.

seek Move the file pointer to a specific location. This does not return any information, but it does have a side-effect. Imagine that some protected local function was looking for information in a file and stepping through it line by line with the **gets** command. This means that it is not specifically checking its location. If an agent is able to inject a **seek** command that moves the pointer in the file, then it could redirect the reading process and screw up the local command.

source

tell Finds the current position of the file pointer. This is only information. There are no side-effects. There is no reason, though, why an agent might need to know this information unless it was using the file system. Why let it in?

time This is used to time the performance of TCL scripts. It could be thought of as just a debugging device. This does execute a script.

unknown This command allows a programmer to patch up holes in commands. It is invoked by the TCL interpreter if it can't find a particular command that was requested. The **unknown** function is responsible for looking for this and satisfying the request. Normally, TCL comes with a default version of **unknown** that will exploit a number of stop-gap measures in the hope of getting the command to run. It will search for the file in other TCL libraries, check to see if it is a shell command and even look for abbreviations.

How can this be used for ill? The default unknown function in Safe-TCL may check certain libraries for functions. If a programmer can invoke a new unknown command, then it could remove some of this filtering. Or, it could confound the operation of a local command. Imagine that this local command invoked another command by some abbreviation that was normally caught by the unknown function. Suppose that the unknown function seized control of the execution chain for a moment. A rogue version of the unknown could grab control in that fleeting moment.

This list is conservative. In many cases, some functions are excluded that only provide the most benign information to the incoming agent. Borenstein and Rose took an extreme approach when they decided what shouldn't be available. This is a good policy because computer security is such a slippery process. Seemingly benign tools can often be used for dangerous ends and the simplest approach is often to bar the door to all comers.

Some programmers might be tempted to allow some of these functions under the same types of reasoning that holds that a single bullet isn't dangerous without a gun. This is a fair assertion. It's does not really seem possible to cause that much damage with the pid command. A programmer might be tempted to let incoming agents execute this command so they can check to see if some local information server is running. This is a fair approach. Why bother to define an entirely new TCL command Is_Info_Server_Running when an agent could execute pid InfoMeister to see if it owns a process id?

The answer, unfortunately, is often unclear. If there is a known way to abuse a command like pid, then it is easy to exclude it. But there may be other hidden ways to exploit the process identifier that may not seem obvious. Host programmers must often make tough choices in matters like this. They may choose to allow the command because the promise is greater than the potential for pain.

Host programmers must make similar choices whenever a new command is added to the collection. Commands can have strange side-effects in the most unexpected places. Any command that is available to the incoming agent could be used in unexpectedly dangerous ways.

12.3   Two Interpreters

If the main file functions are blocked, then how can any local commands use the file system if they need to do so? One solution is to parse all of the incoming code and check to make sure that it isn't calling a restricted command. This is one approach that is used in the basic XLISP example given in Chapter 10. The local, "trusted" commands would still have access to the file functions and the other dangerous commands. This solution may work, but it could easily be tricked with the `eval` function. An incoming TCL script could create a string with the restricted commands in it and `eval` it. The `eval` command could be added to the list of restricted commands, but this could be a severe inconvenience. At the very least, the command is often needed to do type casting and string gluing when the syntax makes it impossible to do some things normally. This is one example of how important it is to design languages so they act cleanly and don't rely upon shortcuts or side-effects.

Borenstein and Rose designed Safe-TCL to use two interpreters: one for the untrusted code and one for the trusted. This is relatively easy to do because the TCL code is written in C. Each interpreter is just a data structure with pointers to the main state of the interpreter. The Safe-TCL C program creates two interpreters and blocks out the offending commands in the version responsible for running the "untrusted" incoming agent. The local commands that might be used to provide data or answers run in the "trusted" interpreter. There are also two commands that let each interpreter evaluate a script in the other.

This structure has enormous advantages. There is no need to check each script and the strings that it `eval`s to ensure that they are free of offending commands. The standard TCL mechanism returns an error if the bad commands are called because the commands aren't defined in the "untrusted" interpreter.

When the Safe-TCL process begins, it loads any new local functions into the trusted interpreter. If any of the functions are to be made open to the incoming agents, then this library should execute `DeclareHarmless` with the name of the command. This does not cause the command to be installed in the untrusted interpreter— it just tells Safe-TCL to install a new command in the untrusted interpreter that points across the barrier. The command is executed in the trusted interpreter and then the result is returned.

12.4   In with the New

If all of the functions that cause side-effects are removed from the reach of the incoming agent, then something must take their place. After all, side-effects and information transfer are the only way that an agent interacts with its host and there must be some interaction to make the trip worthwhile. The trick is to offer very filtered access that cannot be misused by the incoming agent.

Normally, new functions that offer services would be added by the local host programmer. This is not a hard task, but it is one that could introduce new security holes. TCL is filled with dangers like this because the only data structure is a string and these strings are occasionally turned into commands with the `eval` command. Some of these problems can be avoided using some of these guidelines:

Use `eval` *judiciously.* This command converts a string into action. Before using the command, carefully consider where the string came from. Could it contain some data that began as part of an agent? If so, don't allow it. The string might be used to transfer a string like "DeclareHarmless open". If this is evaluated, it allows the incoming agent to use the command `open` with no trouble. Remember that the `eval` command is often used to typecast lists.

Don't offer general access. Set up a list of local tags that an incoming agent can use to request data. Don't let it specify data with a general file name. This is just an invitation to trouble. You may be sure that the

file command is blocked off and there is no way an agent can scan
the file system, but the incoming agent might know enough about the
system to guess the nomenclature and cause trouble.

Offer primitive functions. Several small functions that can be combined to
    do the task are better than a large, omnibus function. This is the TCL
    way that Ousterhout endorses. It also makes good sense for a security
    conscious Safe-TCL programmer. Small commands are easier to check
    for dangerous behavior. See the next entry for an exception.

If small is dangerous, choose large commands. Many smaller commands
    might be more flexible, but they can also be dangerous if they leave
    crucial data in the hands of the agent. Imagine that there is a func-
    tion Return_Data_File key that takes the key and finds the path
    to the right data file containing that information. Anyone after the
    data would then feed the path to Read_File file_name and get the
    data. Ordinarily, this is a good architectural decision. The agent
    might choose to run Return_Data_File on several different keys and
    then intersect the results before calling Read_File. But, the command
    structure also leaves the file names in the hands of the agent, who can
    munge them into any name they want in the interim. A safer solution,
    alas, is to build a bigger function that takes requests, parses them and
    does all of the boolean interaction internally.

These suggestions are just guidelines. Some of them even contradict each
other. There will be times when it makes sense to break the rules. Just try
to imagine what a hacker would do in your place.

12.5   Safe-TCL Extensions

Safe-TCL is an extended subset. Section 12.2 discussed what functions need
to be excluded make it safe. This section examines what extra functions
must be added to make it work. At the very least, some replacement must
be found for the file system because it is the traditional way that a TCL
script interacts with its environment and finds the data it needs to get its

job done. The typical solution is to define new safe commands that provide the information. Safe-TCL provides a standard interface for new agents looking for information about the local environment. The commands that implement this interface are:

SafeTcl_setconfigdata key value Associates value with key in the database. This is generally used to set up preferences or customization strings. This is a standard repository for the information that might normally be stored in a .rc file on a Unix system.

SafeTcl_getconfigdata key ?default? ?prompt? This simply returns a string that is matched with a particular key. This might be used to set up all sorts of local preferences. It could also be used to provide information for the incoming agent in a standard format.

SafeTcl_loadlibrary library_name Load a particular library. There are some advantages in allowing the agent to load up different libraries of functions that may be needed occasionally. This is, however, a dangerous process, so this function loads the libraries into the trusted interpreter and only makes commands available when the command DeclareHarmless is executed.

It would be nice if all users of Safe-TCL adopted the convention of returning a list of local functions in response to the function call

SafeTcl_getconfigdata local-function-list.

Other convenient functions might be

SafeTcl_getconfigdata owner-information

to describe the name and phone number of the local caretaker, and

SafeTcl_getconfigdata local-highlights

to describe how to accomplish the most popular tasks at this site.

There are also a number of functions that accomplish minor feats. They are:

SafeTcl_evaluation_time This is a string that is either set to be `delivery` indicating that the function is running when it arrives, or `activation` indicating that the script is running when someone started reading their mail.

SafeTcl_originator A string containing the name of the creator of the message found in the "From:" field of the header. If the software is hooked up with PGP, this can indicate that the message was authenticated correctly.

SafeTcl_recipient The name of the recipient in the "To:" field of the header. PGP can be used to decode this message using the local secret key.

SafeTcl_random minimum maximum Finds a random number between minimum and maximum.

SafeTcl_genid Creates a string less than 14 characters long that is a locally unique string. It can be used in mail messages and file names to prevent name collisions.

12.5.1   Tearing Apart Mail

Safe-TCL comes with a number of functions for attacking its messenger, the e-mail message that brought it. They were mainly included because the designers hope that Safe- TCL will be used to create cool e-mail using the MIME standard. These hooks are intended to encourage the Safe-TCL programmer to store pictures, artwork and music in the correct part of a MIME message. This allows a mailer without Safe-TCL functionality to get at this data and display it successfully.

The mail functions are:

SafeTcl_getaddrs This finds all of the addresses in the header of the message. They are returned in a list.

SafeTcl_getaddrprop address property Takes an address apart and determines whether it conforms to the address standards circulated in

RFC 822/1123. The property might be, for instance, the host name or the user name.

SafeTcl_getdateprop date property Takes apart a date string sent in RFC 822/1123 format and finds particular parts of it. If property is set to **sec** then the function returns the number of seconds in the date string.

SafeTcl_getheader field ?body? Field specified a field in the header like "To:" or "From:". This function finds the string after this field tag.

SafeTcl_getheaders ?body? This command returns a list of pairs. Each pair contains the field name and the data that follows it. All fields in the header are listed here.

SafeTcl_makebody If you have a block of data that you want to bundle into a MIME message, you can use this function to do the job. The call specifies the type of the data, some additional parameters and the data itself.

SafeTcl_getparts This returns a list of all of the parts in a MIME message and their estimated sizes.

SafeTcl_getbodyprop part property ?body? Find a particular part of the MIME message and determine the property for it. This might be size, type, id or encoding.

SafeTcl_encode encoding data Perform a particular encoding on a block of data to prepare it for transmittal.

SafeTcl_decode encoding data Decode the data so it is readable.

SafeTcl_sendmessage Send a message in an electronic mail form. The additional parameters allow you to specify to whom it is going, the subject, the body and any additional header information.

SafeTcl_printtext Print out text at a local printer.

`SafeTcl_savemessage type ?destination?` Type specifies whether to save the message in a `file` or `folder`. Any `destination` sets the actual name. The underlying Safe-TCL implementation has the responsibility for figuring out where to put this information and it may approach it in a highly individualized way. This function provides a good example of how to allow the user to specify different locations in the file system without actually providing them access. Machine and operating system independence is another good side-effect of this design decision.

These descriptions of the MIME mail capabilities of Safe-TCL are not complete. If you want to use these functions, you should explore the documentation in detail. You will probably also want to find out more information about MIME itself.

The MIME mail functions are intended to be used in the context of enhanced mail. Do they add any functionality to a world of agents? At the very least, the MIME structure of a message can be used as a sort of resource file for the agent that bundles data in a standard format. Some Microsoft Windows programs and all Macintosh programs store data in standard resources. The standard MIME format is supported in many other contexts and this would allow developers and agent programmers to use these pieces of software to create the agents.

The MIME software hooks also allow the developer of the agent realm to escape many of the tedious details of negotiating the network. This is all handled by the underlying Internet standard mail transfer protocol. After the hooks and transfer commands are created, the creator of a Safe-TCL agent realm doesn't need to create a network travel plan. Everything is bundled in.

The MIME standard also allows other software programs to be integrated with Safe-TCL. Additional features like encryption are easy to add if the software is MIME compliant. PGP, the encryption software described in Chapter 14, is also MIME compliant. Integrating it with Safe-TCL is straight forward and easy to do. Almost every major form of data on the network is likely to become MIME compliant as more and more Internet mailers begin to accept the format. For the near term, it is bound to be one of the major standards.

There are, though, significant limitations to embracing MIME level mail as the transfer engine for any agent realm. The largest is it's provincial nature. The Internet may be the biggest network around, but it is far from the only standard available. Other standards promulgated by IBM, Novell and Apple exist in many domains. New versions of the Internet protocol are bound to emerge in the near future.

A more robust solution would include another layer of indirection. Any function for mail or network data transfer would include an additional field that set the network. One of the choices would be Internet, but others could also be included. The main functions like `SafeTcl_sendmessage` would be shells that called special functions for each defined network. New networks could be included over time by installing driver software for them. This flexibility is a good idea. Telescript, the network agent language created by General Magic (Mountain View, CA), contains this indirection level. Any serious, commercially ready version of Safe-TCL should also include it.

12.6 User Interaction

The entire world of software agents often seems to exist on a very abstract plane. This may be because the hard questions addressed by this book involve how to keep the agents from running amok. The answers involve abstract problems like encryption and language design. But even if the agents shuffle around the network executing functions and doing their business, they will still need to interact with humans. Safe-TCL contains several simple commands that let scripts interact with the user if the script is marked to run at `activation`.

The goal of interacting with a human is an interesting reversal of the metaphor of agent as it is often used in this book. The Safe-TCL message is not an agent sent out to gather information— it is an agent sent to bring a message to a person. This is an important enough job that it makes sense to include a set of extra functions that offer a standard way to interact with humans. The basic commands presented here are the lowest common denominator that Borenstein and Rose thought existed on the network. There is little reason why they can't be extended to include more features for various other media.

The standard Safe-TCL human interaction functions are:

SafeTcl_displaytext string Write a string to the screen. The standard version of Safe-TCL does not try to do a competent job displaying this information. There is no provisions for strings that overflow either single lines or the screen. A better version would pause the display and wait for a return key before proceeding.

SafeTcl_displayline string Display only as much string as will fit on one line. The size of a line varies from computer to computer and more often from window to window.

SafeTcl_gettext prompt ?default? Issue a prompt and return with the response. **default** is the default response.

SafeTcl_getline prompt ?default? Just like **SafeTcl_gettext** but it gets only one line of text.

SafeTcl_displaybody body Grab this one particular part of a MIME message and do the right thing with it. This may pose problems if the MIME functionality is not available on the current machine. The empty string comes back if there is success and an error message comes back on failure.

These basic functions, which may seem benign, also introduce new security concerns of their own. Borenstein and Rose warn off Safe-TCL agents that might take over a screen, erase it and start asking for logins and passwords. They suggest that any messages generated by an incoming script be displayed in a window that explicitly warns that the messages are coming from a potentially malicious agent. Giving the agent control over the entire screen is a mistake. They also warn that some terminals react to escape codes that allow distant computers to program the terminals remotely. They suggest filtering out all non-ASCII text from the strings being displayed on the screen to prevent this breach from occurring. The number of security holes that can be introduced by these "features" is surprising. It is also sad how many features must be avoided in the name of security.

12.7 Safe-Tk

Safe-TCL's human interface can also be extended to include more robust user-interfaces. A natural place to begin is with the Tk Toolkit, a collection of user interface widgets built on top of TCL and often distributed with it. The current version of Tk, number 3.6, runs on all X-windows supporting UNIX boxes. Several other versions for both Windows and the Macintosh are reputedly in the works.

The safe Tk extensions to Safe-TCL include all of the standard Tk3.6 functions except **send**, a function that sends a script to a remote process and asks it to execute it, and **toplevel**, a function that creates a new window. The **send** process is inherently dangerous and can't be fixed. The **toplevel** function, though, is replaced by the **mkwindow** command that produces a new window that clearly indicates that a potentially malicious program is in charge of the screen.

The rest of Tk is essential secure. The only side-effect the functions have is on the screen, which is their purpose. Malicious mischief can still be achieved. Four-letter words can be sent scrolling across a screen. In fact, even more obscene messages can be created using the MIME extensions. But there are no solid algorithms for detecting these attacks. You can delete all of the four-letter words, but anyone with any talent can still manage to offend someone.

Rose and Borenstein are careful enough to detect potential problems in the implementation of Tk. They note that there are simple ways to elude the window-drawing functions. A clever agent could redefine many of the smaller functions used to draw data on the screen and either obscure any warning messages about potentially malicious agents or cause trouble on their own. The incoming agent could make a window dance across the screen by playing with the details of the drawing code.

These are just some of the dangers of letting the incoming agent get control of the screen. Although there may be many more GUI toolkits in the future, every new implementation of Safe-TCL that makes some of these features available to the incoming agent must be prepared to deal with the consequences.

12.8   Plugging More Holes

Removing a number of commands is a simple way to plug holes in the TCL framework, but it is also an extreme solution. Occasionally commands are dangerous as well as almost impossible to live without. Slicing them out of TCL is not a solution.

Rose and Borenstein choose to replace **rename**, **proc** and **exit** with shell versions that try to filter out dangerous attempts at mischief. The **rename** and **proc** commands can be used to install new commands in the place of others. This is not seriously dangerous because these new commands don't have infinite power. There is no way to install a new set of file writing commands with the **proc**. You could create the commands with the right names, but these commands would just be strings of Safe-TCL commands. There is no way that they could reach over the walls because all Safe-TCL commands are presumably safe.

The **rename** and **proc** commands, though, can be used to rename anything happening in the untrusted interpreter. The most vulnerable functions executed here are the Tk commands used for display. Everything else are commands brought in by the incoming agent. If the agent wanted to cause havoc, it could rename parts of the display code and install it's own code in its place. (This is discussed in section 12.7.)

The versions of **rename** and **proc** will search a list of names that are forbidden to be renamed. If an agent tries to rename a procedure from this list, the Safe-TCL interpreter will sound an alarm and stop execution. The functions on this list should include many of the display functions as well as **rename** and **proc** themselves. (Otherwise, the agent could rename **rename** or **proc** and install their own command that circumvents the list of forbidden names.)

Safe-TCL also blocks incoming agents from renaming **exit**, the command used to terminate a script. The Safe-TCL version of **exit** does more than just end the execution. It also bundles up all of the messages that might be ready to leave. These should be mailed to the right destinations. Safe-TCL's `exit` does not end the execution of Safe-TCL itself. It just makes it ready to hand execution back to the mailer that might have invoked Safe-TCL in the first place.

If a rogue agent tried to rename `exit`, it could create a minor amount of havoc by screwing up the ending process. The simplest trick to play would be to create a phoenix-like agent that would rebound from termination and begin life again. This endless looping would not be able to do anything particularly dangerous, but it could consume plenty of cycles if the agent is running in a noninteractive mode. A better version of Safe-TCL would contain the ability to time the evaluation and ensure that an incoming agent doesn't consume too much of the system's time.

12.9 Summary

Safe-TCL is a nice modification of TCL that goes a long way toward developing a strong agent realm on the network. It's greatest features are the seamless integration with the MIME standard. This allows it good access to network mobility and a solid foundation for leveraging the past standard. Other software and computers are MIME compliant and more are bound to be in the future.

Safe-TCL also illustrates how easy it is to create new interpreted structures from software designed to be incorporated into other programs. TCL was originally designed to exist as a small part of a larger program that would make it easy to spin together user interfaces and other very high-level code. This structure makes it simple to create two versions in place and segregate trusted and untrusted behavior. This would be easy to do with other small, very-high-level languages designed to take their place in a larger program.

Safe-TCL is limited, though, in one crucial area. It does not regulate the consumption of time and memory. This may be a substantial problem in some cases. The lack of regulation makes it difficult to charge for a service that consumes variable amounts of CPU cycles. These jobs may

become popular if some specialized computers offer computation services
on the Net. Even non-number-crunching hosts might choose to use CPU
cycles to measure the strain on their systems because it is a nice, abstract
measure of the consumption of system resources. A long text search with
many conjunctions and intersections would naturally consume more than a
simple one-word search. It would be possible to meter the number of words
selected and other appropriate primitive search operations, but it may be
simpler to count cycles.

The lack of regulation also opens the door to abuse. "Long-winded"
agents that never stop executing are a real problem for any host. But so
is any agent if the host is besieged by requests for its services. Many of
the popular Internet ftp sites limit the number of incoming connections,
because too many requests bog down the file server and make the response
time impossibly slow for everyone. These ftp servers don't regulate the
number of bytes downloaded once someone gets a connection. This may
be acceptable, but it might be fairer to limit the amount consumed so that
some people to do not maintain long connections all day. The same process
would be ideal for an agent host. Just limiting the number of agents running
might not be enough. It would be better to curtail the long-winded agents
to distribute the services more equitably. Once they get their slice of time,
they could come back later and get back in line.

Modifying Safe-TCL to regulate the time consumed by an incoming agent
is a simple process. If the time consumed by the evaluation is checked
before the execution of each command by the untrusted interpreter, then the
evaluation can be cut off if it oversteps its bounds. This check is often enough
to catch most breaches before they go too far. Checking the time expended
before each command is executed won't be able to catch commands that
run for hours. Host programmers should be careful when they design local
commands so that long-running commands don't circumvent the time check
if they spend hours inside the command. If you're going to create a long-
running command like number factoring, you should check the execution
time and provide a mechanism for breaking out if the time limit is crossed.

Chapter 13

Other Languages

———————————————— The Hype ————————————————

Variety is the spice of life.

———————————————— Political Cynicism ————————————————

The economic overclass always conspires to motivate the masses by constructing an "other" in which it vests almost all possible manifestations of evil.

———————————————— The Buzzwords ————————————————

A multilingual, linkable development system would reduce all language wars.

This book concentrates upon two major languages, LISP and TCL. LISP was chosen as the basis for the example included here because it is easy to extend and there are several good public domain versions available. TCL made the cut because it is quite popular and some have already experimented with turning it into a language for agents. There are still many other languages that are available. Some, like Telescript, may be better because they are commercially supported and aimed directly at building agents. This chapter will explore some of the other options.

13.1 Telescript

One fashion magazine once described the ideal wardrobe in different parts of the country and stated that a T-shirt from General Magic was the coolest shirt to wear in Silicon Valley. The company invested wisely in cute logos and a clever persona that echoed the well-known dictum that any sufficiently advanced technology is indistinguishable from magic. This technically hip charm combined with the deep pockets of major corporations and name-brand principles, made General Magic one of the surest startup companies in Silicon Valley at the time.

At this writing in the Fall of 1994, General Magic still hasn't released much public information about its agent language known as Telescript. The language is being used as part of the operating system of AT&T's PersonaLink, an ambitious project to offer enhanced electronic mail and shopping experiences to the world. At present, users can access the network through a portable, digital assistant made by Sony that incorporates General Magic's Magic Cap user interface. The network uses Telescript to issue commands that float between the devices and the information brokers on the AT&T network.

In my experiments with the system, I discovered several good examples of how the Telescript language is probably being used in Magic Cap. You can distribute software for Magic Cap that comes bundled into an e-mail message. When you click on a button in the middle of the e-mail note, the software installs itself. It is also possible to include many different animated gadgets that don't do anything more than wiggle on the screen.

At this point, it is difficult to gauge the depth and quality of Telescript. It may not be vaporware, but it isn't something that can be touched. This may change by the time you read this book. General Magic plans to make Telescript a general language for the general public. A commercially supported language can often be richer and more robust than many of the experimental, public-domain solutions discussed here.

13.1.1 The Basic Architecture

There is some public information about Telescript that covers some of the most important details at a high level [Way]. While this look might not be enough to generate your own Telescript agent or create your own clone, it can be enough for good inspiration. In fact, some of the approaches taken in this book are based, in some part, on the vision created by Jim White [Whi94] and the others at General Magic.

The system is a completely object-oriented system in the original sense of the word, that is, it is very much like Smalltalk. The language itself is interpreted and this circumvents many of the problems that might emerge when the Telescript agents roam among machines with different CPU architectures. The interpreter is known as the *Telescript engine* and it runs on each machine.

The class structure is slightly different from what many people who use object-oriented systems may be used to using.(Figure 13.1 shows a small part of the Telescript class hierarchy.) The basic element is a *process*, which is a standard object with a list of instructions, an instruction pointer, and a list of data objects. The Telescript engine is responsible for preemptively switching among the different processes and arranging for messages to flow between them. It is also implicitly required to maintain security by confining each process to its own data objects. Any new information must flow in through the Telescript engine. (See Figure 13.2.)

The structure of the interpreter and its collection of objects makes it possible for the Telescript engine to let the agents be "persistent". This may mean that an agent maintains its data at all times and locations. An agent can pick up and move between locations without losing local data.

There are two types of Telescript code called *High Telescript* and *Low*

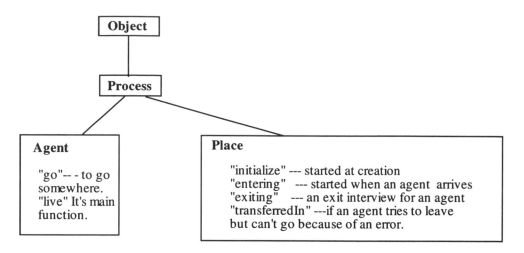

Figure 13.1: A skeleton view of the major elements in the Tele-script class hierarchy and some of its major methods.

Telescript. The high version resembles a mixture of Smalltalk and C. This can be compiled into the lower version which is a stack-based language not unlike PostScript. The lower version is interpreted, but it runs faster because many of the keywords and other details are decoded and converted into tokens.

There are two major types of processes known as *agents* and *places.* A place passes communications between agents. An agent can move from place to place as it sees fit using the **go** command. If you wanted to send out an information request, you would create an agent that would go to the place running on the Telescript engine and converse with another agent there to make the request. The agent might travel to multiple places to service its request. When a Telescript engine encouters a **go** command, it bundles up the agent, its internal state and its instruction pointer and sends it to the new place where execution begins at the next instruction. If the new place lives on the same engine, then the transfer is straightforward. If the new place is on the network, then the underlying network management software bundles up the agent and ships it off.

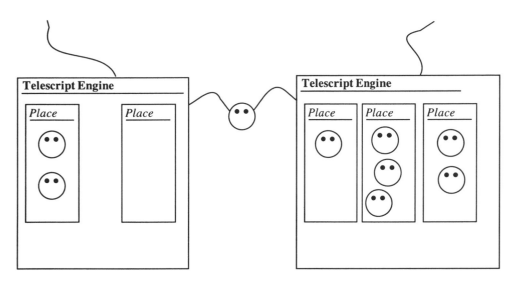

Figure 13.2: A view of the telescript world. Each Telescript engine has a set of places and each agent roams from place to place.

When two agents find each other at a particular place, they can set up a communication channel. This happens when a particular agent executes a **meet** command. The **meet** command can ask for another agent by name, by origin (which is called its *authority*) or by the service it provides (its *class*). This flexibility allows places to provide classes for say, dinner reservations or sports trivia information. The incoming agent doesn't need to know the correct name of the agent receiving reservations at a restaurant's *place*, it just asks for the reservation agent, which might be known universally as the maitre d'hotel.

This channel is really created by granting the agents the ability to execute methods owned by the other agent. That is, it receives a pointer to the other agent and it can invoke whatever commands are available for communication.

The **go** command also lets the agent choose how to specify the destination. This might be as simple as an address or as sophisticated as a request for a location that supports a specific class of service. The underlying Telescript engine is responsible for finding the right location.

Telescript also includes a number of different security measures to ensure the authenticity of agents. Each agent comes with a particular *authority* or identification of its owner or person responsible for it. This can be guaranteed by a digital signature mechanism that may include RSA's technology.

13.2   Python

Python is an object-oriented, very-high level programming language designed in the Netherlands by Guido van Rossum (guido@cwi.nl) to act as a module-linking programming language like TCL. There are numerous differences, however, because Python includes many different extensions that make it a more well-rounded programming language than TCL. The language has been ported to many of the major types of machines including UNIX boxes, Macintoshes and MS-DOS machines.

There are many similarities between TCL and Python. (TCL is only being used as a comparison here because it is described in great detail in Chapter 11.) The language is interpreted. Users can create their own well-written, generalized modules in C and then use Python to link up the routines for specific applications.

The major difference, though, is in the structure of the data. TCL stores everything in a string. This leads to inefficiencies in evaluating numerical data and prevents the user from creating even the simplest data structures which might make a big difference in processing time. Some might argue that anything that requires these complex maneuvers should be written in C and included as a basic module. TCL is just the glue.

Python does not conform to this minimalist definition. Programmers can create objects with well-defined, dynamically changing types that include the basic numbers as well as strings and more complicated higher-order structures like lists. The language contains a garbage collector that allocates memory for the object and cleans up the data by looking for objects that are no longer referenced.

The syntax of Python itself is very flexible and C-like, but there are several notable differences. The most jarring may be the lack of any brackets to specify nesting. Python relies upon indentation of lines to indicate the beginning and the ending of blocks. There are several other subtle differences, but they won't be covered here.

There should be little trouble extending Python to act as an agent language. The C code for the language can be found in several on-line archives described in Chapter 21. Some of the modifications that would be necessary are:

1. The most important step is to add a way to set the security clearance of objects. One potentially useful system would be to assign a security grade between 0 and n. Each function could only access objects with a security number less than its own. In a simple situation, there would be two grades: 0 for the object the agent can see and 1 for the objects the agent can't see. It might be desirable to use higher grades for nested systems. It is not clear that is necessary to add these higher grades, but most machines can compare two numbers in the time it takes to test one bit. The only additional cost is memory.

2. Blocking off file access to prevent wholesale damage.

3. Extending the security system to functions so that some functions or methods can only be invoked by hosts.

13.2.1 Sample Code

Here is some sample code from the Python tutorial written by Guido von Rossum. This example shows a short program entered into an interactive Python session. The code scans through the numbers between 2 and 10 and determines which ones are primes. If it finds a composite, it prints the first pair of factors it discovers and then exits the loop. The output of the code is printed below. Note also that three dots start out all but the first line of the program. The interactive session adds these because Python requires that the nesting be used to explicitly delineate the blocks of the code.

```
>>> for n in range(2, 10):
...     for x in range(2, n):
...         if n % x == 0:
...             print n, 'equals', x, '*', n/x
...             break
...     else:
...         print n, 'is a prime number'
...
is a prime number
is a prime number
equals 2 * 2
is a prime number
equals 2 * 3
is a prime number
equals 2 * 4
equals 3 * 3
>>>
```

Here is another piece of code from the tutorial that defines a function for computing Fibonacci numbers. Notice the parallel assignment statements that change the values of a and b. There are no definitions for local variables in this function because Python allows all variables to be defined dynamically. In this case, all new variables like a and b are entered into the local variable tables. This means that you cannot change the value of a global variable without an explicit global instruction.

```
>>> def fib(n):    # write Fibonacci series up to n
...     a, b = 0, 1
...     while b <= n:
...             print b,
...             a, b = b, a+b
...
>>> # Now call the function we just defined:
... fib(2000)
 1 2 3 5 8 13 21 34 55 89 144 233 377 610 987 1597
>>>
```

13.3 Smalltalk

This book has largely ignored object-oriented approaches because they do not offer direct solutions to the security problems of using agents. An agent can be written in LISP, C or almost any language as long as steps are taken to keep the incoming agent from causing trouble.

In many ways, the most popular implementation of an object-oriented system, C++, doesn't come close to solving the problem. The programmer can still manipulate pointers and the underlying memory with almost as much freedom as they had before. The object-oriented structures can be used to create nice hierarchies, but they don't seem to provide any general solutions for agents.

This does not need to be the case. In a simple and clean object-oriented system like Smalltalk, the programmer is only allowed to handle the objects. All communications between objects must go through messages. There is no direct way to access memory with pointers, nor is there any need to do so. This is why many people consider Telescript to be very similar to Smalltalk. The Telescript agents are objects and they can only speak to objects when they have permission to do so.

Many companies are building Smalltalk systems.[1] Each of them can be a good beginning for creating a flexible agent system. The language offers many of the necessary features because it began as a dynamically created

---

[1]Some reviews can be found in [BW94] and [Gal94].

language. The object-oriented structure that infuses the entire system also makes it easy to spin off agents as separate objects.

Adding security features requires some extra work. Many new implementations allow multiple packages to run namespaces so there are no inadvertent conflicts between the names for the methods in different packages. Although there are many possible combinations of letters, programmers always seem to choose method names like `foo-bar` or `add-to-list`. Running each program in its own namespace ensures that there will be no collisions between two methods with the same name. This is a natural solution for providing agent security. Each incoming agent runs in its own namespace.

Preventing the incoming agent from accessing other parts of the system can take place on two levels. The message dispatcher can intercept each of the messages and stop ones that are leaving the namespace improperly. This access mechanism would allow the host to publish the names of appropriate methods to the agent by signaling the message dispatcher to let the messages through.

The access can also be controlled at a deeper level on some systems. Quasar Knowledge Systems Inc. (QWS) is beginning to market Smalltalk-Agents, a fully formed Smalltalk development system intended to make it simple for programmers to develop applications that run on a distributed network of machines with different CPUs.

The company solved the problem of running their Smalltalk programs on multiple machines by creating a low-level device-independent language. All of the Smalltalk programs are effectively compiled into this lower-level language. On each machine, the company creates a native machine code equivalent for each of the instructions in the lower-level language. The code is executed in much the same way that toolbox traps or microcode are implemented.

Security can be enforced because each execution thread can be given its own table of traps or native code. Normally, all of the threads would be the same. But you could remove the native code entries for potentially damaging operations. So if there was an `RM` command that erased disk files, you could cripple that instruction by replacing its entry in the table with null operations (NOPS).

This is a nice solution in many ways, but it may not be as clean a solution as Telescript. The normal job of SmalltalkAgents is to allow the developers to create very capable programs that roam throughout a distributed network.

13.4   Nextstep, DSOM and Object Systems

Many of the creators of mainstream operating systems like MS-DOS, Windows, OS/2, Solaris and Nextstep are also exploring object-oriented operating systems that allow objects to move about the network and migrate from machine to machine. This is the natural extension of the industry's love affair with object-oriented programming, and there is no reason why the metaphor and the structure it inspires will not continue to shape how we think about distributing work and information about the network.

Any distributed operating system should be designed with security concerns in mind. The federal government and the financial industries are some of the largest consumers of information-processing equipment and they have hefty requirements for secrecy. This is why the developers of the next generation of object-oriented operating systems are looking carefully at ways to allow objects to migrate from machine to machine without creating a hazard. This is the same problem that has been examined in detail in this book and it is not surprising that many of the same ideas are also found in the work of the major companies working in this arena.

The simularities between the work on agents and the work in the object realms should not come as a surprise. The main goal is to be able to control the access of objects to other objects. In many cases, the software used to link objects and control how they bind with each other becomes responsible for stopping security breaches. The operating system already finds, say, the print object for a local document object when it wants to kill a tree. Adding an additional layer of code to determine whether incoming objects can access the print object does not overthrow the entire structure of the system. This additional layer does, though, slow down the process immensely.

13.5   Summary

This is only a partial list of the agent software available. Many other options are bound to emerge from both big companies and the small. The large companies will extend their current software packages with agent technology. Oracle (Redwood City, CA) is extending their very popular database system to include agents. The package called, Oracle in Motion, allows users to develop agent software in C++, Microsoft's Visual Basic, PowerBuilder and Microsoft's Excel. This product is a perfect example of how a large, mainstream can be extended by allowing agent software.

Smaller companies will also contribute to this change. Telescript and SmalltalkAgents come from these smaller companies. This technology might not make its way into the general marketplace. In many cases, it will be integrated into the larger systems through behind-the-scenes licensing agreements.

Chapter 14

Security and Encryption

————————————— The Hype —————————————

Imagine a box made of the strongest adamantine and locked by unpickable locks.

————————————— Political Cynicism —————————————

Encryption allows us to subvert the authoritarian impulses in society by distributing the power of privacy to everyone. It also encourages authoritarianism because it allows small groups to tightly coordinate their schemes for the domination of the underclass.

————————————— The Buzzwords —————————————

A good cipher is a nonlinear, surjective automorphism designed to resist inversion.

Any agent realm must solve two security problems. First, there must be a way for hosts to check out the credentials of agents so that bills can be addressed properly and access can be denied if necessary. Second, there must be a way for the agents to travel in secret across the network. Some agents and hosts may operate without these extra features, but they are necessary in many cases.

The solution to these problems can be found in a collection of encryption algorithms developed using a variety of mathematical tricks. These algorithms make it possible for someone to scramble a computer file or mail message into a form that is only readable by someone possessing the correct computer key. Other algorithms can create digital signatures that are practically unforgeable by anyone who doesn't hold the secret key. The combination of these two tricks will solve the basic security problems of creating an agent space.

This chapter begins with a basic introduction to encryption then discusses the actual techniques and implementations used to create the agents operating in this realm. Finally, the chapter will highlight the Pretty Good Privacy(PGP) software initially written by Phil Zimmerman to provide a concrete implementation for experimentation.

Readers who would like a more complete discussion can turn to *Applied Cryptography* by Bruce Schneier. [Sch94a]

14.1   The Basics of Cryptography

Archimedes once boasted that if he had a lever long enough and a spot to stand, he could use it to move the Earth. Of course, it is easy to see that he would need a very long lever and it would not be enough for him to stand in one place to budge the Earth. He would probably need to move his end of the lever many miles for every millimeter the earth would budge. The size of the quantities involved are tremendous.

The goal of cryptography is to harness mathematics to act as a lever for the memory and let us protect a large collection of data by remembering a small password. This leverage is possible because there are some mathematical algorithms that are easy to compute but difficult to reverse. The

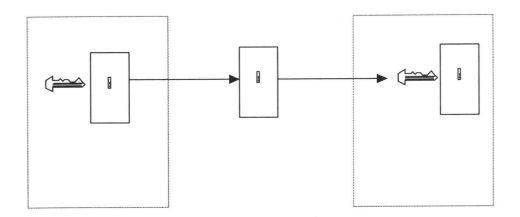

Figure 14.1: In private-key encryption, the document is locked with a particular key. After it arrives at its destination, a copy of the same key must be used to unlock the contents. Normally, this key must find its way to the separate location by another trusted channel.

algorithms let you keep that key a secret and use it to unlock the files when you want them. The mathematical key is needed to work the algorithm as a lever. The numbers involved in this proposition are also phenomenal, but computers make all of this easy.

The most straightforward use of encryption is known as either *single-key* or *private-key* encryption. Figure 14.1 illustrates how the same key is used on both end of the communication link. These algorithms use one key that is kept secret and shared by all the parties who are going to need access to the information. As long as the key is secret, the data is generally safe. If it is discovered, then everything is compromised. DES (Data Encryption Standard), IDEA(Internation Data Encryption Algorithm), and triple-DES which uses three passes of DES are some of the most common single-key encryption algorithms.

Single-key algorithms are good approaches by themselves, but they are only part of a security solution. They work well if you're going to lock up a file on your disk from everyone else or if you and a friend are able to meet and agree upon a secret key. The algorithms are more difficult to use, though, when you want to communicate with someone you've never met. How can you find a way to exchange the key? You can't encrypt it because you don't know a shared key. If you announce the key across the channel, then any eavesdropper would be able to decrypt your communications.

The solution to this problem emerged in the late 1970's from a handful of clever computer scientists including Martin Hellman, Whitfield Diffie, Ralph Merkle, Ron Rivest, Adi Shamir and Len Adleman. They developed a class of algorithms called *public-key* algorithms that need two keys. These algorithms don't have a physical analogy like single-key encryption because the two keys do not work in the same way that, say, the double locks on a safe deposit work. In public-key encryption, one key is used to encrypt the message and the other is used to decrypt it. Once you encrypt a message with one key you can't decrypt it unless you have the other. Figure 14.2 illustrates this.

There are a number of public key algorithms described in the literature and the records of the U.S. Patent Office, but the most well-known effort is the RSA system named for its discoverers Ron Rivest, Adi Shamir and Len Adleman[RSA83, RSA78].   The system is patented and licensing is controlled by a company known as Public Key Partners in Cupertino, CA. Another closely related company known as RSA Data Security produces software that uses these algorithms.

These two keys can be used in very simple ways to solve many problems in key distribution. The solution is to make one key public by publishing it in a public directory much like an electronic phone book. The other key is kept secret by its owner. Every person or host in the agent realm gets its own set of keys and publishes one of them.

Now, secrets can travel successfully through the realm in two ways. If you want to send a message or agent to one particular host, you simply look up the public key of that host in the directory and use that key to encrypt the message. The message can only be unlocked by the holder of the other key. The publicly available key doesn't help. In practice, most people use

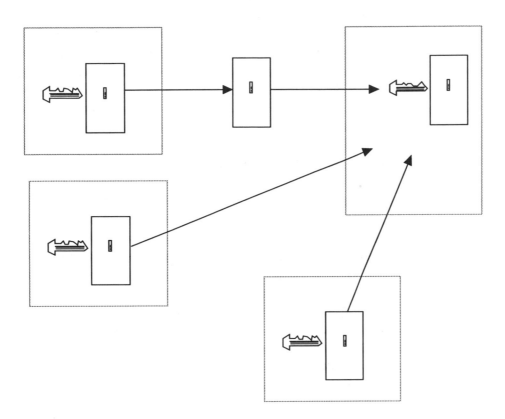

Figure 14.2: Public-key encryption uses two different keys. One locks the message and the other one unlocks it. Normally, the user distributes one key, the public one, to the world and keeps the second one private. Anyone who wants to send a message uses the public key, but only the owner of the private key can read them.

the public-key algorithm to exchange a key for a single-key algorithm like DES. Why? Because DES runs much faster in practice than the implementations of RSA. Splitting the work like this allows us to get the best of both algorithms.

Public-key algorithms also provide a way to generate digital signatures. If some entity wants to verify that it created a particular message, it can encrypt the message with its own hidden key. Everyone can decrypt this message by looking up the entity in the directory and using the public-key to decrypt it. Only the holder of that secret key could have generated the message. These digital signatures are even stronger than their paper analogs. They can't be compromised or forged unless someone discovers that secret key.

Is it necessary to encrypt the entire message with the secret key to sign it? No. A third type of algorithm known as a *cryptographically secure hash function* is an important addition. These are mathematical blenders that take a file and reduce it to some short number in such a way that it is hard to find a file that generates a particular number. Figure 14.3 gives an allegorical impression of the process.

The goal is to use this short number as a surrogate for the entire file. Let's say you sent a long file to your friend. You could call him up after the file arrived and verify that it was, in all probability, unchanged by comparing the hash function on both files. If both of you computed the same number on both ends, then there is little chance that anything went awry.

Hash functions are commonly used in many tasks like file transfer that require errors to be detected. They are often called checksums because the earliest algorithm was simply to add up all of the bytes in a file. This may be a perfectly good defense against random errors, but it is not a good defense against malicious errors. Imagine that someone has a digital copy of a check. They find the two bytes that represent the value of the check for $383.00 to be 01 and 7F in hexadecimal. What if the hacker simply rearranged these two bytes to read 7F 01? Now the check would be worth $32,513.00. The checksum would not detect this change because the sum of all of the bytes in the file would remain the same.

A cryptographically secure hash function is designed to detect this tam-

~

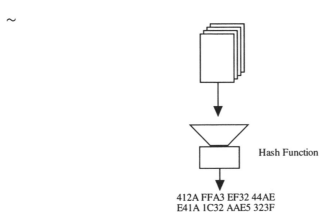

412A FFA3 EF32 44AE
E41A 1C32 AAE5 323F

Figure 14.3: Hash functions convert long files into short numbers. Information may be lost in the process, but cryptographically secure hash functions are designed to make it difficult to reconstruct any file that generates the hash value.

pering. The best algorithms make it practically impossible for you to find another file that generates the same hash value. The algorithms are modifications of standard encryption algorithms that effectively break the file into small blocks and encrypt the blocks in turn using the result from the previous block as the key for the next one. Some of the more common cryptographically secure hash functions are Ralph Merkle's Khufu[Mer91, Mer90a], Ron Rivest's MD-5[Riv90, Riv91, Riv92, dBB92, dBB94, Kal92] and its variant, the Secure Hash Algorithm [Rob94, XX91, 18093] ratified as a government standard by the National Institute of Standards and Technology (NIST, Gaithersburg, MD). Also, any standard block encryption algorithm can be modified to act as a hash function. [Mer90b] The process can also be inverted to convert a hash function into an encryption algorithm.

These three types of algorithms provide all of the security solutions for the agent realm. Each agent creator and each agent host will have their own public-keys published in a directory. These public keys will be used to verify the authenticity of the agents because each creator will sign the cryptographically secure hash value of their agents with their hidden key. The hosts will be able to verify the origin of the agent by using the corresponding public key to check the signature. Single-key encryption may also be used to hide the main text of the agent against eavesdroppers.

The rest of this chapter will discuss some of the technical details of the different algorithms and then delve into the actual implementation used in this book.

14.2   DES and IDEA

The most popular single-key encryption algorithm today emerged from IBM in the 1970's and was ratified as the governmental Data Encryption Standard (DES).[1] Many of the details about the design of the algorithm, though, were classified and this led many people to wonder whether the government had deliberately injected some weakness into the system. Over the years, though, no one has been able to find any weakness. In fact, the most intriguing research shows that DES is actually as strong as it could possibly be against some attacks[BS91a, BS91b].

This success means that many people are still using DES today. The only reason why people are beginning to distrust it is because the keyspace is becoming too small. Each key is 56 bits long and it is becoming increasingly possible to build a very large computer that will cycle through all 2^{55} possible keys in a reasonable amount of time. (Only 2^{55} keys, not 2^{56} keys are necessary because of symmetry.) [Way92, Wie93, GO91]

One solution to this problem is to use *triple-DES* [Kal94, vOW91] which consists of using three different encryption passes using two different 56 bit keys. First encrypt with key K_1, then decrypt with key K_2 then encrypt again with key K_1. Or if you want to be extra careful, you can use an third key instead of reusing the first one. This multiple encryption process either doubles or triples the length of the key and places the security well outside the limits of brute force attacks.

---

[1]The latest note in the Federal Register about the recertification of DES can be found in [NIS92]. Some ANSI Standard details about implementation are [X3.83, X3.81]. [Ban82, DDG+85, Ebe92] show details about fast implementations of DES. Other code can be found in [Sch94a] and the disk of source code that accompanies it.

$000000 \rightarrow 1110$	$000001 \rightarrow 0100$	$000010 \rightarrow 1101$	$000011 \rightarrow 0001$
$000100 \rightarrow 0010$	$000101 \rightarrow 1110$	$000110 \rightarrow 1011$	$000111 \rightarrow 1000$
$001000 \rightarrow 0011$	$001001 \rightarrow 1010$	$001010 \rightarrow 0110$	$001011 \rightarrow 1100$
$001100 \rightarrow 0101$	$001101 \rightarrow 1001$	$001110 \rightarrow 0000$	$001111 \rightarrow 0111$
$010000 \rightarrow 0000$	$010001 \rightarrow 1111$	$010010 \rightarrow 0111$	$010011 \rightarrow 0100$
$010100 \rightarrow 1110$	$010101 \rightarrow 0010$	$010110 \rightarrow 1101$	$010111 \rightarrow 0001$
$011000 \rightarrow 1010$	$011001 \rightarrow 0110$	$011010 \rightarrow 1100$	$011011 \rightarrow 1011$
$011100 \rightarrow 1001$	$011101 \rightarrow 0101$	$011110 \rightarrow 0011$	$011111 \rightarrow 1000$
$100000 \rightarrow 0100$	$100001 \rightarrow 0001$	$100010 \rightarrow 1110$	$100011 \rightarrow 1000$
$100100 \rightarrow 1101$	$100101 \rightarrow 0110$	$100110 \rightarrow 0010$	$100111 \rightarrow 1011$
$101000 \rightarrow 1111$	$101001 \rightarrow 1100$	$101010 \rightarrow 1001$	$101011 \rightarrow 0111$
$101100 \rightarrow 0011$	$101101 \rightarrow 1010$	$101110 \rightarrow 0101$	$101111 \rightarrow 0000$
$110000 \rightarrow 1111$	$110001 \rightarrow 1100$	$110010 \rightarrow 1000$	$110011 \rightarrow 0010$
$110100 \rightarrow 0100$	$110101 \rightarrow 1001$	$110110 \rightarrow 0001$	$110111 \rightarrow 0111$
$111000 \rightarrow 0101$	$111001 \rightarrow 1011$	$111010 \rightarrow 0011$	$111011 \rightarrow 1110$
$111100 \rightarrow 1010$	$111101 \rightarrow 0000$	$111110 \rightarrow 0110$	$111111 \rightarrow 1101$

Figure 14.4: This table shows how the first DES S box converts six-bit values into four-bit ones. Note that a change in one input bit will generally change two output bits. The function is also nonlinear and difficult to approximate with linear functions.

Another relatively popular algorithm is known as IDEA, an acronym for International Data Encryption Algorithm. This algorithm, developed by Xuejia Lai and James Massey, emerged from Switzerland. [LM91, CS92, DGV94] It received a boost in popularity because software with DES cannot be legally exported from the United States. IDEA is one alternative.

Both DES and IDEA are block ciphers that operate by repeatedly using two simple mathematical operations that alternately "confuse" the data and "diffuse" this confusion into the rest of the block. DES operates on 64-bit blocks and divides these blocks into two 32-bit halves. The confusion is created with a collection of seemingly random permutations called *S boxes*. These are actually functions that take 6 bits as input and output 4 bits. Figure 14.4 shows the input and output for the first S box. Although they appear random, their structure is specially designed to be highly nonlinear. The details of the design of these boxes are what was classified. Subsequent work shows that the S boxes must be carefully choosen to avoid linear approximation.[2]

The diffusion in DES occurs by alternately mixing one half with the other. First, one half is "confused" by adding in part of the key. Then it is passed through several S boxes to add more confusion. Finally the result of this is added into the other half using an XOR function, effectively diffusing the confusion from the first half into the second. Then the process is repeated 15 more times. The roles of the halves are exchanged with each repetition.

In Figure 14.5, the sixteen rounds of DES are shown. This repetitive structure made it easy to implement the design in early hardware because it was possible to use microcode to run a loop 16 times. The latest implementations suggest that a pipeline with 16 stages is now economical. The structure is also symmetrical. The same hardware or software implementation can be used to decrypt the data as well. This is a nice, clean approach.

In the figure, the function f is used to provide "confusion". The function f is made up of these steps:

1. The 32-bit input R_{i-1} is *expanded* into 48 bits by repeating some of the bits. More specifically, the 32-bit block is broken up into 8 four-bit blocks. Every four-bit block is replaced with a six-bit block consisting of the last bit of the block before it, the four bits and the first bit of the block that comes after it. More specifically,

$$\{b_i, b_{i+1}, b_{i+2}, b_{i+3}\} \rightarrow \{b_{i-1}, b_i, b_{i+1}, b_{i+2}, b_{i+3}, b_{i+4}\}.$$

The net effect is to repeat the bits on the boundaries of the blocks. This will increase the diffusion between blocks in the S-box step. Call this $E(R_{i-1})$.

---

[2]The latest work on "linearizing" the internal structure of DES can be found in the work of Biham and Shamir.[BS91b, BS91a, BB94, Bih92a, BS93b, BS93a] Other work can be found in [Mat94, Bih95]. This duplicates work that IBM says it did when designing DES. Other work on designing S boxes can be found in [DT91a, DT91b, GR83, KLP94, KPL93, Knu93, Mat95, Nyb91b, Nyb91a].

$$L_0 \qquad\qquad R_0$$
$$L_1 = R_0 \qquad R_1 = L_0 + f(R_0, K_1)$$
$$L_2 = R_1 \qquad R_2 = L_1 + f(R_1, K_2)$$
$$L_3 = R_2 \qquad R_3 = L_2 + f(R_2, K_3)$$
$$L_4 = R_3 \qquad R_4 = L_3 + f(R_3, K_4)$$
$$L_5 = R_4 \qquad R_5 = L_4 + f(R_4, K_5)$$
$$L_6 = R_5 \qquad R_6 = L_5 + f(R_5, K_6)$$
$$L_7 = R_6 \qquad R_7 = L_6 + f(R_6, K_7)$$
$$L_8 = R_7 \qquad R_8 = L_7 + f(R_7, K_8)$$
$$L_9 = R_8 \qquad R_9 = L_8 + f(R_8, K_9)$$
$$L_{10} = R_9 \qquad R_{10} = L_9 + f(R_9, K_{10})$$
$$L_{11} = R_{10} \qquad R_{11} = L_{10} + f(R_{10}, K_{11})$$
$$L_{12} = R_{11} \qquad R_{12} = L_{11} + f(R_{11}, K_{12})$$
$$L_{13} = R_{12} \qquad R_{13} = L_{12} + f(R_{12}, K_{13})$$
$$L_{14} = R_{13} \qquad R_{14} = L_{13} + f(R_{13}, K_{14})$$
$$L_{15} = R_{14} \qquad R_{15} = L_{14} + f(R_{14}, K_{15})$$
$$L_{16} = R_{15} \qquad R_{16} = L_{15} + f(R_{15}, K_{16})$$

Figure 14.5: This figure shows how 16 rounds encrypt the two 32-bit halves of the message L_0 and R_0. Initially, L_0 and R_0 are assembled using the initial permutation. At the end, they are disassembled using the inverse of this permutation.

2. 48 bits are selected from the 56 bits of the key. This is K_i. The key bits are selected each round by rotating the key a select amount and then pulling out a subset of the necessary bits.

3. The 48 bits of K_i and the 48 expanded bits of R_{i-1} are XORed together.

4. The 48 bits of $K_i + E(R_{i-1})$ are passed through a set of S-boxes to yield $S(K_i + E(R_{i-1}))$. The s-boxes are nonlinear functions that take six bits and return four bits. This produces 32 bits. Note that the four-bit blocks of R_{i-1} were expanded to 6 bits, mixed with some key bits and then reduced back to four bits here. Each of these four-bit blocks gets its own s-box and the results are concatenated to yield the final 32-bit section. The actual details of the s-box design are still classified, but it is possible to discover some important features. For instance, they were designed to ensure that any one-bit change in the input would change at least two of the bits of the output.

5. The 32 bits are permuted by a straight permutation.

6. The result is added together with L_{i-1} to give the new R_i.

The computation of this function is repeated 16 different times and each set of four bits goes through the s-boxes eight times. In between each of the passes through the s-boxes, the bits are mixed thoroughly with other bits. It is quite reasonable to expect that changing one bit of the input block will affect many of the output bits.

14.2.1   IDEA

IDEA uses a similar iterated network, but it uses different functions for confusion and diffusion. Instead of an S box, it uses multiplication and addition modulo $2^{16} + 1$. This modulo number was chosen because it is easy to perform the operation by ignoring everything except the 16 least significant bits. This means that the cipher can run quickly even on machines that only do 16-bit mathematics— something that is becoming increasingly

K_A	K_B	K_C	K_D	K_E	K_F
K_0	K_{16}	K_{32}	K_{48}	K_{64}	K_{80}
K_{96}	K_{112}	K_{25}	K_{41}	K_{57}	K_{73}
K_{89}	K_{105}	K_{121}	K_9	K_{50}	K_{66}
K_{82}	K_{98}	K_{114}	K_2	K_{18}	K_{34}
K_{75}	K_{91}	K_{107}	K_{123}	K_{11}	K_{27}
K_{43}	K_{59}	K_{100}	K_{116}	K_4	K_{20}
K_{36}	K_{52}	K_{68}	K_{84}	K_{125}	K_{13}
K_{29}	K_{45}	K_{61}	K_{77}	K_{93}	K_{109}

Figure 14.6: This is the key schedule for IDEA keys. K_i refers to a sixteen-bit block that begins at bit i. There are eight rounds of the algorithm. The six blocks on each row are used in each round.

uncommon. $2^{16} + 1$ is also prime. This means that the behavior of much of the multiplication can be inverted successfully.

The IDEA cipher encrypts 64-bit blocks using 128 bits of key. Each 64-bit block is broken into four 16-bit parts, A, B, C and D and the key is broken into eight 16-bit parts. Let K_i stand for a block of 16 bits of the key that begins with bit i. The bits wrap around so K_{120} would include bits 120 through 127 as well bits 0 through 7. This notation is used because the key-scheduling algorithm includes several 25-bit shifts. Only six blocks are used each of the eight rounds. The structure of these blocks is given in Figure 14.6.

Each of the eight rounds of IDEA consists of a complicated mixture of multiplication modulo $2^{16} + 1$ (represented as normal arithmetic without a modulo mark for brevity), addition modulo $2^{16} + 1$ (also represented with a "+" without a modulo value for brevity) and a bitwise exclusive or (represented as $\odot$).

The steps in each round are broken into intermediate operations because the encryption process uses the same intermediate values multiple times. These temporary values are listed as t_i. The steps are:

1. $t_1 \leftarrow AK_A$

2. $t_2 \leftarrow B + K_B$

3. $t_3 \leftarrow C + K_C$

4. $t_4 \leftarrow DK_D$

5. $t_5 \leftarrow (t_1 \odot t_3)K_E$

6. $t_6 \leftarrow t_2 \odot t_4$

7. $t_7 \leftarrow (t_5 + (t_2 \odot t_4))K_F$

8. $t_8 \leftarrow t_5 + t_7$

9. $A \leftarrow t_1 \odot t_7$

10. $B \leftarrow t_3 \odot t_7$

11. $C \leftarrow t_2 \odot t_8$

12. $D \leftarrow t_4 \odot t_8$

This process is repeated eight times with different values of K_A through K_F chosen from Figure 14.6. There is also an additional final round in which four final keys, K_{29}, K_{45}, K_{61} and K_{77} are mixed with the final values of A, B, C and D. K_{29} and K_{77} are multiplied with A and D respectively and K_{45} and K_{61} are added with C and D respectively.

The decryption processes uses the same network of functional mixing. It just uses different keys that are either the multiplicative or additive inverses modulo $2^{16} + 1$. The entire structure of the network was designed to be symmetrical so that encryption and decryption could take place with the same process.

The best description for this algorithm can be found in the code itself which is distributed with the PGP encryption software. At the time of this writing, there are no known holes in the IDEA algorithm. Anyone who uses the algorithm should remain aware of any weaknesses that might be discovered. IDEA, unlike the DES, was not developed with the supervision of the National Security Agency. Some people may consider this to be a strength and others may consider it a weakness. I feel that it was in the U.S. government's best interest to provide a secure cipher for their citizens and this led them to assist IBM to develop a very strong system. Private efforts do not have the benefits and the experience of a well-funded bureaucracy devoted to breaking codes.

Ascom-Tech AG holds a European patent on the IDEA cipher and does not charge a licensing fee for noncommercial use. Licensing information can be obtained from

```
Dr. Dieter Profos\index{Profos\,Dieter}
Ascom-Tech AG, Solothurn Lab
Postfach 151
4502 Solothurn, Switzerland
Tel: 41 65 242885
```

There are a number of other interesting ciphers evolving using this same framework. Merkle's Khafre is one example. Schneier's Blowfish is another. [Sch94, Sch94b] Many others are evolving through time. Each of these algorithms is the object of much study and there is little doubt that the knowledge in the area is growing.

14.3 RSA

The public-key system known as RSA works with large prime numbers and modulo arithmetic. Prime numbers are numbers that can only be evenly divided by 1 and themselves. The first five prime numbers are 2, 3, 5, 7 and 11. A message is encrypted in RSA by converting it into a number, n, and then computing $n^d \bmod pq$ where p and q are two large primes and d is one of the two keys. Modulo arithmetic operates by dividing everything by one number, in this case pq, and keeping only the remainder.

The world of modular arithmetic has many intriguing patterns. If $p = 5$ and $q = 7$, then $pq = 35$, and there are effectively only 35 values of interest: $0, 1, \ldots, 34$. Any number larger than this will be converted into a smaller one. For instance, $4 \times 9 = 36$ in regular arithmetic. In modulo arithmetic, $4 \times 9 \bmod 35 = 1$ because 36 divided by 35 leaves 1 as the remainder. The values of the set wrap around each other and form a ring of values with no particular beginning or end. This circular structure is the key to RSA's success. This modular arithmetic can be done modulo any integer. I've just used an integer with two prime factors because this is the key to the success of RSA.

Most of the standard arithmetic operations can be done successfully in modular arithmetic. Addition, multiplication and exponentiation all work correctly. Exponentiation, though, leads to an especially nice pattern. For instance, the powers of 2 modulo 11 yield this pattern:

$$2, 4, 8, 5, 10, 9, 7, 3, 6, 1, 2, 4, \ldots.$$

The number 2 is called a *generator* because the successive powers of it will generate all numbers except 0. These generators exist only in modulo arithmetic using a single prime number, in this case 11.

Figure 14.7 shows the values of the powers of 2 modulo 11 arranged around a circle. (Call this Circ(2).) Multiplication by a particular value can also be thought of as moving over a number of notches dictated by the position of the number. So multiplying a value by 2 is the same as moving over one notch clockwise because the value 2 is found one notch clockwise from the value of unity, 1. Multiplying by 4 is equivalent to moving over two notches. Since there are ten elements in this cycle, and ten is divisible by two, then the powers of 4 have only five values:

$$4, 5, 9, 3, 1.$$

The multiple exponentiation still yields interesting patterns. For instance, the powers of 3 modulo 35 are:

$$3, 9, 12, 1, 3, \ldots.$$

The successive powers of 6 modulo 35 only form a cycle with one number: $6 \times 6 \ modulo \ 35 = 1$.

The length and pattern of these cycles are the key to the hidden strength of RSA. It turns out that it is pretty easy to raise some number to a power, but it is difficult to take the inverse of this operation or the log. So given n,

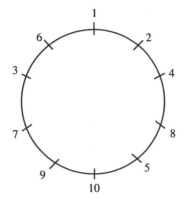

Figure 14.7: The successive powers of 2 modulo 11 arranged counterclockwise in a circle. They start at the top of the circle.

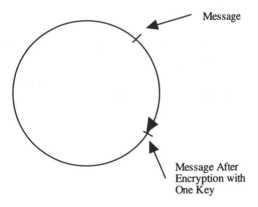

Figure 14.8: A message or key value is encrypted with RSA by converting it into a number in the system modulo pq and then raising it to a power. If the powers of the message are arranged in a circle like Figure 14.7, then the encryption is just a shift along the circle.

d, p and q it is simple to compute $n^d \bmod pq$, but if you receive m it is hard to find an e or an n such that $m = n^e \bmod pq$. The difference between the execution time is significant enough to support a good algorithm like RSA. Encryption will be done by exponentiation. The security depends upon how hard it is to reverse the process. This book won't discuss the details of how people have tried to solve this problem and failed. This doesn't mean that there is no solution out there, but it does mean that many people would be surprised when one is found.

Figure 14.8 shows the circle formed by raising the message to all of the powers modulo pq, i.e. Circ(message). Encryption is equivalent to moving over the same amount for each particular Circ(message).

If exponentiation will be used for encryption and reversing the exponentation is supposed to be so hard, then how can *anyone* decrypt the answer? The reason is that a trapdoor can be constructed using the two prime numbers p and q. The solution is based upon the Euler *Totient* function, $\psi(x)$, which counts the number of positive integers less than x that are relatively prime to x. So if x is prime, then $\psi(x) = x - 1$. It is easy to prove that $\psi(pq) = \psi(p)\psi(q)$ which means that $\psi(pq) = pq - p - q + 1$ if p and q are prime.

Why does this matter? Because $n^{\psi(pq)} \bmod pq = 1$. This means that the maximum length for any cycle formed by exponentiation in this system is $\psi(x)$. It also means that the length of any shorter cycle will divide $\psi(x)$. How can we find a trapdoor for an encrypting key d? Simple. Find an e such that $d \times e = 1 \bmod \psi(pq)$. This can be done using Euclid's algorithm which is beyond the scope of this book.

How does e work as the decryption key? Simple, if you receive $n^d \bmod pq$ in the mail, then you compute

$$\left(n^d\right)^e \bmod pq = n^{(d \times e)} \, modulo \, pq = n^1 modulo \, pq = n.$$

Figure 14.9 shows the decryption process on Circ(encrypted message). When it is created, the actual message will lie at the same spot the same number of notches from unity.

Why can't some eavesdropper come up with e? Because the only efficient algorithm people know for computing $\psi(pq)$ requires you to know both p and

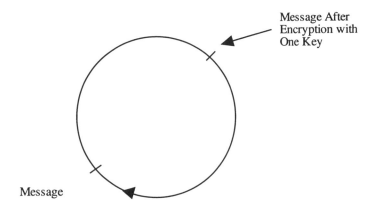

Message After
Encryption with
One Key

Message

Figure 14.9: When RSA decrypts a message, the message will always lie a fixed number of steps around the circle created from the powers of the encrypted message.

q. If you only know the product pq, then you must first factor it into the prime factors. No one knows an efficient way to do this if p and q are both large .

The basic mechanism for using RSA can be summarized:

1. Find two large prime numbers p and q. The larger the better. There are additional criteria not mentioned here that contribute to security.

2. Choose a random number d. Compute e such that $d \times e$ *modulo* $\psi(pq) = 1$.

3. Compute pq and optionally destroy the individual numbers p and q. Publish pq and d as the public key.

4. Anyone sending a message n to you will encrypt it by computing $m = n^d \bmod pq$.

5. You decrypt it by computing $n = m^e \bmod pq$.

6. You sign a message n by computing $m = n^e \bmod pq$.

7. Anyone can decrypt this and recover n by computing $n = m^d \mod pq$.

There are many details left out of this presentation because they involve deep discussion. Another good source of information about these systems is Neal Koblitz's *Public-Key Encryption*[Kob87]. The book also describes less well-known public-key systems using mathematical systems known as eliptical curves.

14.4 MD-4, MD-5 and SHA

MD-4 and its derivative, the Secure Hash Algorithm (SHA), are two of the more popular hash functions available today. MD-4 emerged from Ron Rivest's lab at MIT in 1990. Later work by Eli Biham, B. den Boer and A. Bosselaers [Bih92b, dBB92] produced an attack that could generate two files with the same hash value if a shortened, two-round version of MD-4 was used. Although this did not compromise the entire version, Rivest published an extended version called MD-5 that used different functions as the basic scrambling or confusion methods and then used the scrambling functions for four rounds.

In the same time frame, the National Institute of Standards and Technology was searching for a hash algorithm to include with their Digital Signature Standard (DSS). They chose MD-4 as a model and made their own set of changes. The final version is known as the SHA and is recognized as part of the Digital Signature Standard.

The MD-5 algorithm operates upon 512-bit blocks of data and produces a 128-bit hash value. To ensure the file is a multiple of 512 bits long, MD-5 adds a single 1-bit and all 0 bits until it is 64 bits shy of a multiple of 512. Then a 64-bit number representing the length of the file before padding is appended, extending it to 512 bits. The 512-bit block is treated as sixteen 32-bit integers $M[0] \ldots M[15]$.

The process begins with four 32-bit numbers, A, B, C and D, initialized to set constants. During each step, MD-5 will use in the information in the 512-bit block of file data to permute these four numbers. When all of the scrambling and confusion action is finished, the values in A, B, C and D will be concatenated and output as the 128-bit message digest.

The basic scrambling functions are:

$$F(X, Y, Z) = (X \otimes Y) \oplus ((not X) and Z)$$
$$G(X, Y, Z) = (X \otimes Z) \oplus (Y \otimes (not Z))$$
$$H(X, Y, Z) = X \odot Y \odot Z$$
$$I(X, Y, Z) = Y \odot (X \oplus (not Z))$$

These four functions serve as the basis for confusion. Each of the functions is used in its own separate round to permute the values of A, B, C and D. The four functions are used by taking three of the four A, B, C or D, passing them through of the F, G, H or I functions. Then a strange constant is added to this result and shifted a seemingly random amount. This value is added back to the value of the one of the set A, B, C and D that was not passed through the function. Rivest says the shifting values and the strange constant were chosen to maximize the scrambling effect, and he used empirical tests to settle on the values. The strange constants for instance, are chosen from the 33rd to 64th bits of the absolute value of the sine of the integers.

This scrambling procedure can be summarized in equations as:

$$FF(a, b, c, d, j, s, t) = a := a + (F(b, c, d) + M[j] + t) << s$$
$$GG(a, b, c, d, j, s, t) = a := a + (G(b, c, d) + M[j] + t) << s$$
$$HH(a, b, c, d, j, s, t) = a := a + (H(b, c, d) + M[j] + t) << s$$
$$II(a, b, c, d, j, s, t) = a := a + (I(b, c, d) + M[j] + t) << s$$

The "$<<$" stands for left shift.

These four functions are applied in their own round. In each round, the one function is applied sixteen times to different combinations of A, B, C and D and one of the sixteen values of M. The combinations are chosen to scramble up the values as much as possible. For instance, the first application of a function in the first round is:

$$F(A, B, C, D, 0, 7, 0xd76aa478).$$

That is to say that the value of $F(B, C, D)$, $M[0]$, A and *0xd76aa478* are added together, shifted 7 bits to the left and then placed back in A. This step is repeated 15 more times in the first round with different blocks of M and different permutations of A, B, C and D. There is not enough space to describe the 64 different applications of the functions FF, GG, HH and II and several other details from the implementation. Interested readers should look up the source code.

14.4.1 SHA

The Secure Hash Algorithm is quite similar to MD-5 because it is also descended from MD-4. One major difference is that it produces a 160-bit hash value instead of a 128-bit value. This 160-bit length is necessary because the Digital Signature Standard uses 160-bit values. The SHA creates this 160-bit hash by using five 32-bit variables, A, B, C, D and E and permuting them in much the same way that MD-5 does it.

In this case, the basic scrambling functions are:

$$
\begin{aligned}
F(X, Y, Z) &= (X \otimes Y) \oplus ((notX)andZ) \\
G(X, Y, Z) &= X \odot Y \odot Z \\
H(X, Y, Z) &= (X \otimes Y) \oplus (X \otimes Z) \oplus (Y \otimes Z) \\
I(X, Y, Z) &= X \odot Y \odot Z
\end{aligned}
$$

Notice that G and I are the same function in this case. These are applied in four rounds of 20 applications to ensure that each of the five A, B, C, D and E get the roughly the same amount of scrambling. In this case, the SHA also uses fixed additive constants instead of the bits extracted from the sines. The algorithm also does not use the 512-bit block of data verbatim after the first 16 rounds. After that, it sets the M values to be the sum of four other M values.

Although there are substantial similarities between MD-5 and the SHA, there are also significant differences. The basic structure is the same, but there are significant changes in the way that the functions are applied.

14.5   Digital Signature Standard

The Digital Signature Standard emerged from the National Institute of Standards and Technology (NIST, Gaithersburg, MD) in 1991 with the federal government's express hope that it would become widely used to authenticate documents. The standand consisted of the Secure Hash Algorithm, discussed in section 14.4.1, and a Digital Signature Algorithm (DSA), which is similar in the most abstract sense to RSA. The most significant difference, though, between RSA and the DSA was that the DSA could *not* be used to keep secrets. The algorithm won't lock something away, it will just allow you to verify that it is unchanged. This distinction is an important one to a government that maintains that cryptography is a munition that might be used against the state. Any implementation of DSA can be exported but RSA can't.

The DSA is discussed here for several reasons. One, people may want to create agent systems that can ship information across the U.S. borders. This is theoretically possible today with RSA. Two, governmental standards often become defacto general standards. It is entirely possible that, say, the IRS could set up a digital signature infrastructure that people could use to sign their tax forms. If they made the directory of public keys available to the world, then this might become the standard for the country. A trusted public-key infrastructure is needed before these signatures can become widely used. The third reason the DSA is included here is because a variant of it can be used in some forms of digital cash described in Chapter 15.

Anyone considering using the DSA should be aware that many of the same questions about patent infringement still hold. The holders of the RSA patents, the Public Key Partners, maintain that the use of the DSA falls under the basic claims of the patents they hold. Anyone using the algorithm should pay them for the rights. The government, however, seems willing to fight this battle in court. At this writing in December 1994, there are no details about any settlement, so the public may want to lay low and wait for something to happen.

14.5.1 Digital Signature Algorithm

The DSA is based upon the Schnorr and El Gamal signature algorithms [ElG85a, ElG85b] which both use the discrete log function as the basis of their security. That is, they rely upon the fact that it is easy to compute $x^n \bmod p$ given x,n, and some prime p but hard to invert this and find n if you start with x,p and $x^n \bmod p$. Many people worked seriously on solving this problem and the current opinion is that prime numbers p of about 512 bits long are strong enough to resist attacks at this time. Longer primes will be needed soon.

The DSA begins with:

- p— a prime number between 512 and 1024 bits long. NIST suggests increasing the lengths in quantized amounts, but this is not necessary.

- q— a 160-bit prime factor of $p - 1$.

- $g = h^{\frac{p-1}{q}}$ such that $h \leq p - 1$ and $h^{\frac{p-1}{q}} > 1$.

- x is any number $< q$.

- $y = g^x \bmod p$

To sign a message,

1. The sender computes the hash value of the message, call it $H(m)$, and selects a random number k.

2. The sender computes $r = (g^k \bmod p) \bmod q$ and $s = (k^{-1}(H(m) + xr)) \bmod q$. r and s constitute the signature. They're bound up with the message in an appropriate way.

The signature is verified by computing:

1. $w = s^{-1} \bmod q$

2. $u1 = (H(m) \times w) \bmod q$

3. $u2 = (r \times w) \bmod q$

4. $v = ((g^{u1} \times y^{u2}) \bmod p) \bmod q$

5. if $v = r$ then the signatures match and the document is verified.

There are several ways that the DSA can be circumvented to include subliminal secret messages. The easiest way to understand how this can be done is to imagine trying to send a single bit. This can be accomplished by simply keep choosing a new random k until the output has a least-significant bit that matches the message. Doing this with larger messages is more complicated but is well documented in the work of Gus Simmons [Sim84, Sim85, Sim85, Sim93, Sim94].

Finally, readers might want to note that there is a Digital Signature Standard(DSS) that describes how to use the Digital Signature Algorithm. The terms are often used interchangeably even there are some differences. The algorithm is a mathematical construct. The standard is a guide for people in the federal government.

14.6 More Signature Schemes

There are many different ways to sign documents electronically. Section 14.3 showed how to use RSA encryption to do the job. This is a popular standard used in the system software distributed by Apple, Novell and Sun among others. Section 14.5 describes DSA, a proposed federal standard that NIST would like to be widely adopted. These are just the beginning. There are several other schemes that are worth describing because they make it possible to create more robust versions of digital cash described in Chapter 15.

These signatures, like the DSA, rely upon the intractability of the discrete log problem for their security. The problem is often used to exchange keys, but it is not used as often for signatures because the structure of the problem leads to the complex equations like the ones used for the DSA. RSA-based signatures don't need this complexity because the equations allow a trapdoor that can only be exploited by someone knowing the secret key. Systems using the discrete log can't use a trapdoor because there isn't one. This structure, though, has its advantages because it allows us to construct a better cash system.

The best place to begin might be with the standard Diffie-Hellman key exchange. [DH76a, DH76b, Lab93] This shows how the basic discrete log problem can be used to set up secrets on both sides of an insecure channel. The first step is getting both parties to agree upon p, a large prime number (512 bits or greater), and a generator for that prime. The process is simple:

1. You choose a random number x and your potential communications partner chooses their own random number y. Neither of you know the other's number.

2. You and the partner compute $k^a\ mod\ p$ and $k^b\ mod\ p$ respectively and mail these values to each other. Anyone listening in will be able to see these numbers but they won't be able to calculate a or b. The difficulty of the discrete log problem prevents this from happening.

3. You take the $k^b\ mod\ p$ you receive in the mail and calculate $(k^b)^a\ mod\ p$. Your partner calculates $(k^a)^b\ mod\ p$. These are equal. Anyone listening in could not do this calculation because they do not know x or y.

4. Now you and your partner share a secret number that no one else knows. You can use the number itself for a key to an encryption system like DES or you can pass it through a hash function for additional security.

The Diffie-Hellman key exchange allows two parties who haven't met to set up a unique channel. (See Figure 14.10) The same basic equations can be used to create a signature that can be checked interactively. That means that if a person receives a document with a digital signature, they need to interact with the signer to check the validity of the signature. Ordinarily, this is not a feature but a problem because signature schemes like the DSS or RSA do not require this. The algorithm is just presented here because it makes the next algorithm easier to understand. The steps in the protocol are:

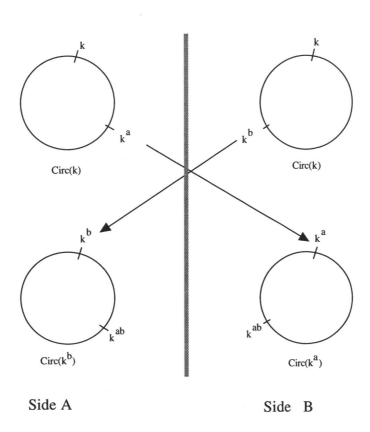

Figure 14.10: An illustration of Diffie-Hellman key exchange using the Circ diagrams. Side A and Side B only know the values of a and b respectively. That is the number of notches to move along their diagram. The same number, k^{ab} ends up in the right spot of each diagram.

1. You create a document with hash m and sign it by computing $m^x \bmod p$. x is the secret key that generated this signature. You also distribute g, p and $g^x \bmod p$.

2. Someone arrives and asks you to validate the signature. You create a random number w and send this person $g^w \bmod p$ and $m^w \bmod p$ where g is a generator as before.

3. The challenger to the signature creates a random number c and sends it to you.

4. You calculate $r = cx + w$ and send this back. This calculation does not reveal x or w. Even if an attacker had you verify a signature many times, he could not recover the values of x and w because w is randomly created each time.

5. The challenger computes $g^r \bmod p$ and verifies that it is the same as $(g^x)^c \times (g^w) \bmod p$. The challenger can also verify $m^r \bmod p$ is equal to $(m^x)^c \times (m^w) \bmod p$.

The same calculations are done for both g and m as a check. The value of $g^x \bmod p$ is circulated publicly in the same manner as the public key half in RSA. This forces the signer to use the same x when $m^x \bmod p$ is created. If this parallel track of confirmation wasn't available, then the signer could choose any random y, complete the signer's half of the protocol and merely show that they knew the value of this random y. The publicly known $g^x \bmod p$ is the check against anyone making up a number.

The interactive component of this signature scheme can be eliminated if you use a cryptographically secure hash function. In this case, the protocol looks like this:

1. You create a document with hash value m and sign it by computing $m^x \bmod p$. Then you choose a random w and compute $m^w \bmod p$ and $g^w \bmod p$.

2. Instead of waiting for a challenger to generate their own c, you compute an indisputable c by hashing up the values of m, $m^x \bmod p$, $g^w \bmod p$

and $m^w \bmod p$. You can do this by placing all of their values in a file and setting c to the result of hashing the file. This value of c could not be faked by you because the cryptographically secure hash function can not be manipulated to output a certain value.

3. You calculate $r = cx + w$ as before and publish the four numbers r, $m^x \bmod p$, $g^w \bmod p$ and $m^w \bmod p$ as the signature.

4. Any challenger can check this signature by computing c by hashing the four numbers m, $m^x \bmod p$, $g^w \bmod p$ and $m^w \bmod p$ and then computing $(g^x)^c \times (g^w) \bmod p$ and $(m^x)^c \times (m^w) \bmod p$.

The hash function removes the requirement for interactivity by choosing an impartial c. If a forger wanted to create a fake signature, he could create a c that did the job. Using a hash function closes this option.

There are few practical reasons why anyone would want to use a signature like this. It may require the same number of exchanges of data that RSA requires, but it is more complicated to implement. The extra numbers are also more cumbersome. The style of signature, though, will be more useful in constructing the version of digital cash described in section 15.7.

14.7 PGP 2.6.1

Pretty Good Privacy (PGP) is certainly one of the most contentious pieces of software to emerge in recent years. The author, Phil Zimmerman, was attacked by both the Public-Key Partners (PKP) who hold the patents for RSA, and the U.S. government. PKP went after him because the software uses the RSA algorithm and in many cases the users never paid royalties. This was settled over time after the software became so ubiquitous that PKP was forced to make peace in order to colonize the user base. The latest version (2.6) of PGP comes with a license from PKP to use the software for noncommercial purposes. If you want to use the software for commercial purposes, PKP can arrange that for you easily because the latest version of PGP is upwardly compatible with PKP's toolkit.

The U.S. government presumably went after Phil Zimmerman because the State Department has the authority to regulate the export of munitions technology, and it considers encryption software to be munitions. Given that copies of PGP made their way out of the country, there is little doubt that *someone* was responsible for exporting them. Although no charges were filed as of this writing, the press widely reported that an investigation was launched into Zimmerman's work.

Despite all of this contention, there is no dispute that PGP is a good piece of software that solves many of the problems for implementing RSA. Zimmerman came up with solid solutions for how to take a text message, encrypt it and append a digital signature. The file formats are all text-based and they are able to move freely across the network. The software handles many of the tricky details of key generation so that the average user does not need to worry about how to find large prime numbers of the right format. Finally, Zimmerman freely distributes the source code for the implementations so that users can both check the code to make sure it is free of loopholes and change and adapt the system to their needs.

The latest version of PGP at this writing number is 2.6.2 and it represents the fruit of the compromise between Zimmerman and PKP. It was developed at MIT and it is available to U.S. addresses through anonymous FTP. (See Chapter 21 for more sources.) The only major difference is that it does not operate cleanly with earlier versions of the software that were implemented without PKP's permission.

14.7.1 PGP Details

Although many programmers understand how to use RSA in a theoretical sense, there are many important details to be solved before it can be used practically. Any implementation must construct a standard file format that will be readable by any particular machine on the network. PGP rests upon a complex and flexible file format that is designed to make it simple to handle the many levels of processing that might be requested for each file. The format allows files to be compressed, encrypted, signed and turned into ASCII text in any combination.The details of the file format are not given here because they are a bit too involved. They can be found inside the documentation for the PGP software.

PGP encrypts each file with IDEA and then bundles the key used in this encryption in a packet encrypted with the recipient's public key. If a signature is added, PGP uses MD-5 to compute a cryptographically secure hash value and then it encrypts this hash value with the sender's secret key. This generates the signature.

PGP stores all of the public keys available to it in a keyring file. This includes your own personal key as well as the keys of anyone with whom you correspond. The most novel feature in PGP is the Web of Trust it uses to authenticate the keys. Although it is simple to say that you can check a digital signature by looking up the correct public key in a directory, it is an entirely different manner to generate this directory in a trustworthy way. How can anyone be certain that the key listed for a certain individual is *really* the correct key?

Many implementations of RSA rely upon a centralized, trusted company that issues certificates. If you purchase Apple's latest version of MacOS called System 7 Pro, it comes with a procedure to create your own digital signature that is certified by Apple. After you type in the right phrases and make a trip to your local notary public, a document containing your public key is sent to a central processing center which signs it with its public key. All signatures created by you will contain a copy of the public key and a public-key certificate issued by Apple attesting that this public key is authentic. This certificate is yet another public-key signature using the public-key of the central authority.

Let's say you receive a document that was signed by X using Apple's System 7 Pro. What is the chain of trust that binds this document? You are trusting that:

1. The signature was not forged. The Apple software protects X's private key by encrypting it. X must type in a password that decrypts it before the signature can be created.

2. The certificate from Apple is correct. This means that only Apple knows the corresponding private key that generated this public key.

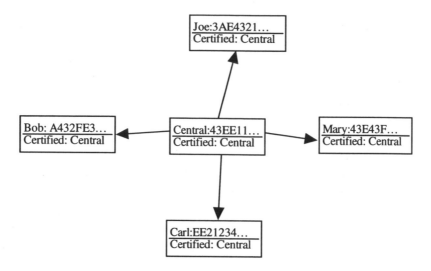

Figure 14.11: This illustrates the trust network that is used in RSA's implementation for Apple's System 7. The arrows point in the direction that trust "flows". That is, the keys of each of the four people is certified by the central agency. The number next to the name simulates the public key of the owner.

They signed it with this private key. Your software is using the matching public key to check this certificate

3. When Apple received X's public key, it was properly processed. This means that the notary checked three forms of identification before signing it themselves.

This is a fairly solid chain of authenticity. A signature generated in this fashion is certain to be more secure than any paper chain. The responsibility, though, rests upon Apple's central key certification facility. If it is compromised or the private key that they use to create their certifications is made public, then everything falls apart.

Figure 14.11 shows the trust network developed using the Apple system. Only one central authority certifies each key, but this central authority is a company that is presumably going to take the job seriously enough to stay in business. In this example, you would use the central authority's public key to test the signature it has given to the public key of Bob before validating his signature.

PGP is based upon a Web of Trust. This means that there is no central authority. All the keys contain certificates generated by other PGP users. This means that you can, and probably will, be asked to vouch for the signature of a friend or colleague. When you do this, you use your private key to sign a copy of that friend's public key. Your signature now travels around with this public key and vouches for it.

Now imagine that you receive a document supposedly signed by X using PGP. If you know X personally, you will probably have a copy of X's public key in your keyring certified by yourself. This is very easy to trust. But what happens if X is a friend of a friend? X's public key might come with a signature using a public key certified by your friend Y. If you have a copy of Y's public key signed by yourself, then you can be certain that the chain of trust extends to X and X's signature is valid.

An example of a simple Web of Trust can be found in Figure 14.12. In this example, there is no central authority. Some keys are certified by one other person, but most are certified by more. In real-life PGP usage, many people have keys that are certified by many different people. Let's say that you receive a message from Carl. If you know Carl and exchanged public keys face-to-face, then you can be certain that the signature is valid because you've got his public key in your trusted file.

If you've never met Carl before, however, you can rely upon the Web of Trust to certify the signature. Imagine you know Alan, who's vouched for Carl. Then you can trust his signature without meeting him. If you've never met Mary, but you know both Alan and Joe, then you know you can trust Mary's key.

Is such a Web of Trust successful? Only if a large number of people routinely certify their circle of friends and acquaintances. A popular theory that is perhaps apocryphal states that everyone in the world is no more than six hops away from another. If this turns out to be true, then you should, in theory, be able to build a significant web.

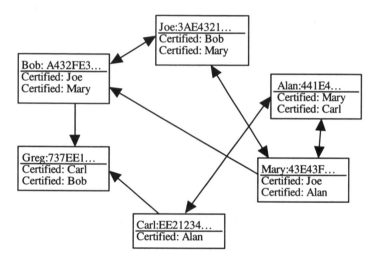

Figure 14.12: This illustrates the trust network that is used in PGP's implementation. The arrows point in the direction that trust "flows". So Carl's key is certified by Alan and Alan's key is certified by Mary and Carl. The number next to the name simulates the public key of the owner.

In practice, I predict that multiple PGP users will begin to act as certification authorities by certifying as many different people as they can. Their signatures will become widespread and be responsible for authenticating most of the keys in the world. If this occurs, then PGP can have all of the advantages of a centralized system with the extra flexibility available to handle different solutions.

14.8 Adapting PGP for Agents

PGP already handles all of the tasks that an agent realm would require. It can sign and seal messages and even compress them. Since agents are really programs written in text, there is no problem fitting their egos into an encrypted form.

The PGP technology can be glued into the agent technology in two different ways. The easiest solution is to use a higher-order scripting language to interact with PGP separately. When an agent arrives in the mail, it is saved in a file and the name of the file is passed to PGP. After PGP decodes it and verifies that the signature is valid, then it returns this information to the scripting program which fires up the agent host. The agent host then does its job and sends it on. Using a scripting language is easy to do in UNIX or a PC. It is somewhat more complicated in the Macintosh OS, but this is only because there are so many more parameters to set.

The other solution is take the PGP source code an integrate it with the rest of the agent software. That is, create one huge program with all of the features compiled into it. This can be more efficient because there is no need to use the disk drive as a temporary repository. It can be more problematic, though, if there is any reason to upgrade the software. Version 2.6.1 is the most current version of PGP at this writing, but it is entirely possible that a new version will emerge. Compiling everything over again is a painful process that slows the process of change.

A more practical problem that argues for using PGP with a scripting language is that PGP is considered to be a munitions product. Although PGP is widely available outside the United States, it is illegal to export it from the U.S. where this book is being written. This means that some people may not be able to use PGP. The best solution seems to be to leave it as a separate module that can be included if people desire to use it.

This book does not include PGP because it would complicate the marketting of the book. Unfortunately, I need to leave this integration for you.

Another advantage to leaving the encryption as a separate process is that it can be replaced by a different algorithm. There may be times when you want to use a different encryption algorithm than the one offered by PGP. A separate module allows these features to be interchanged successfully.

14.9   Royalties

The publicly available version of PGP 2.6.1 can be freely distributed and used for non- commercial purposes. If you want use the PGP software for commercial purposes or if you want to create an agent realm that does commercial things, then you must negotiate a license with PKP. Their license terms are fairly general. For details contact:

```
Robert Fougner
Director of Licensing
Public-Key Partners
130B Kifer Court
Sunnyvale, CA 94086
(408) 735 6779
```

14.10   Judging Security

Security is a very important problem for any agent realm. It allows a host to control access and prevent wayward agents from strolling through an open door. The digital signature scheme described in this chapter won't stop viruses or malicious attacks, but it does let you track down the culprit.

Some may feel that the actual details of an agent are not as necessary to encrypt. This depends upon how much you trust your communications medium. Most messages or agents are innocuous enough to travel in the clear and rely upon blending in for security. This is an okay solution, but it is not a long-term one. Many people like to assume that privacy is just a shield for illegal activity. Any secret must be hiding the work of a cabal or a network of crooks. Phil Zimmerman, for instance, states that some of the reasons that you might want to encrypt something are because you're "conducting an illicit affair" or "doing something that you feel shouldn't be illegal but is." These reasons for privacy are romantic in the same way that Bonnie and Clyde were romantic and obscure the largely legitimate reasons for maintaining privacy. There must be millions of cases recorded where criminals used privileged information to defraud or steal. Good security is a good practical defense against crime.

It is a good idea to get in the practice of routinely encrypting data when it travels on the network. This encourages the development of tools that maintain privacy. These tools should be widely available. The only way to do this is to use encryption in routine matters.

A larger problem is maintaining a central repository of signatures. The PGP Web of Trust model can work effectively for smaller communities of hackers and enthusiasts. It may run into more problems in a larger commercial or campus setting. If there is going to be a widespread network of agents running around a network, then a central authority should begin to offer to serve as a clearinghouse for all signatures. This is easy to accomplish within the PGP framework if one group or person does the job.

14.11 Summary

Encryption is probably one of the most important technologies to bind a network. Computer agents will not be able to work for very long in a serious environment if there can't be some way to extend trust across the network.

Of course, there are also great problems with the technology. Some consider encryption to be the greatest threat to law enforcement that ever came along. The problem is that the codes are potentially unbreakable. Anyone can encrypt information and be fairly sure that the information can't be used to incriminate them unless the key is discovered. Some of the traditional ways to gather evidence like wiretaps and searches are now rendered worthless. Unreliable methods like finding someone to turn a witness for the prosecution in return for a lighter sentence grow more and more important.

There is also a strong case for encryption. Information is very valuable. Businesses need to be wary of industrial espionage. People need to guard personal financial records like credit card numbers because fraud is easy for anyone who gains access to the records. Encryption is a technology that can help people protect private information.

The tension between the branches of the U.S. government like the National Security Agency and the Federal Bureau of Investigations and the average citizen that wants to use encryption are sure to grow in the next several years. The U.S. government seems determined to maintain access to every form of communication that it can find. It also seems determined to stop the export of any security software that could be used by a non-American.

This battle is bound to lead to disaster. Bureaucratic inertia will prevent companies from developing well-written, solid implementations of secure software because they won't be able to export it. It will be impossible for companies to create agent software that truly links people around the globe because they won't be able to include strong encryption software. The net result will be a world for agents that is hardly secure and barely protected. The irony is that this will probably encourage more crime by sophisticated computer hackers. Theft of cellular phone services is already a huge business and the phone companies are finding it difficult to stop. This is just a small part of people's lives. If agents do more, then the crime loss will be staggering.

At this writing, the FBI and the NSA have made it obvious through their actions that they will continue to campaign against secure communications that threaten their ability to routinely intercept and gather data. Readers are encouraged to decide for themselves whether encryption is a net win or a net loss for society and then make their opinions known to Congress.

Chapter 15

Cash

——————————————— The Hype ———————————————

*There is a profound elegance to the way that cash slips throughout
the economy, joining the lives of two different people together in
a bond of wonderful commerce, if not for their lives, at least for
a few blissful moments.*

——————————————— Political Cynicism ———————————————

*If we're going to escape the bounds of capitalism, we must keep
the corrosive influence of cash and its second cousin cultural domination out of the electronic Eden known as the Net.*

——————————————— The Buzzwords ———————————————

*Blinding signatures and RSA technology instantiate a unit for
exchanging computational resources.*

The parodists of the Beatles known as the "Ruttles" sang, "All you need is cash." Nothing could be more true for any on-line agent realm if the agents are going to do something truly useful. Software agents need to be able to traffic in money to get the jobs done.

One intermediate solution is invoicing. Any host can send a bill or invoice to the owner of the agent that uses time or data. This is quite possible to do using digital signatures because the signature is a pretty good way to track down the debtor. The invoice may even be the preferred method of doing business among businesses that regularly assume that they'll be able to pay invoices within 30 days after receiving them. Many businesses need that much time to process the paperwork.

This solution is fine, but it requires plenty of preliminary work before the agent arrives. The agent's sender must arrange for an account to be opened at the agent host. At the very least, this means arranging for the public keys with digital signatures attached. It also means extending credit. In many cases, a business must check out a credit history and decide whether to extend credit or require an outside agency like a credit card company.

Invoicing and credit work, but they're slow. They require plenty of pre-negotiation and a large amount of trust. Some businesses routinely go by the motto, "In God We Trust. All others pay cash." How is such a business going to move into the electronic realm? How are we going to demand payment up front for some services? The goal is to find a way to give the agent some electronic cash to negotiate payment when it arrives.

Some problems appear immediately. How can an agent carry cash? If an agent is just a file full of characters, then the cash would need to be represented as some sort of words, numbers or bits. Someone could just duplicate the agent and rob it stripping out the right data. Then they could make thousands of copies of this cash and go on a big spending spree. Copies of digital items are easy to make.

The solution is to use all of the clever cryptographic algorithms described in Chapter 14 to sign and date cashiers checks that can act like money. These digitally signed versions are even more secure than the average bank check, which is relatively easy to forge with a laser printer and a good replica of a signature. The algorithms can also be used to create digital cash that is, like regular cash, potentially anonymous.

This chapter describes a wide variety of digital cash algorithms. The approaches get more complex as they acquire more features. The simplest ones are not anonymous, while the most complex ones are anonymous and allow the bank to track down any malicious user. The best ones are complex and efficient. Several commercial systems are described in Chapter 16. [1]

15.1 Digital Cashier's Checks

A common way to carry a large chunk of cash is to bring a cashier's check. [Cha90b] When the bank creates such a check, it places a hold on the money so that the check will always clear. This effectively allows the checks to act as a surrogate for cash. Although people may not be conscious of it, they are effectively treating the special printing and appearance of the check as proof that it is authentic. Forging such a check is easy if you have access to another copy and the right tools.

A digital version is just as easy to create. The client goes to his bank which creates a block of data like this:

(Bank Name, Account Number, Check Number, Amount).

Then the bank signs it with its own digital signature. It can also encrypt the account number and the check number if it wants to do so for extra security. When such a packet is presented to someone else, they can take the packet to the bank and cash it. The bank must keep a record of the check, maintain a hold on the amount and check this record before it cashes the check.

This approach produces something very similar to cash. Any user could go to the bank and routinely request a collection of checks in standard denominations like $10. This money could be parceled out and spent as necessary although it would not be very efficient if someone needed to make change. This system would require plenty of $.01 checks and it is entirely possible that the disk space at the bank required to keep track of this check

---

[1] Much of the work on digital cash began with David Chaum. These papers include [Cha81, Cha83, Cha85b] and they culminate in patents like [Cha85a, Cha88a, Cha88b, Cha90a, Cha90d, Cha90c, Cha92b]. The article [Cha92a] gives a good summary of the work. Other cash systems include [Bra94, Hay90, LL93, OO90, OO92, Ant90, YLR93].

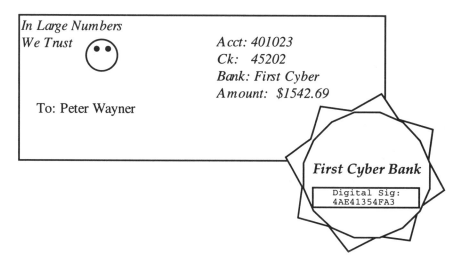

Figure 15.1: A basic digital cashier's check. The bank creates a digital signature for the note by hashing the recipient, the account number, the check number, and the amount and then encrypting this value with its private key.

would cost more than a penny.

15.2   Endorsed Digital Cashier's Checks

One potential hazard with the digital cashier's check is that the holder is
the owner. This might be desirable in some situations where it would be
nice to exchange the digital cashier's check multiple times before someone
takes it to the bank. The only problem is that copies are simple to make.
In fact, everyone along the chain of exchange would have a copy. The first
one to cash the check gets the money. There is no audit trail available. In
fact, someone could be getting a copy of the check and think it is valid long
after it was cashed by someone else.

A better solution is to require the owner of the account to endorse the
check. The owner takes a standard digital cashier's check for a certain
amount and adds the name of the person who gets the money. Then the
owner signs the entire packet with its own digital signature. When the check
arrives at the bank, the bank checks to make sure that the endorsing signature is a valid signature for the account. Then it makes sure that the person
depositing the check matches the name on the check.

This solution is much safer. If someone tries to cheat by using the same
check twice, then both copies of the check will arrive at the bank with the
endorsing signature. The only person who could have done this is the account
holder with the private key used to generate the signature.

One problem with a system like this is overhead. Each dollar bill might go
through thousands of hands in its life in the economy. Every time someone
gets a dollar bill, they can respend it without sending it off to the bank.
Another problem is anonymity. Many people like to keep their personal
business private. Now, every single financial transaction in the agent realm
would leave a trail.

The holder of a digital cashier's check can add more security by adding
another layer of encryption. After endorsing this check with their digital
signature, they can encrypt this block with the public key of the check's
recipient. Now, only the recipient holds the private key needed to decode
the endorsement.

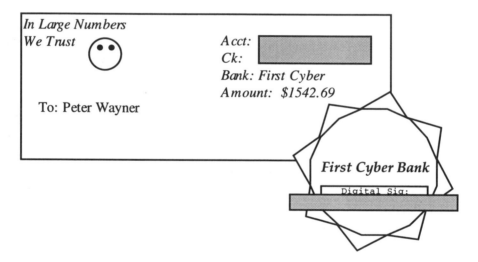

Figure 15.2: An enhanced digital cashier's check. The account and check number are encrypted with a secret key by the bank. It's signature is encrypted with the public key of the recipient so only the recipient can cash it.

This approach is secure because only the holder could have generated the digital signature endorsing the check to the recipient and only the recipient could have decrypted this endorsement before presenting it to the bank. Figure 15.2 gives an allegorical interpretation of the scheme.

15.3 Blinded Signatures

Anonymous digital cash requires a new cryptographic technique known as *blinded signatures*. David Chaum, a cryptographer in Holland, created the technique and used it as the base of many of the digital cash algorithms. [Cha83, Cha85b] The goal is to find a way for a bank to validate a cashier's check without being able to keep track of the serial numbers inside. This prevents them from tracking the cash flow.

If the bank uses RSA signatures, it has it's public key, e, it's private key d, and the modulus $n = pq$. Ordinarily, the bank would sign the message m by computing $m^d \bmod n$. The value of m would be a cryptographic hash of the packet of check information. The trick to getting the bank to sign something without knowing what it is signing is to blind the quantity using a random number k ($1 \leq k \leq n$) called a *blinding factor*. You send the bank the value:

$$r = mk^e \bmod n.$$

The bank signs this by computing:

$$r^d = (mk^e)^d \bmod n.$$

Ordinarily, the bank would keep a record of this value r because it contains all of the information. In this case, all of the information is hidden by the blinding factor.

When you receive the signed value r^d back from the bank, you remove the blinding factor by computing:

$$t = r^d k^{-1} \bmod n = m^d \bmod n.$$

This solution works because $(k^e)^d \bmod n = k^{de} \bmod n = k$. You've now got a signature on something without letting the bank know what they're signing. Figure 15.3 illustrates the scheme.

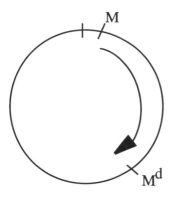 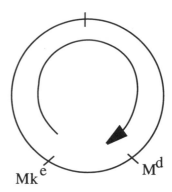

Figure 15.3: **Blinded digital signatures can be created using a blinding factor k^e. This hides the value being signed, M. The blinding factor disappears because $k^{d \times e} = 1$.**

15.4   Simple Anonymous Cash

Blinded signatures are the first step to creating anonymous cash. The second step is convincing a bank, or anyone else for that matter, that they should just blithely apply their signature guaranteeing payment to something they've never seen.

The simple solution is to use a process called *cut and choose* that is useful for stopping people from bluffing. When a customer wants one unit of anonymous cash, the bank asks him to prepare i bank notes with blinded signatures. The bank checks $i - 1$ of them to ensure that they're okay and then signs the one that's left. (See Figure 15.4) There is still one chance in i that fraud will occur, but if the bank has penalties that are greater than i times the value of the note then most people won't play the losing game. Indictments for fraud can tilt the balance even further.

When a customer wants one unit of anonymous digital cash, the bank requires him to prepare i anonymous bank notes or checks for a signature:

$$B_1, B_2, \ldots B_i.$$

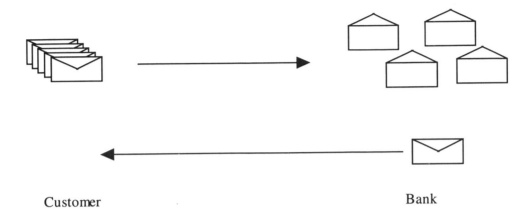

Figure 15.4: A customer who wants to create anonymous cash must create i sealed bills, shown here as envelopes. The bank opens up $i - 1$ "envelopes" to check for fraud and returns the last one.

Each note contains the amount, the bank's name and a random serial number chosen from a selection of numbers large enough to prevent duplication. The customer encrypts these notes with i keys:

$$f(B_1, key_1), f(B_2, key_2), \ldots f(B_i, key_i).$$

The customer also prepares the i different hash values of the different bills:

$$hash(B_1), hash(B_2) \ldots hash(B_i)$$

and blinds them using i blinding factors, $k_1, k_2, \ldots k_i$. This produces:

$$h_1 = k_1^e hash(B_1), h_2 = k_2^e hash(B_2) \ldots h_i = k_i^e hash(B_i).$$

When the bank receives the package of encrypted bank notes and their blinded hash values asking for a signature, it chooses $i - 1$ bank notes and asks for their keys and their blinding factors. The customer supplies them and the bank removes the blinding factor by computing $h_j^d k^{-1} \bmod n$ for each bank note B_j being challenged. Then it decrypts the notes and checks their hash value. Ideally, everything will match up. If it does, the bank sends back the blinded signature of the one note left unchallenged and deducts the value of this bill from the applicant's account.

The cut and choose protocol is a favorite part of many cryptograpic protocols because it allows people to check facts without revealing all of the information. In highly structured cases, proofs exist that that no knowledge is exchanged. These protocols, often known as *zero-knowledge proofs*, may be of interest in some cases.[2]

The bank notes produced by this method are now anonymous. They make their way around the network and can be traded like the digital cashier's checks described earlier. When someone finally decides to convert them into regular cash or gold by calling the bank, the bank can't trace where the cash came from. It knows that it is authentic. The signature is valid and it only applied that signature to bank notes. Therefore it can cash it.

The bank couldn't keep a record if it tried. Even though it knows the identity of everyone who took out money, it can't keep track of the various signatures it applies to bills because they're worthless. By the time the bill arrives for repayment, the blinding factor is gone.

Although much of this information is gone, there is still enough left to corral fraud. The bank defends against someone trying to spend the note twice by keeping a record of all of the serial numbers of the bills it cashes. This number won't tie the note back to the creator because the number was only seen in an encrypted form. It will allow the bank to stop the second customer who tries to cash it. If this person is someone who thought they were getting a valid note, then that person is out of luck. There is no way to trace the note. They will presumably go to the person who gave them

---

[2]The notion of a zero-knowledge proof is straightforward, even though the execution of the protocol is intended to be perfectly elusive and elliptical. The theoretical work from the 1980's ([BC86, BC87, Cr87, FFS87, FFS88]) culminated with the paper [BOGG+90] that showed that everything provable could be done while revealing "zero knowledge." These results are not necessarily applicable to efficient implementations. Some papers exploring more practical details are [GQ88, Bet88, BSMP91, BFL90, FS90, Kil91]. Finally, these papers provide an overview of the topic: [JJea90, Gol93, BC90]. Schneier [Sch94a] also explores the topic in depth.

$$
\begin{aligned}
Id_1 &= 10011010110 \\
Id_2 &= 01110100100 \\
Id_3 &= 10110010001 \\
Id_4 &= 11010100110 \\
Id_{total} &= 10001000101
\end{aligned}
$$

Figure 15.5: Here is an example of a secret number (Id_{total}) split into four parts (Id_1, Id_2, Id_3 and Id_4) that can be XORed together to reveal the secret.

the note and try to track the fraud that way.

15.5 Secret Sharing

An ideal form of digital cash would remain anonymous until someone tried to spend the cash twice. Then, there would be enough information for the bank to swoop down and catch the bad seed. The solution to this problem uses a cryptographic technique called *secret sharing* that allows someone to split up a value into n parts. In some of the simple implementations, all n parts are necessary to decrypt the data. The more sophisticated algorithms allow the secret value to be recovered if some subset of k parts are also known, but they won't be used here. The goal is to hide the identity of the person who created the bank notes so that it can be recovered if the bill is spent twice.

The simple solution to splitting some value Id into n parts is to create $n-1$ random numbers, $Id_1 \ldots Id_{n-1}$ of the same number of bits as Id. Finally, set $Id_n = Id_1 \odot Id_2 \odot \ldots Id_{n-1} \odot Id$. Now, $Id = Id_1 \odot Id_2 \odot \ldots Id_{n-1} \odot Id_n$ and these are the n parts of the secret value Id. ("$\odot$" stands for bitwise XOR).

The anonymous traceable digital cash will require one additional feature. The secrets will be encrypted in a packet that can only be decrypted in one way. This technique, often called *bit commitment*, is often used when people want to prove that a particular piece of data existed at one time. In this case, a second well-known string is attached to the end of each secret. This might be the phrase "Bob's Bank is Best" or it might be a number. In any case, it must be recognizable at the end. Let's assume the bank's value is the number G.

In the next section, the n parts of the secret Id will be sealed into n bit-commited packets by encrypting them:

$$f(Id_1G, IdKey_1), f(Id_2G, IdKey_2), \ldots, f(Id_nG, IdKey_n).$$

Id_iG is formed by concatenating the two values into a data structure. This protocol might be used in a case where the n holders of the parts couldn't be trusted by each other. In this case, the n parts are dispersed to the n holders who choose their own key, encrypt it and return their part back to a neutral observer. When the time comes to open up the secrets in the future, the neutral observer requests the n keys and then decrypts the packets. If each holds the distinctive message G at the end, then it is presumed that the keys were correct and the secret could successfully be reassembled from the parts.

This procedure relies upon the encryption algorithm to thoroughly mix the bits being encrypted. That is, if one bit in the packet is changed, any bit in the encrypted version might be changed. In practice, many algorithms only do a limited amount of mixing. The most basic form of DES uses 64-bit blocks and any changes in one block do not affect the results of an other. If someone used a version like this and set both Id_i and G to be 64-bit blocks, it would be possible for a cheater to change Id_i without affecting the encrypted version of G.

More sophisticated versions of DES use block chaining to do deeper mixing by using the result of each block as the initialization vector of the next block. Many of the newest encryption algorithms have adopted DES's scheme for chaining the blocks together. Versions with a feature like this should be used. Although these algorithms work serially and changes in one block only affect the encrypted value of subsequent blocks, this effect will still preserve the integrity of the system because Id_i is placed before the spe-

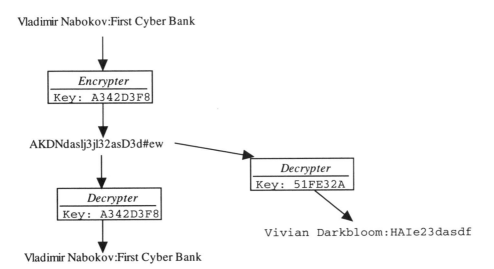

Figure 15.6: Vladimir Nabokov creates a bit-committed packet for some cash issued by "First Cyber Bank" by adding his name to the special phrase G and encrypting it. If he tries to deny this was created by him, he may find a key that, by some miracle, decrypted to the name "Vivian Darkbloom" and framed her. In this case, it is highly unlikely that the name of the bank would survive correctly.

cial value G. If some are attempts to tamper with the encrypted version of ld_i, then the special value of G will not emerge.

15.6 Traceable Anonymous Cash

What if someone spends the cash twice? It would be nice to track down the crook. This is easy to do with digital cashier's checks, but how would it work with anonymous cash? Just add another field into each note that contains the identity of the original customer creating the cash, but lock this up in a bit-commited shared secret. Let this identity be split into two parts:

$$f(Id_1G, IdKey_1) and f(Id_2G, IdKey_2).$$

This is added to the text of each of the notes that is hashed and encrypted before being presented to the bank for signing. Splitting the identity into just two values won't be enough for a robust system, but it is enough to reveal how the system works. Figure 15.7 shows a diagram of a traceable anonymous cash system.

When a customer wants an anonymous bank note, it creates i notes as usual. The bank checks $i - 1$ notes for correctness. It checks the identity string by asking the customer to present the two keys $IdKey_1$ and $IdKey_2$. This allows it to decrypt the two halves of the identity, $f(Id_1G, IdKey_1)$ and $f(Id_2G, IdKey_2)$. Then it verifies that the special slogan or number G is present and that Id_1 and Id_2 can be XOR'ed together to reveal the customer successfully. If everything checks out on all $i - 1$ bills, the bank assumes that the customer's last bill is okay and signs it.

Now, when the customer goes to spend the note, the store flips a coin and asks the customer to reveal $IdKey_1$ or $IdKey_2$. The store can determine that the special slogan G is present which verifies that the note hasn't been tampered with, but it can't determine the identity because it only decoded one of the two parts. If the G is okay, then it accepts the note, completes the purchase and eventually returns to the bank to cash it.

When the bank accepts the note, it can check to see that the identification number is not recorded as being spent. If it has, then there is trouble. The bank must try to figure out who is cheating. It pulls out its copy of the old

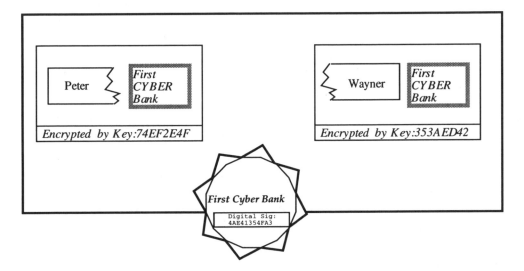

Figure 15.7: A schematic diagram of traceable anonymous digital cash The identity is split between two puzzle pieces. Both are locked in a bit-committed box with the logo phrase of the bank. The entire package is signed by the bank with a blinded digital signature.

note. If $IdKey_1$ was used to unlock half of the identity string on one note and $IdKey_2$ was used on the other note, then the double spending could only have been done by the customer. The unlocked halves can be combined to reveal the identity of the customer.

If the same half of the identity was unlocked on both bills when the store flipped the coin, then the result is ambiguous. The store might be secretly duplicating the bill and presenting it twice or the customer could have been spending it at different stores. This is why one pair isn't enough for a robust system. It will only catch a bad customer half of the time.

The solution is to add many identity pairs to each note. See Figure 15.8. The more there are, the safer the system will be. When the notes are presented to the bank for signing, the bank asks for both halves of each pair on each note and checks them all. When the customer spends the note, the store flips the coin for each pair and asks for one half of each pair.

Now, if the same serial number appears at the bank twice, the bank can be certain who is the troublemaker. If the same halves of each identity were revealed in both notes, then the store must be the one turning in the bill twice. Only the customer can unlock halves of the identity by revealing the $IdKey$'s. The store can't unlock more.

On the other hand, if the customer was spending the bill twice at different stores, then the odds are quite good that the customer will reveal different halves of the same identity string to each store. If there are p pairs of identity strings, then the odds are only 1 in 2^p that the same halves of the pairs will be revealed to both stores. The bank only needs one pair to reveal the secret identity and send the customer packing.

This solution is quite novel and very robust. It allows the bank to protect itself against double spending and identify any customer or store that tries to cheat the bank by spending the cash twice. It does not, however, allow any fraud to be caught if the cash travels between several hands in the path. In fact, it is practically impossible to use this last system for transferable cash because the creating customer must be able to unlock halves of the identity string for the final customer.

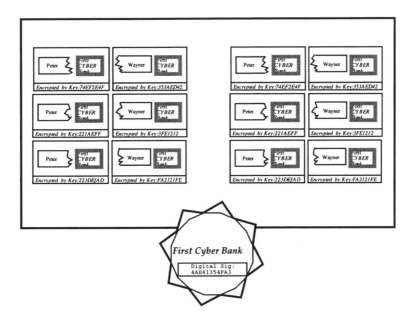

Figure 15.8: A true anonymous cash item will contain many bit-commited packets that split the identity into two halves. Here six packets ensure that a double spending person will be able to be identified in all but 1 out of 2^6 cases on average.

15.7   Cash without Choices

The cash protocols defined so far need each cash creator to generate n potential bills or checks and let the bank open up $n - 1$ of them to look for cheating. The value of n controls the efficiency of the scheme. If it is small, then the applications to create new bills can be much shorter but the chances of cheating will rise. An ideal cash system would avoid this waste.

Stefan Brands [Bra93, Bra94] developed such a system using the discrete log based signature schemes described in section 14.6. The system works because the bank will only sign documents of a set form. Anyone can present a potential note in any form, but they will not be able to spend it later. The protocol only works if cash is in the right format.

In this system, there are three systemwide numbers: p, the prime modulus, g, a generator from the set; and d, a number from the bank that represents the bank. Each bank might use several values of d and let them encode different denominations. These numbers are widely circulated from public sources. Each bank also creates an individual identity tag for each user. This is Id. It may be a bank account number, a general id number like the social security number or even an alphanumerically encoded name.

The bank avoids choosing between n different potential notes by only signing a note that is in the form $d(g^{Id})\ mod\ p$. A bad user might present any number, but they will not be able to spend the cash effectively. A note is generated like this:

1. The potential note holder creates $d(g^{Id})\ mod\ p$. d represents the bank and it includes a serial number for the bill.

2. The note holder blinds this value with a random number s by raising it to the s power, i.e calculating $d^s(g^{(s \times Id)}\ mod\ p$.

3. The note holder presents this value to the bank for a signature. The bank signs it with whatever signature algorithm it chooses. It should be a version of the discrete log based signature scheme described in section 14.6 for security reasons.

4. The note holder creates two values, A and B such that

$$AB = d^s(g^{(s \times Id)} \bmod p.$$

The holder does this by splitting s into two parts, x_1 and x_2, such that $x_1 + x_2 = s$ and $s \times Id$ into two parts y_1 and y_2 such that $y_1 + y_2 = s \times Id$. This means that $A = d^{x_1} g^{y_1} \bmod p$ and $B = d^{x_2} g^{y^2} \bmod p$.

The bank now created a new note, but it cannot use its records to keep track of the note itself because of the blinding factor s. This obscures the result from the bank and preserves the anonymity.

The cash is spent in a more elaborate ritual. The store must force the spender to reveal enough about its identity so that any attempt at double spending can be caught. In an earlier version of cash, the identity was obscured by breaking it into two halves that added together to reveal the identity. (See section 15.5.) Now, the identity will be encoded by converting the identity into a point in a domain and forcing the spender to draw a line through the identity point. This line does not reveal the identity because there are an infinity number of points on the line. It will reveal the identity, however, if the spender uses the cash twice and creates two lines. The identity lies at the intersection of the points.

Here is the spending protocol in a less abstract format:

1. The spender offers up $d^s(g^{(s \times Id)} \bmod p$, the banks signature on that number as well as A and B.

2. The store challenges the spender with a random number c.

3. The spender responds with $x_1 + cx_2$ and $y_1 + cy_2$. This is the information that could catch the double spender. Anyone can deduce the values of x_1, x_2, y_1 and y_2 if they can get a second copy generated with a different value of c. This reveals the value of s and $s \times Id$ which is enough to calculate Id.

4. The store checks this response by calculating

$$A(B^c) and d^{(x_1 + cx_2)} g^{(y_1 + cy_2)}.$$

These two numbers should be equal. If they are not, then the spender is trying to cheat by using fake values of A and B.

5. The store also checks the signature on $d^s(g^{(s \times Id)} \bmod p$. It confirms that the bank issued that note.

This protocol only works if the cash is created in a specific format. If the note spender tries to create a note in the wrong format, it will not work when it is split into A and B. If the spender tries to spend the cash twice, then the system reveals the values of Id in a nice, elegant way.

There is one hole to fix. The spender could create different versions of A and B for each trip to the store. Each of them would check out, but the combination of the two would not reveal the identity because different values of x_1, x_2, y_1 and y_2 were used. This problem can be solved by changing the way that the bank computes its signature. It will use the discrete log based system described in section 14.6 because this system can force the bank into making a signature that depends upon a particular challenge.

The protocol works like this:

1. The bank propagates the public part of its signature, g, $g^x \bmod p$ and p.

2. The future note holder presents a note to be signed by the bank. $m = d^s(g^{(s \times Id)} \bmod p$.

3. The bank creates a random number w and computes $m^x \bmod p$, $m^w \bmod p$ and $g^w \bmod p$.

4. The note holder presents a number c. In an interactive discrete log signature scheme, this would be a random number. Here, the future note holder computes it by hashing together m, $m^x \bmod p$, $g^w \bmod p$, $m^w \bmod p$ as well as the A and B that it will use to spend the cash later. The future note holder gives this to the bank. Notice that this does not reveal the A and B to the bank.

5. The bank computes $r = cx + w$ and creates the signature consisting of the number $m^x \bmod p$, $m^w \bmod p$, $g^w \bmod p$ and r.

When the cash is later spent, the store checks the signature by:

1. Computing c, the hash value of m, $m^x \bmod p$, $g^w \bmod p$, $m^w \bmod p$ as well as the A and B.

2. Computing $m^r \bmod p$ and checking that it is equal to $(m^x)^c \times (m^w) \bmod p$.

3. Computing $g^r \bmod p$ and checking that it is equal to $(g^x)^c \times (g^w) \bmod p$.

This signature cannot be adjusted by the note spender because he does not know the values of x and w and can't compute them unless he knows how to take a discrete logarithm. The hash value is the most important part of this measure because it forces the note creator/spender to lock in a value of A and B at the beginning. It cannot switch them without invalidating the digital signature from the bank that guarantees the note.

The advantages of this cash system are obvious. The amount of information that must be transfered between the note creator and the bank are much smaller now. There is no need to send n notes and open up $n-1$ to guard against cheating. The structure of the note itself and the bank's digital signature help prevent double spending.

The notes are also substantially smaller. There is no need to maintain m different versions of half of the identity and force each spender to reveal a random set of m halves. This reduces both the size of the note itself and the amount of information the bank must keep on hand to guard against double spending.

There are some limitations to these signatures. The protocol is much more complicated for programmers. The software must hash values in a consistent and reproducible way. If network and storage costs aren't too high, it may be simpler to pay the transfer fees to create n bills. This is, however, unlikely because any efficient implementation of digital cash will require large, large banks to issue large numbers of bills to keep operating overhead to a minimum. At these sizes, even saving 10% of the size of the note is enough.

15.8   Summary

The digital cash systems discussed in this chapter are quite intriguing because they allow people to transfer money without transferring anything physical. The only support for any check or bank note is the reputation of the bank. Although this digital transfer seems somewhat eerie and divorced from reality, it is not much different from our old gold-backed currency system. At that time, we just had faith that everyone would still be interested in gold in the future. Given that so little of the gold is ever destroyed or used in industry, this is a pretty large leap of faith.

There are still large practical problems with using the digital cash systems described here. Basic digital cashier's checks are relatively simple to use. The signature does not add too much overhead. Anonymity, though, can cost plenty if the bank intends to track down the fraud.

Another major problem is brought about by the patent claims. All of the digital signature schemes described here are claimed by someone and occasionally several people. The Public Key Partners claims that its wide variety of patents covers processes like using exponentiation to implement secure communication. Unfortunately, the courts are responsible for deciding how narrowly or broadly the claims of a patent can be construed, and getting an opinion from the court system requires a good team of lawyers who won't work for free (or digital cash that might infringe on a patent). The easiest solution is often just to license the software.

There are other legal problems as well. It is not entirely clear who can issue bank notes. In the not-so-distant past, many banks issued their own currency which they backed with a corresponding amount of gold kept in the vault. Bad banks quickly took advantage of the opportunity to print money and this contributed to the monetary troubles that led to the creation of the Federal Reserve System controlled by an independent agency based in Washington, DC. They issue the currency for the country and ensure that it is backed by the good faith of the U.S. government. At the very least, it may not be politically possible to issue notes that compete with the green bills.

The best solution may be to find regulatory niches that permit companies to issue their own scrip or cash. Traveler's checks are a popular form of cash for some people. Prepaid telephone calling cards are another form of digital cash that masquerades as a simple calling chit. Both of these realms might offer companies the chance to create digital cash and offer it successfully to the world. But even these can cause problems. Some governments are sure to view these cards as a form of currency and decide that the government alone has the right to issue currency.

These problems are certain to be resolved in the near future. Chapter 16 describes many of the new commercial cash systems emerging on the market. Many banks, credit card companies and other financial entities are sure to rush into this field. They see the electronic network as a frontier to be colonized.

Anonymity can also cause problems. Criminals are some of the biggest fans of anonymity. Cash transactions help support illicit businesses. The blinded signing process can easily be used for anonymous extortion. The approach is commonly described as involving a kidnapped child. [vSN92, Sch94a] When the kidnappers have the child, they send in the blinded hash values for a long list of $100 notes. The bank signs them and prints the values in an advertisement in a newspaper. The kidnappers buy a newspaper, unblind the notes and spend their cool million dollars. If they're lucky, the newspaper is published electronically and the criminals won't need to spend the time typing in the answers. There is no troublesome cash exchange in the physical world and the cops won't be able to catch them.

Chapter 16

Commercial Cash

––––––––––––––––––– The Hype –––––––––––––––––––

Why work hard for money if you can just print it?

––––––––––––––– Political Cynicism –––––––––––––––

If the power to create currency is vested in a small class of people, they will use their power to dominate the underclass.

––––––––––––––––– The Buzzwords –––––––––––––––––

Digital signatures, zero-knowledge proofs and encryption rolled into one system.

When this book was being written in the fall of 1994, many companies both small and large began offering different digital payment schemes to the world. Although there will certainly be some shake out in the market between the time that I write this and the time that you read this, there is still some advantage in going over the different products available and discussing some of their technical strengths and weaknesses. This may help you structure your own digital payment method and, perhaps, choose between the plans on the market.

The challenge is simple: exchange payment over the network. Many companies, however, are choosing widely different parameters for their solutions. Some are explicitly mimicking credit cards, which offer little privacy or anonymity, but may be functionally easier to develop. Others are creating full-fledged anonymous cash systems that will enable anyone to exchange payment with anyone else. Some companies are using specialized hardware to guard against counterfeiting. Others are using only software because it is cheaper. All of the approaches have some merit and only time and the marketplace will determine which wins.

No one should interpret the discussion of the products in this section as an endorsement or even a thorough product review. Many of the approaches and systems are new, and it is not possible to guarantee anything about the companies. Merchants interested in the technology should conduct their own investigation of the companies offering digital cash using all of the diligence that they feel the topic is due.

16.1   NetCash

NetCash is a trademark of a digital cash product offered by NetBank, which is run by Software Agents, Inc., a company in Germantown, Maryland. They are trying to supply the network with a simple way to pay for shareware and other information-based products. The company maintains an electronic catalog of all of the merchants that accept their NetCash and distribute it freely in the hope that others will choose to make this system their choice for payments.

NetCash bills looks like this:

```
NetCash US$ 5.00 B234567C789012D
NetCash US$ 10.00 A123456B789012C
```

The bills are just tags identifying the currency type, a denomination and a serial number. The NetBank maintains a list of all valid serial numbers and ensures that they are not spent twice. There are no built-in digital signatures or other encryption.

Anyone can purchase NetCash through two different methods. The first is to telephone a 900 number with a modem. When the connection is established, the NetBank will send you a copy of a $10 bill and the phone company will charge you $10.00 for the phone call on your monthly bill. The bills purchased in this way look slightly different:

```
NetCash $ 10.00 A1234B5678C.
```

The serial numbers are shorter and there is no "US" in the tag. If you receive one of these bills, you will pay a 20% surcharge to cash it. This pays for the phone company's 900 charge.

The second method does not have such a stiff surcharge. You can purchase the regular NetCash bills by either mailing or faxing a check to the company's office in Maryland. Then, they will electronically mail you back the bills in any denomination. The faxed checks are legal tender and the NetBank is able to send them through the Federal Reserve system.

You must set up a merchant account at the bank to convert the bills back into "real" money. Once you've done that, you send in the bills and deposit them into your account. At the end of each month, the NetBank will write you a check for this cash. When these bills are exchanged, the NetBank will take a 2% charge.

The NetBank also maintains an electronic change server that will make change for your bills. It is quite possible to convert a $10 bill into two $5 bills to make spending easier. When you mail in a bill to change it, the server will destroy the old bill and create new ones.

The limitations of this system are obvious. The serial numbers of the bills must be kept secret. (The NetBank will accept PGP-encrypted messages to protect the electronic mail.) There are no digital signatures that allow a merchant to check a bill's authenticity when it arrives. The merchant must deposit the NetCash and wait to see if it clears at the bank. If the electronic mail exchange system allows the NetCash to clear quickly and easily, then the company will probably be able to do without the signatures. Anyone with NetCash will be able to find out right away whether it is worth anything.

The advantages, however, are more subtle. NetCash is easy to exchange. You just clip and paste it into a text document. There is no need to use complicated formatting software to exchange long messages. The freedom from digital signatures also means that the company doesn't need to negotiate licensing agreements with companies like PKP that have patents that might cover these signatures. This lowers their operating costs, which they should be able to pass on to the merchant in lower transaction fees.

The greatest problem will be collecting the money from customers who are purchasing NetCash. Many people aren't used to faxing checks, and mailing the check to the NetBank is probably just as fast as mailing a check to the merchant. It may be possible to buy the NetCash with a credit or debit card, but this might be adding an unnecessary step. You could simply send the credit or debit card number to the vendor.

Software Agents maintains that it is safer to send NetCash across the network than it is to send a credit card account number. This is because the size of the loss is limited by the size of the NetCash denomination. Anyone who intercepts the message won't be able to use the number to go on a wild spending spree.

As of this writing, the best place to reach NetCash is:

Software Agents, Inc.
NetBank Merchant P.O. Box 541
Germantown, MD 20875

They can also be reached electronically by sending e-mail to

`netbank-info@agents.com`

with the following keyword(s) in the message:

Keyword	Topic
netbank-intro	Introduction to the NetBank system
buying-netcash	How to buy NetCash from the NetBank
netbank-faq	Answers to frequently asked questions

16.2   First Virtual

First Virtual is a company that links up several diverse people who have had a large impact on the protocols that bind the Internet. Some of the principal members of the team include Nathaniel Borenstein and Marshall Rose , who created the Safe-TCL version described in Chapter 12. Now, the company is trying to create an information market that will allow users to buy and sell copies of data through their central clearinghouse. Their central system mediates all transactions to protect against fraud.

The basic structure of the system is explained in a document called the "Green Commerce Model" that is available via anonymous ftp from `ftp.fv.com` or through their WWW server at `http://www.fv.com`. This document lays out the basic structure of transactions between participants in their system. The technical details of the actual format of the exchanges are spelled out in the documents "The Simple Green Commerce Protocol" and "The application/green-commerce MIME Content-type".

The goal of the system is to create a level network of information traders. Everyone who sets up an account can operate at the same level. Ideally, each person will both make money by writing and disseminating information and spend money by reading what others create on the system. The system, though, supports methods for people to add and subtract "real" money from their account with credit cards, electronic transfers or checks.

The Green model solves several problems in exchange by shifting the risk of nonpayment to the merchant of information. That means that if the merchant mails out a big block of information and the check never comes back through the system, it is the merchant's tough luck. This saves First Virtual from guaranteeing the transactions by providing real digital cash. In essence, they are acting just like credit card companies, which also do not guarantee that the user will pay for the item. Many people may not be aware of the fact that they can refuse to pay for an item on their credit card bill and negotiate directly with the merchant to give them payment. This process, known as "charge-back," can annoy merchants, so the card companies try to ensure that it is only used in cases of legitimate problems with service or overcharging.

The steps of the basic payment protocol are straightforward:

1. Each user creates an account that is identified by a unique number or character string. The account contains information for how money is paid into the account and how it is taken out of it. The most important part is an electronic mail address that is used to confirm purchases.

2. The buyer starts the transaction by providing the account number. This works in the same way that the buyer might give a credit card number of the phone.

3. The merchant sends a "transfer-request" message containing the account number and the transaction amount to the central computer. The message can either be in the MIME format or be created using an interactive TCP protocol.

4. The central computer sends a "transfer-query" message with the transaction details to the buyer by connecting with the e-mail address listed on the account. This message includes all of the details of the transaction including the price of the product and any currency exchange transactions. This is equivalent to a pizza parlor calling back the person who placed an order to check to see if it is valid.

5. The central computer waits until the buyer acknowledges the transaction. Ideally, this will happen quickly. In the worst case, the buyer will ignore the responses. First Virtual will cut off accounts after a certain amount of time elapses. They will probably experiment with the length of these grace periods.

6. When the reply arrives, the central computer notifies the merchant of the decision of the buyer. Ideally, this will be "Yes", but it could also be "No" or "Potential Fraud". First Virtual seems prepared to encourage people to sell the material on an "approval" basis. They only pay if they like the information and destroy it if they don't. This will mean that merchants using this system may see more charge-backs then those who sell with credit cards. Some merchants may choose to

send the product once the authorization to charge is approved. First Virtual also intends to charge the buyer a service charge for a "No" reply and cut off the accounts of those who do this too often.

7. The merchant pays $.29 and 2% of the transaction cost when the amount is finally added to their account.

8. The accounts are settled up every set period of time. If an account is negative, the central computer sends out a charge to the account's pay-in method. This could be a credit card or a debit card. It might be a bill. If it is positive, the central computer might issue a check or transfer the money elsewhere.

There are many features of this system that work like the credit card network in our country. The accounting and the assumption of risk are identical. The major difference is the confirmation message. Ordinarily, a credit card holder only certifies a transaction with a signature that is easily forged. This isn't even used in phone transactions. The additional message could significantly reduce the potential for fraud on the network. It could also gum up the works if people delay authorizing transactions in the same way that they delay paying their bills. First Virtual will need to watch the psychological aspects of each transaction to encourage people to authorize transactions as soon as possible.

The potential for fraud is still here. Many people understand how to create fake electronic mail messages on the Internet. Is it possible for a criminal to start a transaction and then fake an acknowledgment from the owner of an account? Yes. The Green Commerce model guards against this by numbering each transaction with a unique number. This number is sent in the "transfer-query" to the owner of the buyer's account and the buyer must include the number in the return message authorizing the charge. Anyone trying to fake an authorization message would need to have access to this unique number, and this may be difficult to get. It may be possible if someone has access to a person's account, but it is unlikely to be available to random hackers on the net. First Virtual may be counting on the fact that credit card fraud is a huge but manageable cost for the banks that run credit card companies.

This system, like the NetCash system described in section 16.1, does not use digital signatures. In fact, the literature cites this as a feature because there is no reason to pay licensing fees to the patent holders. It seems clear that these fees are a complex problem for anyone trying to set up such a system and at least two companies feel ready to live without digital signatures and deal with potential for greater fraud.

16.3   DigiCash

A robust, cryptographically secure version of digital cash is being marketed by a Dutch firm set up with the cooperation of David Chaum, the inventor of many of the algorithms described in Chapter 15. The company, DigiCash BV is offering software for Windows, the Macintosh and UNIX workstations that allow these computers to transfer funds successfully. This software is highly integrated and user friendly. You can use the system to drag and drop coins which represent digital cash numbers underneath. Figure 16.1 shows a screenshot from some of their software.

There is no reason to go into great detail here because there is substantial documentation of the approach in Chapter 15. The system does not include many of the cleverest algorithms for catching double spending described in Chapter 15 because many of them are not efficient enough for practical uses. In the end, the DigiCash company chose to implement a simpler set of algorithms for their first version.

You can contact the company at `info@digicash.nl` or at:

```
DigiCash BV
Kruislaan 419
1098 VA Amsterdam
Netherlands.
```

16.4   CommerceNet

Another commercial venture known as CommerceNet operates out of Palo Alto, California. The company is working with a closely related firm known

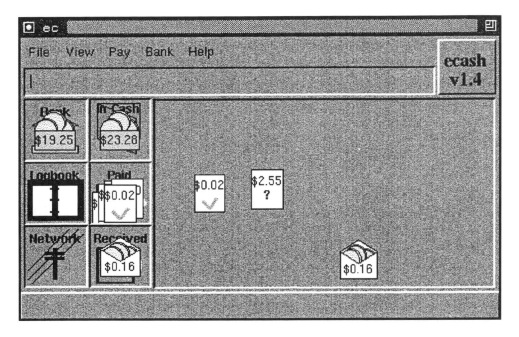

Figure 16.1: A screen shot of the Digi-Cash system. The actual version is in color. A user can exchange cash and verify it by dragging the little cash simulacra.

as Enterprise Integration Technologies to to provide a secure foundation for companies using the well-known World-Wide Web (WWW) or Mosaic technology. They hope to convert the enthusiasm for this net-based hypertext into netbased commerce by creating a way for the WWW server and the client to set up secure communications.

The structure of the underlying technology is described in an Internet Request For Comments (RFC), issued by E. Rescorla and A. Schiffman of Enterprise Integration Technology in June 1994. The goal is to extend the standard HTTP (Hyper Text Transfer Protocol) that drives most WWW interaction with a set of commands that will allow the server and client to offer different modes of access. A trusted client offering the right password could get access to documents that others could not get. The connection between the two could also be used to exchange data about credit card numbers or other sensitive financial data.

Their version of HTTP, called S-HTTP (for Secure HTTP), relies upon RSA public-key technology to preserve security. The system is designed to integrate with the various public-key certificate generators that may come to inhabit the network. This will allow people to use RSA-based digital signatures to sign their messages that flow between the S-HTTP server and the client.

The system is open ended, though, because it will allow secure connections to be established between an unknown, uncertified party and an S-HTTP server. A new client logs in by encrypting the session key with the public key of the S-HTTP server. The client and server can also use keys from a prearranged list of keys that may have been distributed by trusted courier or other means.

The S-HTTP RFC suggests that both the Internet-based Privacy Enhanced Mail (PEM) format and the PGP format (see section 14.7) will be supported to encrypt the messages. One particular problem with allowing messages to be encrypted with the public key of the S-HTTP server is that another party can interpose itself and sneak in fake replies from a client. This is because both parties have access to the public key of the client. The S-HTTP suggests that software use *Nonces*, another word for a random transaction id like the one used in First Virtual's system described in section 16.2 and the concept known as bit commitment described in section 15.5. One half of the pair sends a message and appends it with a particular random nonce. The other half responds and includes this number proving that it was the one that received the original communication. Someone else will not be able to send a fake message with different numbers because they will not have access to the nonce.

16.5 Conclusions

At the time this survey was written, there were already many announcements from companies of systems. Many of the announcements give little detail. They might be the tip of a large system that is sure to emerge or they could just be vaporware. This survey of digital cash systems is sure to be incomplete and almost certain to be out of date by the time you read it. Such emerging exciting markets are often dominated by small companies that soon merge with bigger companies or go out of business. Many of the biggest companies and banks have not offered systems to the Net yet. It will be interesting to see what companies like Visa, Microsoft and Citibank bring to the mix.

Chapter 17

Going Deeper

————————————————— The Hype —————————————————

Agents are just the beginning. We're really interested in finding a way to bundle your mind, heart and soul into a multimedia-enabled, cross-platform-ready object.

————————————————— Political Cynicism —————————————————

Technology always presents itself as the savior for the problems that it creates. Subway too inconvenient? Try a car. Can't get through the traffic jam? Try a magnetically levitating train. The economic overclass never hesitates to create problems and then sell solutions to the disenfranchised.

————————————————— The Buzzwords —————————————————

A self-organizing, group-enabled, transframe, meme-ready, conceptually co-dependent activated semantic network encapsulated into a single object would really make the world a better place.

The bulk of this book concentrated on the practical problems of creating a secure domain for agents to roam. These are important problems to solve and there is little doubt that there will be an economic need for these solutions. But, there are also a great number of more advanced and abstract, blue-sky dreams for agents emerging from academia.

In many cases, these advanced notions of agents in the Net are disappointing when they are viewed in detail. They may promise to encapsulate some form of powerful intelligence into an agent, but when it comes time to deliver the technology, is often more trouble than it is worth. The agent may be able to reason, but it may only do so after you spend hours creating a special if-then-else chart for it to follow. It may be able to learn, but only after you create an elaborate framework for what it is supposed to learn.

Many people who try to implement artificial intelligence ideas outside the laboratory have this adverse reaction. Avoiding AI technology might be a smart move economically, but it can be a mistake intellectually. Even though the grand thoughts and impertinent dreams might never fall to earth, they still can inspire plenty of interesting ideas. Object-oriented programming emerged from the artificial intelligence labs long ago. While the modern class systems that make it easy to build a user interface don't seem to embody any flash of intelligence, they are still quite useful.

This chapter discusses some of the more ambitious and extreme examples of how people are attempting to create "agents". Some of the experimental results will be quite useful on their own and others can serve as an inspiration for other computational schemas. It may be possible, for instance, to take some of the ideas here and use them to inspire simpler solutions for hosts and agents.

17.1   Emotional Agents

Ah, emotion. This is that one great arena where poets and English majors love to feel that computers just can't compete with humans. Machines might be able to do arithmetic correctly, but they'll never understand anger, love or fear.

Despite all of the strong feelings that people have about machines and their ability to feel, some researchers are strolling into the domain of the heart and soul. Some of this is an extreme vision and a quest for a digital friend that will presumably display all of the charm and companionship of a human friend without stealing someone's girlfriend. Woody Bledsoe wrote/spoke of such a friend who could "understand, act automously, think, learn, enjoy, hate" and, perhaps most important of all, "liked to walk and play Ping-Pong, especially with me."[Ble86]

While a companion might be nice, there are more practical reasons for injecting some emotion into agents. Emotions are a big part of how humans communicate. Computers need to communicate with humans. So it makes sense to teach computers some of the rudimentary details of how to use emotions effectively when dealing with humans. This way, future computers will know to inject more urgency into a cry of "Fire" than into an announcement that the mail just arrived.

Joseph Bates, W.S. Reilly and A.B. Loyall at Carnegie Mellon University (Pittsburgh, PA) have been researching the techniques used by master animators to create believable characters on the screen. [Bat94, RB92, BLR92] They studied the writings of master animators at Disney [TJ81] and Warner Brothers [Jon89] who helped recreate popular stories from the past. They abstracted the lessons from these masters and came up with three principles:

1. The emotional state of the character must be clearly defined.

2. The thought process reveals the feeling.

3. Accentuate the emotion. Use time wisely to establish the emotion, to convey it to the viewers and to let them savor the situation.

These three principles were used when the researchers tried to create agents that could portray emotions. They created a list of basic emotional states like fear or sadness. Each agent displayed its emotional state in a different graphical way. For instance, one agent named "Wolf" would display fear by arranging itself into its most aggressive posture. Another agent named "Shrimp" would appear to be alarmed. The way that each of the different agents displayed its emotions was how the individual character of the agent revealed itself. The agents expressed these emotions by changing the way that their eyes and facial features were arranged. Alarmed agents grew wide-eyed. Moping agents moved slowly and drooped. The team drew these drawing techniques that created the appearance of emotion from the animation world.

The possible emotions for an agent were well-defined because they were programmed in the computer. Anyone who attempts to follow this approach will need to be careful in creating the list of possible emotional states. They should be as distinct as possible. Love, hate, fear, loathing and ecstasy are simple examples. Naturally, some people may want to push this to the extreme. Why stop at pure love when you can distinguish between lust, the love of someone who just wants a warm bed, platonic love and the burning, smoldering passion of Heathcliff? Why stop at pure satisfaction if you can distinguish between the polite thank you, the grateful look of someone eating their first meal after leaving a desert island, and the wistful pleasure of someone whose bite of a madeline fills his mind with warm visions of childhood?

At this point, artificial intelligence researchers are often ready to dive deeper and create an architecture for emotional response and find a method for capturing a character inside of this architecture. This may be interesting research, but it goes beyond the practical applications of the work.

There are many practical ways that this research can be used in the simplest situations. Emotional signals cut through the noise. Many of us deal with plenty of information each day, but information that is properly categorized emotionally is easier to process. The ability to portray emotion correctly can also help agents bring their messages to the user.

Television stations have been honing this ability to an art. Urgent news is announced by interrupting the "regularly scheduled program," playing some fast-paced, bass-profundo music and cutting to an announcer who reads the news with a mixture of urgency and gravitas.

More common, but still urgent events are often broadcast by a scrolling banner on the bottom of the screen. In Baltimore, one television station announces a tornado warning by displaying a faint tornado icon in the corner of the screen so that viewers can be aware of the potential for danger. Less urgent news is presented in the news shows, which are carefully designed to include plenty of emotional clues for the viewer. Light material is placed at the end of the show and preceded by some happy banter by newscasters. Important details come at the beginning of the broadcast. These clues make it much easier for the viewer to follow what is happening.

Any agent programmer that wants to allow agents to bring information directly to the user will want to develop these theatrical skills. Actors spend plenty of time polishing the nuances and outwardly apparent clues that signal these emotions. Anyone building an agent system can strive for this accuracy if they're able to come up with good, agreeable means for displaying the results correctly. This may be why the first principle encourages clearly defined emotions. Any agent creator who wants to build agents that display emotions will need to approach the task with the eye of a seasoned dramatic coach and director. Every tick, gesture and motion must be scrutinized to make sure it conveys the right meaning.

17.2 Matters of Taste

Tastes are a very important part of the modern economy. New cars can succeed or fail based upon the shape of their body. Artistic industries like music and publishing rise or fall based on their ability to anticipate and satisfy the tastes of the market. These industries are major parts of the economy and there is every indication that they will grow as the manufacturing and agricultural sections of the economy become more and more adept at providing for our daily needs.

But these taste-driven industries have a major problem. They do not provide commodities so the companies must re-educate each consumer about each product. In fact, the taste-driven industries need to surprise and entertain again and again. The publishing and music industries rely heavily on media coverage from radio and newspapers to create a market for many of their products. A new book might be just the thing for 500,000 people out there, but unless these people know about it they won't be able to buy it. They must be informed, in some manner, that the book has the right mixture of rain, car chases, lovemaking and sudden, unexpected plot reversals that appeals to them.

One techniques that can be used to circumvent this problem is to classify items by other items to which they are stylistically similar. One magazine ran a text box hoping to help babyboomers find the contemporary music they liked based upon the musical tastes that they had in their formative years. If they liked Joni Mitchell, for instance, then they would like Nanci Griffith. Unfortunately, these techniques are still quite limited.

Some computer scientists are actively exploring ways to classify taste numerically despite the admonition that there is "no accounting for taste." The researchers, though, are merely trying to build a statistical model of similarity. This model will take other people's impressions about a product's likeability and feed it back into a likeability matrix.

At MIT's Media Lab, some scientists are experimenting with a collection of agents that learn your likes and dislikes. The first version organized the net news for its readers and used the responses of the other readers as a guide. You would read articles and rate your reaction as positive or negative. The current version only stores your reaction to the content and uses keyword search to rate future articles. Future versions may use the responses of other people to the piece and add this information into the equation.

Interested readers can check out the work on learning agents that schedule meetings [RM93] and filter information [SM93, Fey93]. The article by Pattie Maes [Mae94] is a good introduction to the topic, and the field is expanding rapidly.

17.3   Negotiation

Everything, they say, is open to negotiation. This will certainly be true for agents out on the network. The agents will be negotiating for access to data, for the form of data provided, and practically any other detail of the exchange. Half of the job might be successfully negotiating the information release. This is why some researchers are beginning to examine the interaction between agents and their hosts. There are plenty of rich problems that can be defined and solved in this arena.

There will be some who will be suspicious and cynical about the complexity of negotiation on the network. Most information services will provide very simple solutions for people. They will welcome agents because of their efficiency, but it will be in their economic best interest to make it as simple possible for people to send agents to that particular infomart. The interaction protocols shouldn't be too complex or the agents will never succeed and people will stop sending them. This implies that the hosts will never engage in the psychological games of chicken played in poker games and used car lots.

This careful and stable view will probably prove true for many agents. A good network will develop a stock set of boilerplate programs for negotiating resources. The agents will probably spend at relatively fixed rates and their owners will be relatively certain that their agent won't roll home with a big bill after a crazy night cruising through large databases. Everyone will be able to process data successfully.

But there will still be openings for new techniques even if large parts of the markets standardize on straightforward contracts. For instance, auction houses could offer auctions for the agents. Also, efficient markets will spawn people who make their living buying a bit lower and selling a bit higher. This arbitrage by market makers brings a flexibility and stability to the market and agents could take over a large part of the effort. Anyone can imagine clever autonomous agents prowling the network looking for locations where prices were cheaper and the moment was right for striking it rich.[1]

While there are many good reasons to dream up cool goals for agents in the future, there are some intriguing reasons to study the negotiation process between agents. Why? Because agents aren't human and don't exhibit any of the human idiosyncracies that gum up negotiations. All of the abstract economic theory using linear programming and game theory starts to make perfect sense. When the emotions, worries and ambiguities are gone, it's just math.

In fact, much of this theory can be used to cut right through much of the negotiations. For instance, imagine an auction attended by agents. Many of the big auction houses make a point about encouraging large crowds for their auctions because this builds excitement and suspense. They even begin

---

[1]One investment bank maintained a computer program that scanned the market for takeover targets.

276 CHAPTER 17. GOING DEEPER

raising the prices when no one is bidding. This won't matter to the agents. It would be possible to arrange a network where each person sent their agent with simple instructions to bid up to a cutoff amount and then stop. The host acting as auctioneer could poll each agent in turn to see if they wanted to raise the bid. This would continue until only one agent was left bidding. A simpler approach is to use a *Dutch auction*, which requires each agent to submit a sealed bid. The winner is the one with the highest bid, but that winner only pays the price of the second highest bid. This will achieve exactly the same result as an auction with minimal bid increments.

The solution was used in the Spawn distributed operating system developed at Xerox PARC by Tadd Hogg and Bernardo Huberman. Each agent would submit a bid for the processing cycles on the different machines on the network.

Deeper solutions of complicated games are certainly also possible. The problem is using game theory in the presence of deception. For instance, game theory can predict how resources can be allocated optimally. It can find a theoretical equilibrium between competing parties in a market. But, it often relies upon perfect knowledge about the costs and structure of all of the parties involved. Some good places to begin researching this topic can be found in the books [Bin92, FT92] and the articles [RZ94, GDW, ER93, ER92].

17.4 Conclusion

There are many other interesting and exciting ideas that could affect the way that you create agents. In many cases, the ideas may come from unexpected domains. Robots, for instance, cannot exist without structured ways to interact with the world and other robots. So, it is not surprising that robotists are interested in agent-like technology. [Don95, DJR94] Nor is it surprising that nanotechnologists, who are interested in creating micro machines that will be able to manipulate the world on an atomic level, are also interested in agent-like interactions. Economists have always studied how people interact and make deals. All of their theoretical work could be applied to this agent domain intact.

Chapter 18

Experimenting

───────────────── The Hype ─────────────────

*"This Chemistry Set Supports Over 100 Different Experiments."–
From the box of a Christmas Present.*

───────────────── Political Cynicism ─────────────────

*Ah, experiments. Some like to refer to the Soviet economy as the
great experiment. Its failure proves the failure of communism.
But even experiments that fail teach lessons and communicate
fundamental truths.*

───────────────── The Buzzwords ─────────────────

*An object-based, dynamically linking program in MS-DOS for-
matted ASCII files designed for instantiation on MS-DOS machines, Macintoshes, or other machines supporting XLISP. Portable.*

Talking about agents is fun, but playing with them is even better. This book contains a number of different suggestions and descriptions for agent systems. Many of you will want to fire up the systems and experiment. Good luck. The instructions for how to use the XLISP agents are discussed in this chapter.

The XLISP-Agent project is very much a work-in-progress. Please monitor the Web page: `http://access.digex.net:/pcw/pcwpage.html` for information about new releases, bug fixes and system specific information. Also make sure to send electronic mail to the author at:

`pcw@access.digex.com`

and ask to be added to a mailing list. Please include the four characters "[AU]" in the subject heading. This helps me filter out mail related to this book.

18.1 XLISP Agents

This book discussed many different aspects of developing an agent technology. Some of the chapters on XLISP describe an actual agent/host combination. You can use the enclosed disk and software to experiment with the technology on either a PC or a Macintosh.

The software on this disk, alas, does not provide a network-ready agent system. The number of different mail systems used by PCs and Macintoshes alone are too numerous to mention. The amount of time it would take to support enough different machines did not justify the effort at this time. Perhaps in the near future.

The software on the disk also lacks the ability to interface with PGP. This is largely because it is not possible to export encryption software from the United States. So, if you want to use this book as a base for an agent system, then you'll need to get a copy of this software separately. In many cases, people are actively exploring integrating PGP with mailer software. This is a hot project as this book goes to press.

The enclosed disk contains a number of files that can be used to experiment with an agent system built upon XLISP. These files are:

CORE.LSP The core files for maintaining an agent host.

HOSTSKEL.LSP The basic skeleton for a HOST file. This should be expanded to include the local functions.

AGSKEL.LSP The basic functions for an agent. You will need to expand these yourself.

AIRHOST.LSP The file containing the LISP program for the host component of the airline reservation system example discussed in Chapter 4.

AIRAGENT.LSP The LISP definitions for the agent that travels to this host and makes a reservation.

XL21GWIN.ZIP A version of XLISP for Microsoft's Windows 3.1.

XL21G386.ZIP A version of XLISP for DOS.

XL21GSRC.ZIP The source for XLISP.

XLISP.HQX A version of XLISP for the Macintosh.

If you want to begin, simply load the file LOADER.LSP using the load command on XLISP. Then type `do-agent`.

18.2 Safe-TCL Agents

Safe-TCL is also a floating target. To experiment with it, you will need a copy of the latest distribution of the C-code from Ousterhout's project. At this writing, the code can be found at `ftp.cs.berkeley.edu`, but a new site will probably emerge at Sun Microsystems once they begin releasing newer versions. Version 7.3 of TCL was the latest version available when this chapter was written in late 1994. The distribution from `ftp.cs.berkeley.edu` is intended for UNIX machines.

18.3   LOADER.LSP

This code will load up the parts of the agent, host and core into LISP and
recover from any errors. If you want to experiment with the agent system,
load this file first and execute do-agent.

```lisp
(defun loader-1 ()
  (let ((success nil))
    (setq success (errset (load "agent.lsp")))
      (cond ((null success)
             (print "Failure to load Agent Correctly.")
           (return nil))
        (t (print "Successfully loaded Agent.")))
    (setq success (errset (load "core.lsp")))
    (cond ((null success)
          (print "Failure to load Core code Correctly.")
          (return nil))
          (t (print "Successfully loaded CORE.")))
    (setq success (errset (load "host.lsp")))
    (cond ((null success)
          (print "Failure to load Host code Correctly.")
          (return nil))
          (t (print "Successfully loaded HOST.")))
    (setq success (FH-Initialize-Host))
    (cond ((null success)
          (print "Failure to Initialize Host Correctly.")
          (return nil))
          (t (print "Successfully Initialized HOST.")))
    (setq success (FH-Initialize-Security))
    (cond ((null success)
          (print "Failure to Initialize Host Security Correctly.")
          (return nil))
          (t (print "Successfully Initialized Host Security.")))
    (setq success (tb '(FA-Resource-Negotiator) 10000))
    ;; Give it 10000 units
```

```
     (cond ((null success)
           (print "Failure to Negotiate Resources Correctly.")
           (return nil))
           (t (print "Successfully Negotiated Resources.")))
     (setq success (errset (tb3 '(FA-Initialization-Function))))
     (cond ((null success)
           (print "Failure to Initialize Agent Correctly.")
           (return nil))
           (t (print "Successfully Initialized Agent.")))
     (setq success (errset (tb3 '(FA-Main-Function))))
     (cond ((null success)
           (print "Failure to Run Agent Correctly.")
           (return nil))
           (t (print "Successfully Ran Agent.")))
     (setq success (errset (tb3 '(FA-Clean-Up-Function))))
     (cond ((null success)
           (print "Failure to Clean up Agent Correctly.")
           (return nil))
           (t (print "Successfully Cleaned Up Agent.")))
     ))
(defun do-agent ()
  (dribble "Trans")
  (cond ((loader-1)
         (dribble)
         ;; ignore transcript because no error.
         )
         (t (dribble)
            (FH-Mail  FA-Return-Address "Trans")
            (FH-Send-Agent
               FA-Return-Address
               FA-Report-Me-In-Errors))))
```

18.4   AIRAGENT.LSP

This is the sample code for the agent that travels to make an airline reservation. It meets a host defined by AIRHOST.LSP.

```lisp
;;; Sample Agent
;;; It will negotiate for a flight at times with the AirRes Host.
;;;
(defun FA-Initialization-Function ()
  (setq LA-Info-Block (make-info-block
    :first-name "Peter"
    :last-name "Wayner"
    :credit-card-number 01023414223234
    :address "1000110 Whim Drive, Sim, NY 41201"
    :month 'Jun
    :date 14
    :year 1995))
  (setq FA-Agent-Identity (make-agent-ident
    :name "Fred"
    :owner "Peter Wayner"
    :return-address "pcw@access.digex.com"
    :serial-number 1
    ))
  t)
(defvar LA-Triple-List
  '((time greater-than 900) (time less-than 1200)))
;;     (start-city equal charm)
;;     (end-city equal circuit)
;;     (day equal tue)))
(defvar LA-Info-Block nil)
(defun LA-Make-Res (flt)
;; Make a reservation.
  (LH-Make-Reservation
    (flight-number flt)
    'first-aisle
```

```lisp
          LA-Info-Block))
(defun LA-Declare-Success (flt)
;; We found a flight.
  (print "Reservation Made Successfully.")
  (LH-Print-Flight-Info flt))
(defun FA-Main-Function ()
  (let ((answer nil))
    (setq answer (LH-Flights-By-Item-2
                      (car LA-Triple-List)))
  ;;; (setq *time-left* (+ 1000 *time-left*))
    (do ((l (cdr LA-Triple-List) (cdr l))) ((null l))
        (Format t "Starting ~a" (car l))
      (setq answer (LH-Flights-By-Item-2 (car l) answer))
      (Format t "After ~a there are ~a possible flights.~%"
          (car l) (length answer)))
    (cond (answer ;; There is a flight!!
        (do ((l answer (cdr l))) ((null l))
          (cond ((LA-Make-Res (car l))
              (LA-Declare-Success (car l))
              (setq l nil))))))
    ))
(defun FA-Clean-Up-Function  ()
)
(defvar FA-Resource-Requests nil)
(defvar FA-Return-Address "pcw@access.digex.com")
;;; Error Code
(defvar Error-Problems nil)
(defun Report-Error (type body)
  (setq Error-Problems (cons
        (list error-type body (get-internal-run-time)
            *time-left*)
        Report-Error)))
(defun LA-Ask-For-More (bid)
;;; Get some access.
```

```
;;; This is a BASIC version.
(let* (
       (answer t)
       (counter (FH-Negotiate-Resources bid)))
  (print counter)
  (do ()
      ((null counter)) ;; nil means we are there.
    (let ((cost (assoc 'FR-Dollars counter)))
      (cond ((null cost)
             (setq answer nil)
             (setq counter nil)) ;;; Too confusing for now.
            ((>= (cash-on-hand) (cadr cost))
             (setq answer (not (null
                   (Pay-Out-Resource
                    'FR-Dollars (cadr cost))))))
            (t
             (setq answer nil)
             (setq counter nil))))
    (print counter)
    (cond ((not (null counter))
           (setq counter
             (FH-Negotiate-Resources counter)))))
  answer))
(defun FA-Error-Function (error-type &rest body)
;; Handle errors reported by the host.
  (cond ((eq error-type 'FE-Programming-Error)
         (Report-Error error-type body))
        ((eq error-type 'FE-Numerical-Error)
         (Report-Error error-type body))
        ((eq error-type
             'FE-Unauthorized-Function-Call)
         (Report-Error error-type body))
        ((eq error-type 'FE-Unauthorized-Data-Call)
         (Report-Error error-type body))
```

```
            ((eq error-type
                'FE-Unauthorized-Resource-Consumption)
            (Report-Error error-type body))
            ((eq error-type
               'FE-Unauthorized-Resource-Bound-Approaching)
             (cond ((eq body 'FR-Execution-Time)
                    (LA-Ask-For-More
                       '(FR-Execution-time 10000))))
             (Report-Error error-type body))
            ((eq error-type 'FE-Resource-Unavailable)
            (Report-Error error-type body))
            ((eq error-type 'FE-Out-Of-Memory)
            (Report-Error error-type body))
            ((eq error-type 'FE-Host-Shutting-Down-Now)
            (Report-Error error-type body)
            )
            ((eq error-type 'FE-Host-Shutting-Down-Soon)
            (Report-Error error-type body)
            )
    )
)
(defvar FA-Report-Me-In-Errors
    '(Error-Problems)
)
(defun FA-Burn-Some-Cycles (cyc)
  (do ((i 0 (+ 1 i))) ((= i cyc))))
;;; Here is a simple resource negotiator:
(setq FA-Initial-Resource-Bid '((FR-Execution-Time -100000)))
(setq FA-Resource-Supply '((FR-Dollars 2u 1231231 1231321)
                           (FR-Dollars 10 1231231 12312312)
                           (FR-Dollars 15 2123122 231314124)))
 (defun Cash-On-Hand ()
 (let ((answer 0))
   (do ((l FA-Resource-Supply (cdr l))) ((null l))
```

```
          (cond ((eq (caar l) 'FR-Dollars)
                 (setq answer (+ answer (cadr (car l)))))))
     answer))
(defun Pay-Out-Resource (res amount)
;;; Pay out the resource to the Host.
;;; This should be used as spending money
;;; Returns amount paid if successful.
;;; Returns nil if it fails.
(let ((payment nil) (left-over nil) (tot 0) )
  (do ((l FA-Resource-Supply (cdr l)))
      ((or (null l) ))
      (print "resource considering")
      (print (car l))
    (cond ((and (eq (caar l) res) (<= tot amount))
           (setf payment (cons (car l) payment))
           (setq tot (+ tot (cadr (car l)))))
          (t (setf left-over (cons (car l) left-over)))))
          (print (list "payment" payment))
  (cond ((>= tot amount)
         (FH-Give-Resources payment)
         (setf FA-Resource-Supply left-over)
         tot)
        (t nil))))
(defun FA-Resource-Negotiator ()
;;; Get some access.
;;; This is a BASIC version.
(let* ((bid FA-Initial-Resource-Bid)
       (answer t)
       (counter (FH-Negotiate-Resources bid)))
  (print counter)
  (do ()
      ((null counter)) ;; nil means we are there.
    (let ((cost (assoc 'FR-Dollars counter)))
      (cond ((null cost
```

```
                      (setq answer nil)
                      (setq counter nil)) ;;; Too confusing for now.
                ((>= (cash-on-hand) (cadr cost))
                 (setq answer (not (null
                       (Pay-Out-Resource
                        'FR-Dollars (cadr cost))))))
                (t
                 (setq answer nil)
                 (setq counter nil))))
        (print counter)
        (cond ((not (null counter))
               (setq counter
                  (FH-Negotiate-Resources counter)))))
      answer))
```

18.5   AIRHOST.LSP

This is the sample code for the host that accepts the incoming agent defined
in AIRAGENT.LSP.

```
;;; Airline Reservation System for oo7.
;; This simulates a large reservation system like SABRE with
;; a simple flat list of tuples.
;; The structure is:
(defstruct flight
          Airline Day Time Plane Stops
          Number Price-Coach Price-First
          Coach-Aisle-Seats-Available
          Coach-Window-Seats-Available
          First-Aisle-Seats-Available
          Coach-Window-Seats-Available
          Start-City End-City)
;;; This structure is only a toy. There are numerous deficiencies.
;;; For instance, all flights are assumed to be non-smoking. Also,
```

```
;;; there are only seven available days to fly. A more robust
;;; version would include arrays for maintaining this information.
;; Here are some functions for accessing the parts. This would
;; be done well in Common Lisp with the Defstruct command. I've
;; ignored that option here.
(defvar Airline-List '(FlugZug PsychicWings SquareAir))
(defvar Days-List '(Mon Tue Wed Thur Fri Sat Sun))
(defvar Plane-List '(707 727 737 747 767 777 DC-3 DC-9 DC-10))
(defvar City-List '(Emerald Circuit Fat Big Charm ))
(defvar Town-List '(Bean Small Our))
(defun Choose-Random (ls) (nth (random (length ls)) ls))
(defun Make-Random-Flight ()
;; Used to create a random flight. We'll
;; create a random set of flights for testing.
(let ((answer (make-flight  :airline (choose-random airline-list)
        :day (choose-random days-list)
        :time (+ (* 100 (random 24)) (random 60))
        :plane (choose-random plane-list)
        :stops (choose-random town-list)
        :number (random 10000)
        :price-coach (random 400)
        :price-first (random 1200) ;;; It could be cheaper.
        :Coach-Aisle-Seats-Available (random 100)
        :Coach-Window-Seats-Available (random 100)
        :First-Aisle-Seats-Available  (random 10)
        :Coach-Window-Seats-Available (random 10)
        :start-city (choose-random city-list)
        :end-city (choose-random city-list))))
(do () ((not (eq (flight-start-city answer)
                (flight-end-city answer))))
    (setf (flight-end-city answer)
          (choose-random city-list)))
answer))
(defun LH-Print-Flight-Info (flt)
```

```lisp
    (Format t "The Airline is: ~A."
      (flight-Airline flt))
    (Format t "From: ~A to ~A on"
      (flight-start-city flt)
      (flight-end-city flt))
  (Format t "Departing: ~A on a  ~A"
      (flight-time flt)
      (flight-plane flt)))
(defvar LH-Flight-List nil)
(defun Build-Test-Flight-List (&optional (num 100))
;; Build a set of test cases.
  (do ((i 0 (+ 1 i))) ((= i num))
    (setf LH-Flight-List
        (cons (make-random-flight) LH-Flight-List))))
(defun LH-Flights-By-Item-Weak (Search-Func Matcher)
;; Find the flights. This has some security
;; holes because it allows any function to be passed
;; into the function and applied without question to
;; every flight. A terrorist could destroy every flight
;; by passing in a bad lambda expression.
  (let ((answer nil))
    (do ((l LH-Flight-List (cdr l))) ((null l))
      (cond ((eq Matcher
                (apply search-func (list (car l))))
            (setf answer (cons (car l) answer)))))
    answer))
(defvar LH-Item-Function-Map
          '((day #'flight-day)
            (start-city #'flight-start-city)
            (end-city #'flight-end-city)
            (airline #'flight-airline)
            (stops #'flight-stops)
            (number #'flight-number)
            (time #'flight-time)))
```

```
(defun LH-Flights-By-Item (Item Matcher)
  (let ((fun (assoc item LH-Item-Function-Map)))
    (cond (fun
           (LH-Flights-By-Item-Weak (cadadr fun) matcher))
          (t nil))))
(defun LH-Test-Flight (triple FLT )
;;It would be faster to put these decision
;;statements outside of the loop. But then
;;this function wouldn't be as flexible.
  (let ((fun (cadadr (assoc (car triple) LH-Item-Function-Map))))
    (cond    ((eq (cadr triple) 'Greater-Than)
           (cond ((> (apply fun (list FLT)) (caddr triple))
                t)
                (t nil))
          )
          ((eq (cadr triple) 'Less-Than)
           (cond ((< (apply fun (list FLT)) (caddr triple))
                t)
                (t nil))
          )
          ((eq (cadr triple) 'Equal)
           (cond ((eq (apply fun (list FLT)) (caddr triple))
                t)
                (t nil))
          ))))
(defun LH-Flights-By-Item-2 (triple &optional (ls LH-Flight-List))
;; This takes  requests as a triples.
;; The three parts in the triple are:
;;    1 Tag from LH-Item-Function-Map
;;    2 Tag from list ('Greater-Than 'Less-Than 'Equal)
;;    3 Value for comparison.
  (let ((answer nil))
    (do ((l ls (cdr l))) ((null l))
        (cond ((LH-Test-Flight triple (car l)
```

```
                        (setf answer (cons (car l) answer)))))
            answer))
(defstruct Info-Block First-Name Last-Name
                      Credit-Card-Number Address
                      Month Date Year)
(defun Decrement-Seat (seat-class fl)
(cond ((eq seat-class 'first-aisle)
        (setf (flight-First-Aisle-Seats-Available fl)
           (- (flight-First-Aisle-Seats-Available fl) 1)))
      ((eq seat-class 'coach-aisle)
       (setf (flight-coach-Aisle-Seats-Available fl)
          (- (flight-First-Aisle-Seats-Available fl) 1)))
      ((eq seat-class 'first-window)
       (setf (flight-First-window-Seats-Available fl)
          (- (flight-First-window-Seats-Available fl) 1)))
      ((eq seat-class 'first-window)
       (setf (flight-First-window-Seats-Available fl)
          (- (flight-First-window-Seats-Available fl) 1)))
      ))
(defun LH-Make-Reservation (flight-num seat-class info-block)
;;; Makes a reservation.
;;; Seat class is one of
;;; '(first-aisle first-window coach-aisle coach-window)
   (let ((fl (LH-Flights-By-Item-Weak
                  #'flight-number flight-num)))
     (cond (fl
             (Decrement-Seat seat-class (car fl)))
           (t nil))))
(defun FH-Current-Time ()
    ;; Given in seconds.
    ;; Defined by the system this runs upon.
  (round (/ (get-internal-real-time)
    internal-time-units-per-second)))
(defun FH-Host-Speed ()
```

```
;; The standard benchmark.
  (let ((start-time (FH-Current-Time)))
    (do ((i 0 (+ 1 i))) ((= i 200))
      (let ((ls '(1 1)))
        (do ((j 0 (+ 1 j))) ((= j 32))
          (setq ls (cons (* (cadr ls) 2) ls))
          (setq ls (cons (* (cadr ls) .3242) ls)))
        (setq ls (reverse ls))))
  (/ 100000 (- (FH-Current-Time) start-time))))
;; This must be modified to include the benchmark.
(defun FH-Go-To (address)
)
;;;(defun FH-Send-Agent (address agent-parts))
;;; Kept in the core.lsp file.
(defun FH-Save-To-File (name data)
        (FA-Error-Function
            'FE-Resource-Unavailable
            "No file access allowed")
)
(defun FH-Read-From-File (name data)
        (FA-Error-Function
            'FE-Resource-Unavailable
            "No file access allowed")
)
(defun FH-Give-Personality-Description ()
        )
(defun FH-Give-Resource-Description ())
(defun FH-Give-Errors-Description  ())
(defun FH-Get-Next-Event () )
(defun FH-Initialize-Security ()
 (setf *free-functions* (append
      (list 'FH-Mail
      'FH-Initialize-Host
      'LH-Make-Reservation
```

```
            'LH-Flights-By-Item
            'FH-Send-Agent
            'FH-Give-Personality-Description
            'FH-Give-Resource-Description
            'FH-Give-Errors-Description
            'FH-Give-Resources
            'FH-Available-Resources
            'FH-Negotiate-Resources
            'LH-Flights-By-Item
            'LH-Flights-By-Item-2
            )
    *free-functions*))
    (setf *protected-variables* (append
        (list
        'LH-Flight-List
        'FH-Agent-Account
        'Test-Resources-Deposited
        'LH-Item-Function-Map
        )
      *protected-variables*))
    (setf *forbidden-functions* (append
        (list
        'Build-Test-Flight-List
        'LH-Flights-By-Item-Weak
        'FH-Save-To-File
        'FH-Read-From-File
        'FH-Clean-Up-Host
        'FH-Initialize-Host
        'Separate-Resources
        'Test-Resource-Pair
        'Cost-Resource-Pair
        'Determine-Dollar-Cost
        'Determine-Cost
        'Meets-The-Offer
```

```
        'Check-For-Dollars
        'Remove-Unavailable-Resources
        'Are-All-Available
        'No-Costp
        'Accept-Resources
        )
   *forbidden-functions*))
 t ;; Must return true if successful.
 )
(defun FH-Mail (address agent-parts))
(defun FH-Initialize-Host ()
  (Build-Test-Flight-List 100)
  (FH-Initialize-Security)
 ;; Must return true if successful.
)
(defun FH-Clean-Up-Host ()
 t ;; Must return true if successful.
 )
;;; Resource Negotiation Skeleton
(defun Separate-Resources (ls)
;; Pulls out the positive demands
;;(what the agent will supply)
;; and separates them from the negative demands.
(let ((p nil) (s nil))
    (do ((l ls (cdr l)))
        ((null l))
      (if (< 0 (cadr (car l)))
          (setq p (cons  (car l) p))
          (setq s (cons (car l) s))))
    (list p s)))
(defun Test-Resource-Pair (p)
(cond ((eq 'FR-Execution-Time (car p))
       (cond ((and (> 0 (cadr p))
              (< -20000 (cadr p)))
```

```
              t) ;;; if it is less than 20000, then yes.
              (t nil)))
        ((eq 'FR-Execution-Space (car p))
         (cond ((and (> 0 (cadr p))
               (< -10000 (cadr p)))
              t) ;;; if it is less than 10000, then yes.
              (t nil)))
        ((eq 'FR-Execution-Units (car p))
          (cond ((and (> 0 (cadr p))
                (< -10000 (/ (cadr p) FH-Host-Speed)))
               t) ;;; if it is less than 10000, then yes.
               (t nil)))
        ((eq 'FR-Dollars (car p))
          (cond ((< 0 (cadr p)) t)
               (t nil)))
        ))
(defun Cost-Resource-Pair (p)
;; Find the cost
(cond ((equal 'FR-Execution-Time (car p))
        (/ (abs (cadr p)) 10000)) ;; 1 dollar per 1000 units
        ((equal 'FR-Execution-Space (car p))
         0);; No charge now.
        ((eq 'FR-Execution-Units (car p))
          (/ (/ (cadr p) FH-Host-Speed) 10000))
        ((eq 'FR-Dollars (car p))
          0)
        (t 0) ; else zero
        ))
(defun Determine-Dollar-Cost (ls)
;;; Scan down a list and figure out the price.
(let ((cost 0))
    (do ((l ls (cdr l)))
        ((null l))
        (setq cost (+ cost (Cost-Resource-Pair (car l))))))
```

```
       cost))
(defun Determine-Cost (ls)
;; Look at the list, but only trade dollars for now.
  (list (list 'FR-Dollars (Determine-Dollar-Cost ls))))
(defun Meets-The-Offer (cost positive-offers)
  ;;Ensures that the everything in the cost is offered.
  (let ((answer t))
    (do ((l cost (cdr l))) ((null l))
      (let ((found (assoc (caar l) positive-offers)))
        (cond (found ;; Something is there...
               (cond ((> (cadr (car l))
                         (cadr (car positive-offers)))
                      (setq answer nil))))
              (t (setq answer nil)))))
    answer))
(defvar FH-Agent-Account nil)
;;; This is a list of all resources deposited by the agent.
(defun FH-Give-Resources (ls)
;; An agent uses this function to transfer resources.
  (setq FH-Agent-Account (append ls FH-Agent-Account)))
(defun Test-Resources-Deposited ( ls);
;; Once the price is agreed to, make sure the cash is in hand.
  (let ((answer t))
    (do ((l ls (cdr l))) ((null l))
      (cond ((eq (caar l) 'FR-Dollars)
             (cond ((not (Check-For-Dollars
                          FH-Agent-Account
                          (cadr (car l))))
                    (setq answer nil))))
            (t nil) ; Do nothing otherwise
            ))
    answer))
(defun Check-For-Dollars (ls amount)
;;; This is just a shell that does not check
```

```
;;; whether the digital cash tendered is authentic.
;;; Format is ('FR-Dollars amount serialnum signature)
;;; The serialnum and signature are ignored in this shell.
  (let ((tot 0))
    (do ((l ls (cdr l))) ((null l))
      (cond ((eq 'FR-Dollars (car (car l)))
             (setq tot (+ tot (cadr (car l)))))
            (t nil)))
    (cond ((> tot amount)
             t) ;;; Enough is there.
          (t nil))))
(setq FH-Available-Resources
              '(FR-Execution-Time
                FR-Execution-Space
                FR-Execution-Units))
(defun Remove-Unavailable-Resources (ls)
;; Returns ls minus stuff we can't provide.
(let ((answer nil))
  (do ((l ls (cdr l))) ((null l))
    (cond ((member (caar l) FH-Available-Resources)
           (setf answer (cons (car l) answer)))
          ))
  answer))
(defun Are-All-Available (ls)
(let ((answer t))
  (do ((l ls (cdr l))) ((null l))
    (cond ((not (member (caar l) FH-Available-Resources))
           (setq answer nil))))
  answer))
(defun No-Costp (ls)
;; Check a list of resources and make
;; sure it is all positive.
(let ((answer t))
  (do ((l ls (cdr l))) ((null l))
```

```lisp
      (cond ((< 0 (cadr (car l)))
             (setq answer nil))))
    answer))
(defun Accept-Resources (ls)
;;; Alert the rest of the program
;;; that it can consume resources.
(do ((l ls (cdr l))) ((null l))
   (cond ((eq (caar l) 'FR-Execution-Time)
          (setq *time-left* (- (cadr (car l)))))
         ((eq (caar l) 'FR-Execution-Units)
          (setq *time-left* (-
                                (* FH-Host-Speed
                                   (cadr (car l)))))))
         ))) ;; Ignore the rest.
(defun FH-Negotiate-Resources (ls)
;;; Decide on the mode of payment by an agent.
;; ls contains a list of resources to be exchanged.
(let* ((the-list (separate-resources ls))
       (the-cost (Determine-Cost (cadr the-list))))
    (cond ((No-Costp the-cost)
           (Accept-Resources (cadr the-list))
            nil) ;; We accept.
          ((and (Meets-The-Offer the-cost (car the-list))
                (Are-All-Available (cadr the-list))
                (Test-Resources-Deposited the-cost))
           (Accept-Resources (cadr the-list))
            nil) ;; Accept!
          (t ;; Otherwise ask for cash.
            (append the-cost
                    (Remove-Unavailable-Resources
                    (cadr the-list)))))))
```

18.6   CORE.LSP

This is the core functions that make up the XLISP security system. They are loaded with the host to run the agent.

```
;define a C-like iterator.
(defmacro while (test &rest forms)
        '(do () ((not ,test))
        ,@forms))
;create the nesting level counter.
(defparameter *hooklevel* 0)
(defvar *time-end* 0)
(defvar *time-left* 0)
(defmacro timebound ( form    bound  &rest val)
    '(progn
      (setf *hooklevel* 0)            ;init nesting counter
      (setq *time-end* (+ (get-internal-run-time) ,bound))
      (setq *check-count* 0)
      (setq error nil)
      (setf val (evalhook ',form     ;eval, and kick off stepper
                          #'eval-hook-function
                          nil ;;;;;#'apply-hook-function
                          nil))
      val))                          ;and return it
(defun tb (form bound)
  (let  (( *hooklevel 0)
         (*time-end* (+ (get-internal-run-time) bound)))
    (*evalhook* #'eval-hook-function)
    (answer (catch 'error (eval form))))
    answer))
(defun tb2 (form bound)
  (let  ((*hooklevel 0)
              (*time-end* (+ (get-internal-run-time) bound))
    (*evalhook* #'eval-hook-function))
    (eval form)
```

```
        (- (get-internal-run-time) *time-end*)))
(defun tb3 (form)
  (let ((answer nil))
  (setq *time-end* (+ (get-internal-run-time) *time-left*))
  (setq answer (catch 'error (let    ((*hooklevel 0)
        (*evalhook* #'eval-hook-function))
    (evalhook form #'eval-hook-function nil nil))))
    (setq *time-left* (- *time-end* (get-internal-run-time) ))
    answer))
;this is the substitute "eval" routine that gets control when
;a user form is evaluated during stepping.
(defvar *check-count* 0)
(defvar *allow-screen-action* nil)
(defvar *protected-functions*
  (list
    'defun
    'setq
    'setf
    'cond
    'evalhook
    'applyhook
    'eval-hook-function
    'test-form
    'Is-Predefinedp
    'tb
    'timebound
  ))
(defvar *protected-variables*
  (list
    '*evalhook*
    '*applyhook*
    '*gc-hook*
    '*unbound*
    '*breakenable*
```

```
      '*protected-functions*
      '*debug-io*
      '*terminal-io*
      '*standard-input*
      '*standard-output*
      'pi
      '*obarray*
      '*protected-variables*
      '*forbidden-functions*
      '*screen-functions*
      '*time-end*
      '*time-left*
    ))
(defvar *free-functions*
;; This is the list of functions that can be applied
;; without the benefit of eval-hook-function.
  (list
    ))
(defvar *forbidden-functions*
  (list
    'open
    'write-char
    'write-byte
    'read-char
    'peek-char
    'write-char
    'read-line
    'close
    'delete-file
    'truename
    'with-open-file
    'read-byte
    'write-byte
    'file-length
```

```
          'file-position
          'dribble
          'peek
          'poke
          'address-of
          'system
          'get-output-stream-list
          'get-output-stream-string
          'make-string-output-stream
          'make-string-input-stream
                'with-output-to-string
          'with-open-file
          'with-input-from-string
          'error
          'cerror
          'break
          'clean-up
          'continue
          'errset
          'top-level
      ))
(defvar *screen-functions*
    (list
          'goto-xy
          'color
          'move
          'moverel
          'draw
          'drawrel
          'mode
          'cls
          'cleol
          'get-key
          'goto-xy
```

```
  ))
(defun test-form (form)
;;; Tests the form to ensure that it is not breaking any rules.
      ;;; (print (list "in test form" form))
   (cond   ((or (eql (car form) 'defun)
             ;;; DEFUNing old names aren't cool.
                (eql (car form) 'defmacro))
       (cond ((or (member (cadr form) *protected-function*)
              (Is-Predefinedp (car form)))
              (FA-Error-Function 'FE-Unauthorized-Function-Call
                  form)
            nil)
          (t t))
    )
    ((or (eql (car form) 'setq)
        ;;; setq'ing certain variables is bad.
        (eql (car form) 'setf))
      (cond ((member (cadr form) *protected-variables*)
      (FA-Error-Function 'FE-Unauthorized-Data-Call
                 form)
         nil)
         (t t))
    )
    (t
      (cond ((member (car form) *forbidden-functions*)
            (FA-Error-Function 'FE-Unauthorized-Function-Call
                form)
         nil)
        ((and (not *allow-screen-action*)
            (member (car form) *screen-functions*))
            (FA-Error-Function 'FE-Unauthorized-Function-Call
                form)
         nil)
        (t t)
```

```
            ))
    ))
(defun apply-hook-function (func form)
    (print (list "here in applyhook" func))
    (print (list "result of test-form"
        (member func *forbidden-functions*))))
(defun Is-Predefinedp (func)
    (let ((aa (eval '(type-of #',func))))
        (or (eq aa 'FSUBR) (eq aa 'SUBR))))
(defun eval-hook-function (form env &aux val f1)
    (cond ((> (get-internal-run-time) *time-end*)
            (print "OUT OF TIME!")
            (throw 'error 'out-of-time))
          ((< (- *time-end* (get-internal-run-time)) 1000)
            (print "Reached Warning Time")
            (FA-Error-Function 'FE-fred))
          ((consp form)
            (cond ((member (car form) *free-functions*)
                    (print "Going Free with")
                    (print form)
                    (setf val (evalhook form nil nil env)))
                  ((test-form form)
                    (setf val (evalhook form
                                    #'eval-hook-function
                                    nil
                                    env)))
                  (t (print "BAD FUNCTION")
                    (print form)
                    (throw 'error 'bad-function))))
          (t
            (setf val (evalhook form nil nil env))))
          val)
(defun eval-hook-function (form env &aux val f1)
    (cond ((> (get-internal-run-time) *time-end*)
```

```
                    (print "OUT OF TIME!")
                    (throw 'error 'out-of-time))
                   ((< (- *time-end* (get-internal-run-time)) 1000)
                    (print "Reached Warning Time")
                    (FA-Error-Function
                         'FE-Unauthorized-Resource-Bound-Approaching
                         'FR-Execution-Time))
                   ((consp form)
                    (cond ((member (car form) *free-functions*)
                           (print "Going Free with")
                           (print form)
                           (setf val (evalhook form nil nil env)))
                          ((test-form form)
                           (setf val (evalhook form
                                        #'eval-hook-function
                                        nil
                                        env)))
                          (t (print "BAD FUNCTION")
                             (print form)
                             (throw 'error 'bad-function))))
                   (t
                     (setf val (evalhook form nil nil env))))
                   val)
(defun eval-hook-function-short (form env &aux val f1)
    (cond ((< (get-internal-run-time) *time-end*)
           (cond ((consp form)
                    (setf val (evalhook form
                                        #'eval-hook-function
                                        nil
                                        env)))
                   (t
                     (setf val (evalhook form nil nil env))))
                   val)
           (t (throw 'error nil)
```

```
         )))
;;;;;;;;;;;;;;
;; Software for going.
(defun FH-mail (address file)
;;; Hook for mailing file to address. Must be customized for
;;; your system.
)
(defun savefuns (fname funs)
  (let* ((fp (open fname :direction
                :output :if-exists :overwrite)))
    (cond (fp
        (do ((l funs (cdr l))) ((null l))
          (cond ((fboundp (car l))
            (let ((fval (get-lambda-expression
                (symbol-function (car l)))))
              (pprint (cons (if (eq (car fval) 'lambda)
                              'defun
                              'defmacro)
              (cons (car l) (cdr fval))) fp)))
          (t
            (pprint (cons 'setq
                (cons (car l) (eval (car l))) fp)))))
          (close fp)
          fname)
        (t nil))))
(defun FH-Send-Agent (address agent-parts)
  (if (savefuns "OutAgent" agents-parts)
      (FH-mail address "OutAgent")
      nil))
```

```
;;;;;;;;;;;;;;;;;;;;;;;;;;;;;;;;;;;;;;;;;;;;;;;;;
;;; Software for names
(defstruct Agent-Ident
    Name Owner Return-Address Serial-Number Agent-Type)
;; This structure is used by the agent to identify
;; itself.
```

Chapter 19

Back to the Future

———————————————— The Hype ————————————————

"I see a figure five in gold." — William Carlos Williams

———————————————— Political Cynicism ————————————————

Dreams for the future are just another opiate for the people. But liberation is impossible without them. Thus the modern paradox.

———————————————— The Buzzwords ————————————————

Although computer clocks are ticking faster, it doesn't mean the future is getting here any sooner.

This book lays out a simple, experimental agent system designed to explore some of the concepts required to build a domain where agents can roam freely. This effort is, like all first cuts at global projects, quite short of being complete. There are many different topics to explore and many different details that might lead to deeper experimentation.

The rest of this chapter is a list of some of the more important topics that I think will need to be addressed before we reach a world where agents can roam unimpeded.

A Worldwide Object Standard There is little doubt that object-oriented programming is the standard way to approach programming problems in the 1990s and beyond. C++ is the most popular language, and the most exciting smaller languages have object-oriented extensions that make them part of the club. The idea has many limitations, but they can usually be resolved with a bit of forethought and planning.

A standard format for objects that would work on many machines would be an ideal platform for agents. If an object can move from machine to machine and carry data and procedures for manipulating this data, then many of the technical details in this book that are necessary for creating a safe agent world can be avoided. An object-oriented operating system like this would allow agents to do serious work when they arrive because the entire operating system is ready to interact with them. In many ways, implementing an agent in an operating system that facilitated roaming objects would be trivial.

The greatest advantage of using an object-oriented operating system would lie in the creation of agents that interact with the users of the machine. In the implementation of XLISP in Chapter 10, the agent could print out some information and perhaps read some information. The Safe-TCL program described in Chapter 12 only allows a few simple calls to the screen using the Tk toolkit. There are very few ways that an agent can do much on arrival unless the host has been specifically programmed to accept special formatted data. It would be impossible to ship a multimedia presentation embedded with buttons and other selection devices to someone unless the other person had a host for the incoming agent that contained all of the code for interpreting the information.

An object-oriented operating system with a standard set of calls could open all of the power of the embedded commands to the incoming agent. Simple tasks like flashing a menu bar, beeping the speaker, creating icons and using embedded compression software would be easy to do because it all came bundled in the OS.

At this writing, the major computing companies are beginning to roll out their own approaches. Microsoft's OLE (Object Linking Environment) is already in revision 2.0 and it is incorporated into several major products. Apple is pursuing OpenDoc, which promises to offer the same amount of OOP wrapping. Sun is pushing their DOE (Distributed Objects Everywhere). IBM's OS/2 was written around their SOM (System Object Model) that has been extended to include distributed objects. NeXT's Nextstep operating system is highly object-oriented and Taligent, a startup company with major resources, is planning to offer objects to the world soon.

These are just the beginning. Microsoft continues to encourage speculation about the operating systems of the near future. There will be Windows95 and perhaps a few more on the road to an operating system that they say will be fully object-oriented and currently code-named Cairo. The other companies will also continue to develop their products. Apple's OpenDoc grows more and more ambitious with each press release.

Will there be any industry-wide convergence? This is a difficult proposition. If an OS is going to be efficient, it will need to be written in the native code of the host machine. If an agent is going to exist as an object that lives in this OS, it will need to be written in this native machine code and it will only be able to exist on this one brand.

Time will tell. Even an object standard that links one OS, be it Microsoft's, Apple's, Next's, UNIX or whatever, would be a big win for people who own these machines. In many cases, corporations choose one platform and invest heavily in that OS across their network. Even a single OS object standard would let them build an internal agent system that did efficient work.

A Safe Object Space Security was one of the major concerns of this book. An object-oriented operating system might let the agent access all parts of the OS efficiently, but this could be a large security hole. An object-oriented operating system can only be open to incoming agents if there are ways to partition off capabilities.

There are two major solutions to this approach. The first is to create an intermediate class that will stand between the standard full-featured, application-level object and the incoming agent. This intermediate class will contain procedures that will override all of the features of a full-featured object that should be denied to the incoming agent. If the standard application-level object in the system has a procedure called `Erase-All-Files`, then the intermediate class of object would contain it s own `Erase-All-Files` that did nothing. Then, when the incoming agent tried to inherit this behavior, it wouldn't receive a loaded gun.

The second part of the solution is to control the passing of messages between the objects. Each OS has a central dispatch system that finds the destination object, delivers the message and fires up the object so it can execute the message. This central dispatcher must become aware that some objects have different levels of access than others. It must maintain a list of which objects can talk to which others. This might be as complicated as a table that kept track of all pairs of objects, but it would be better arranged according to the class hierarchy.

This approach, though, will only work if the object can't address arbitrary parts of memory. It will be a long time before anyone tells C++ programmers that they can't do that. But there are OO languages that successfully offer this behavior without appearing as crippled as the language here. Smalltalk is just one example.

The major operating system companies will be certain to spend ample time developing this technology. The U.S. government is a major buyer of computers and it often requires that the purchased computers pass a set of security standards that govern how secure a computer can be.

Efficient Emulation Technology At first glance, it might be ideal if every computer would run every program. This would make it easy to write agents in machine code so they could run much faster when they arrived. The problem with this approach, though, is that it leaves no room for improvement in the underlying machine architecture. We get stuck with one forever. Intel should be proud that they're able to generate as much power as they can with their latest chips despite being hobbled by the remnants of an old 16-bit architecture.

The best performance comes out of new architectures, but many people hesitate to change because they lose the investment in their old software. The best solution may be solid technology for emulating one processor on another. Apple's PowerPC is proof that this can be done successfully without losing too much speed. The PowerPC computers run old 680x0 applications faster than many of the 680x0 machines in the Apple line. They run native applications much faster.

One solution for a robust agent realm would be to create a very low-level and simple assembly language for the agents. Each host machine would emulate this code. The agent programmer would write in a high-level language like C that would be compiled into this simple assembler by the compiler. The simple nature of it would prevent much of the slowdown brought about by interpretation. In fact, much of the slowdown would be prevented by precompilation. This simple, assembly language *lingua franca* does not need to be designed from scratch. One of the basic RISC assembly codes might serve quite well. This would have the added advantage of running much faster on the native chips.

The memory architecture would be quite similar to the private address spaces allocated to processes in well-designed multitasking OSs like UNIX. The agent would get a contiguous block of memory beginning at zero. It would be free to use this block as it wished.

The interface with the host would be arranged like the trap mechanism used in computers like Apple's Macintosh. The host would publish a list of trap numbers for each of the local procedures available to the agent. The agent would call these by moving the parameters to the stack and then issuing the instruction and the right trap number for the procedure it wanted to invoke.

This lightweight architecture for the agent may be the best solution to the problems of speed and language. It would be faster than most interpreted code and it would be flexible enough to allow people to program in different languages that were compiled down to this simple agent assembly code.

A Worldwide Digital Signature System The world desperately needs an infrastructure so people can use public-key technology to sign documents. This would allow both agents and electronic commerce to flourish. It may be the place of the government, the phone company or the postal system to set up a nationwide directory of names and public keys for their signatures.

The greatest impediment will probably also be the government. Although NIST and the NSA encourage digital signatures used for authentication, they prefer that these signatures be generated with a crippled system like the DSS. (See section 14.5.) Widespread public key encryption seems to worry them.

This puts the government at odds with two of the best proponents of the technology: RSA Data Security and PGP. Both of these use the RSA algorithm and at least one will make some money if the RSA algorithm becomes the standard. These two forces have also proven to be very good at bringing the technology to the people. RSA Data Security has licensed their technology to Apple, Microsoft and Sun among many others. Apple's digital signature user interface is a model for simplicity and ease of use. Just drag the file to the signature icon, type in a passphrase and the document is signed.

PGP, on the other hand, has provided a solid body of source code that promotes cross-platform interaction. A PGP-encrypted file will be correctly decrypted on any one of a variety of machines. The software is spreading rapidly, in part because it comes so cheaply. In many on-line communities, the PGP web of trust is the defacto standard.

A Worldwide Encryption System While software that implements digital signature standards for authentication only can be readily exported from the United States, solid encryption software can't leave the borders. This prevents anyone from using computer networks for any international commerce that can't be conducted in the clear. Agents may not be human, but I doubt that any court or human agent of the U.S. government would hesitate to prosecute the programmer of the agent that broke these laws.

This presents a serious complication. While the U.S. government may use its ability to eavesdrop to stop crime and terrorism, industrial spies may do the same thing. Unencrypted traffic exposes anyone who tries to use the network for business to eavesdropping. Cellular phone fraud is just one example of how quickly criminals learn to exploit technological holes in the system. No one will be able to use the network and the agents for serious international business.

The prohibition stops agents from doing useful work. Many of the digital cash systems described here require some form of encryption that can't be exported. Even the most rudimentary forms of encryption are needed to seal a credit card number so it can't be stolen by an eavesdropper.

This entire subject illustrates how weak many of the existing governments will become in the face of the now unstoppable internationalization of commerce. If the United States tries to resist distributing its encryption software to the world, it risks becoming an island outside of the world economy. Although it is a large force, there may come a time when U.S. companies will find it difficult to compete abroad because foreign computer networks won't use American solutions.

A Worldwide Appliance Control System In the first chapter of this book, Bondo saves the Big Mac from destruction by sending instructions to the various machines in the kitchen telling them what to do and when to do it. This may not seem particularily far-fetched to anyone who bothers to look behind the counter at the high amount of computerization in these restaurants. Everything is linked together and networked.

Such a plan, though, would be close to impossible in current homes where the only link is through the electric power lines. Many of the appliances include computers, and some of these processors do complicated work. The embedded processor in a bread machine schedules all parts of the baking operation. It seems a shame that these devices can't be linked up to computers. If this was the case, then agents would be able to have true physical "agency" and do work that affected the world.

The best solution would be a single processing chip that sat on the power line and listened for FM signals directed at that particular machine. This chip would be able to feed any incoming messages to the central embedded processor that ran the appliance. The bandwidth of FM signals on power lines is not great, nor is it particularly robust, but these can be solved with some patience and error-correction. Unless someone develops a PostScript-compatible cake baker that accepts PostScript files to describe the final printing on the top of the cake, there will probably be no reason to send large quantities of data to a machine.

There are some companies that are reportedly developing chips like these, but they haven't reached the general market as of this writing. One popular solution known as the X-10 standard is encorporated into products made by Radio Shack, X-10 Powerhouse, and Stanley among others. These are simple switches that allow you to broadcast on and off messages throughout the power wires without running special circuits. There is also the X10 CP290 that interfaces with a basic computer and translates requests from the computer into data that goes out across the power lines.

These products are a good start, but they are a far cry from what may come. In the future, the packaging and the marketing costs for creating an embedded processor will be much greater than the actual costs of fabricating the silicon. This will mean that it will be quite feasible to include a fairly capable computer in each product for much the same cost that it takes to include a chip that runs a microwave oven. It would be ideal if some person or company would take the initiative to find a way to make such a standard with the ability to actually accept incoming agents.

A Worldwide Multimedia Interface Standard One of the best reasons for creating an agent system is for enhanced electronic mail that will carry more than words. The standards already exist for bundling binary data into electronic mail. They are not all compatible, but the differences will disappear over time. The next step is a successful standard for bundling up information to be presented. The Quicktime standard from Apple is one such solution. If such a standard could emerge to cover all computers, then it could allow agents to serve as dancing mailmen and deliver more than just text.

Using agents for this, though, may not be particularly efficient. This structure would require all of the data in the presentation to be bundled into the agent and then sent along the wires. This may be quite wasteful if the reader might only look at a small fraction of it or, alas, toss most of it away.

In some senses, the work on WWW and Mosaic that is exploding across the country is a more efficient approach. Readers only access what they need. If the standard would allow unlimited local processing so WWW and Mosaic servers could send "agents" to present the data, then this might be the best melding of the two approaches. Readers would only download what they chose to access and this would then fire up an agent upon arrival.

A Worldwide Digital Cash Transaction System Some say that money is a wonderful lubricant for social interaction. Of course, many people believe that the generous, free-spirited life of the Internet is only possible because it was generally impractical for anyone to charge anything for their information. So people gave it away. *Sic transit gloria mundi.*

Chapter 16 described several different commercial cash programs that are developing around the world. One of them will probably find a way to become one of the standard systems. This will probably happen when the major banks or financial institutions launch major programs. The Microsoft – Visa deal promises to be a major effort. Other banks like Citibank are sure to follow. In any case, when this happens agents will be able to buy, sell and broker many different ephemeral things.

A Worldwide Wireless Network Desktop computers are great for work. But who wants to spend all day at a desk? There are so many times that we may be sitting down, but aren't in contact with the desktop computer that just happens to be hooked up to the network.

Wireless network applications are already exploding. Pagers that accept up to 2000 letters of data are no bigger than a credit card and fit into a portable computer. When these networks become two-directional and ubiquitous, then agents will be able to serve people in all parts of their day. Large databases, reservation systems and info brokers don't need to be mobile. They can sit happily buried in their regulated climates breathing filtered air. Agents that can come and go from a personal communicator that can be carried about will complete the picture.

A Stronger Legal Foundation Of course, object-oriented operating systems provide wonderful flexibility for people who want to customize their desktop systems to do different things. But parceling out such flexibility makes it much easier for a malicious programmer to hide devious work in other places. If any button can be converted into an arbitrarily complex device then there is no reason why someone won't be able to add a virus to this device. This means that the future may be bright for those who want to play games.

But if agents are good viruses, then the law will need to be very carefully defined to distinguish between agents and viruses. After Robert Morris sent a virus out across the Internet from his post high above the waters of Cayuga Lake at Cornell University, many people wondered whether it was a crime to exploit a loophole in the security system of a computer. His code asked permission to enter and the computer victims were more than happy to let him in.

The basic structures defined in this book go a long way toward eliminating the ambiguity that might emerge in intercomputer interaction. The agents are required to bargain directly for the resources that they will consume. This will prevent people from saying, "I said you could use my computer, but not overload the disk." Good contracts make good neighbors.

The law might choose to recognize this bargaining as a form of legally binding contract in the near future. In fact, lawyers often perform many details by rote using boilerplate contracts that are barely tailored to particular circumstances. It is entirely possible that legal negotiations between people will be replaced by negotiations between lawyer agents that iterate through the different possible contract permutations.

Standard Extendable Personal Databases The *finger* program for the UNIX system was one of the first netwide systems that allowed people to look up personal data about a particular user. This might include prosaic information like name, telephone number, and address, but some people extended it to include more personal information about their jobs, their hobbies, and their reasons for living.

An agent environment would flourish if a good, extendable standard for storing local information emerged. The programs in this book did not try and force the local host for agents to reveal too much about themselves beyond their interface protocols. But, it would be desirable if there was a good way to find out something about who is responsible for a corner of the network.

The finger protocol is a good example of a standard way to make basic information available to people. It would be better if there were a large set of standard elements that could be extracted in an automatic way.

The Internet Config system for the Macintosh is a good example of how many different Internet-ready applications for the Mac can use a central database filled with commonly used information. The Internet Config preferences file contains data like the real name, telephone number, prefered Archie server and WWW home page. The system was written by Quinn "The Eskimo!" (`quinn@cs.uwa.edu.au`) and Peter N Lewis (`peter.lewis@info.curtin.edu.au`). The support address for Internet Config is `internet-config@share.com`.

An Internet Yellow Pages How can you find the lyrics and demo sound files of a band known as "Descartes Blanche"? How can you locate data conversion services? What about reservation agencies that find tickets for concerts? The Internet is already filled with services that allow people to search for information by keyword. The WAIS servers maintain indices of databases by keywords. The various WebCrawlers build huge indices of the WWW and Mosaic pages on the network. So, it is possible to find information if you know a word that happens to be in the name of the service. If you asked for "music", you might get a long list of netservices and one might be called "Music and Concert Reservation System." Bingo. But you would miss "Ticketron" and others with different names.

The solution is a class of service provider directory. You, or your agent, will be able to select the location based upon the class of service that will be offered. Designing such a directory demands a large amount of standardization. The topics must be broad enough way to be useful, but narrow enough way to be effective.

Some preliminary descriptions of the Telescript language include indications that the language includes instructions that allow an agent to request a destination that offers a particular class of service.

So, that's it. There may be more challenges than there are solutions. This is only fair. If everyone solved problems without creating new ones, we would have nothing to do all day.

I hope that the content this book will continue to grow and change. The Internet, anonymous FTP and Web pages make this easy to do. Please feel free to write me at `pcw@access.digex.com` with your comments, corrections or suggestions. Make sure to insert the tag [AU] in the subject line. This allows me to filter your messages out of the dross I collect in my mailbox. If you want to be on the mailing list, make sure to ask explicitly for this feature. I plan on posting adaptions, extensions and fixes for the software described in this book on the Net. Please be in touch.

Finally, `http://access.digex.net:/~pcw/pcwpage.html` is my home page. I plan to keep updated material and other interesting data here. Check in often.

Chapter 20

Glossary

Understanding a word is as easy as looking it up in a dictionary.

————————————— Political Cynicism —————————————

The system of meaning is a network of oppression designed by the insiders to exclude those who are not part of the power matrix that defines the words.

————————————— The Buzzwords —————————————

A one-to-one mapping between words and definitions.

Agent A program sent to run on a different machine. Ideally, this program will run in a protected mode that prevents it from damaging the host. The first examination of the topic is given in Chapter 3.

Cryptographically-Secure Hash Function An algorithm used to create a unique number that represents a large file. Ideally, it is practically impossible to find two different files that have the same hash value. The hash value is used as a surrogate for the entire file when the digital signature is created. This is also refered to as a "message digest".

DES The Digital Encryption Standard (DES) was developed by IBM and approved by the National Bureau of Standards in the 1970s. The design and selection was controversial because many details were kept classified. No subsequent research found any problems with the algorithm and it is in wide use today. The best implementations now use three passes of the algorithm with three keys to ensure greater security.

Digital Cash If agents are going to pay for services in advance, they will need to be able to offer a host some digital cash. This is a special data format using digital signatures that allows banks to offer digital certified checks to the network in such a way that they are unforgeable. Chapter 15 explores the topic in detail.

Digital Signature An additional data field added to a document that can only be created by someone holding a secret key. Anyone can verify that this signature came from that secret key by checking it with a corresponding public key. These algorithms can be used in digital cash (section 15.3) and agent verification.

DSS The Digital Signature Standard (DSS) is an algorithm offered by NIST (National Institute of Standards and Technology, Gaithersburg, MD) for all Federal Agencies that need digital signatures. It is not based directly upon the RSA signature standard although the company that holds the RSA patents (Public Key Partners) claims that DSS infringes on some of its patents.

Dylan Once a variant of LISP developed by Apple Computer Company as part of its research into dynamic languages. Now, it is becoming more C-like. If only in syntax. Dylan is short for "DYnamic LANguage".

Host The machine and its operating system that accept an agent and start it running. The host usually includes an interpreter for parsing and executing the incoming agent and a set of definitions for local functions that offer services to this agent. Chapter 4 describes the basic architecture of a host.

Host Personality Files These files are LISP programs that contain all of the local functions available to an incoming agent at a particular host. Section 4.1.1 describes ow their structure and the rules for creating them.

IDEA The International Data Encryption Algorithm is a modern contender to DES. It is used in PGP because the software and the algorithm were designed outside of the United States. This makes it easy to export the software without violating the export regulations.

Interpreted Language An interpreted language is parsed and decoded at execution time by a program known as an interpreter. Compiled languages are converted into machine code which can run without any interpreter on a particular computer. Interpreted languages are more convenient for creating a world of agents because they are machine-independent, easy to extend and easier to secure. It is much simpler to cripple the language to prevent wayward agents than to watch machine code for errors.

LISP One of the first computer languages, developed in the 1950s. The language is quite popular in the artificial intelligence community because it is flexible and easily extended. This book explores using a version of it (XLISP) as an agent language because it is interpreted and well-known.

MD-4 A cryptographically secure hash function developed by Ron Rivest. It was later adapted to become the federal standard Secure Hash Algorithm. See section 14.4 for details.

MD-5 A derivative of MD-4 with some changes designed to enhance security. See section 14.4 for details.

MIME MIME stands for Multipurpose Internet Mail Extensions. They were created to let people package many different types of data into simple mail messages. Section 12.1 describes the topic briefly as an introduction for Safe-TCL.

PGP PGP stands for "Pretty Good Privacy" and is a collection of encryption routines that can be used to add digital signatures and security to electronic mail. It was first created by Phil Zimmerman. Later versions were developed with the help of many different people. Chapter 14 explores the details of encryption and section 14.7 discuss PGP's implementation.

Object-Oriented X The object-oriented adjective is used in many different ways. In general, it means that software is designed around a cluster of code and data known as an object that is, in many respects, treated like a little person. The programmer does not manipulate the data inside the object directly, the objects sends messages to each other that are run by the internal procedures bound in the object. Many feel that this way of programming produces more flexible and easily extended code. The paradigm is naturally well-suited for the agent domain. Many languages like Smalltalk are trivially agent languages because they build all of their work around objects, which are in many contexts, another word for agents.

Resources A general term used to define items in the digital economy of agents. Digital cash is a resource. So are answers to questions or computation time on a local host. Agents bargain for resources when they arrive at a host and spend their time exchanging them. If a host is going to regulate some behavior of an incoming agent, it should express this regulated commodity as a resource. Chapter 8 defines the concept and makes it real through code.

Scheme A modern, simpler extension of LISP used heavily at MIT. The language is also available on the network in a variety of different formats.

RSA RSA is the name for a public-key encryption system created by Ron Rivest, Adi Shamir and Len Adleman in the late 1970's. Section 14.3 explores it in light detail.

Safe-TCL An extension of TCL written by Nathaniel Borenstein and Marshall Rose that allows a computer mailer to run a TCL script without worrying about it causing damage. Chapter 12 explores how the extensions create a viable domain for incoming agents.

SHA The Secure Hash Algorithm defined by the National Institute of Standards and Technology for use by Federal Agencies that need message digests. It is part of the Digital Signature Standard. Sections 14.4 and 14.4.1 contains details.

Smalltalk A completely object-oriented language developed at Xerox's Palo Alto Research Center in the 1970's. It is, in many respects, a complete agent language without the authentication systems. Creating a new secure version of Smalltalk would be possible without much trouble.

SmalltalkAgents A version of Smalltalk from Quasar Knowledge Systems (Bethesda, MD). The language allows the user to create distributed, dynamic systems for users with of the first famous object-oriented languages. See section 13.3.

TCL TCL stands for Tool Command Language, a very high-level language that emerged from Berkeley in the late 1980s. Chapter 11 describes the basic structure of the language and Chapter 12 explores how the language can be modified to serve agents.

Telescript A company in Mountain View, California offers a commercial agent language called "Telescript." Very few details are available at this writing.

Tk A user interface toolkit that runs with TCL. Section 12.7 describes some of the details for how it is used in Safe-TCL. A scheme-based version, Stk, can also be found on the Internet.

XLISP XLISP is a free version of the Lisp programming language created by Dave Betz. A description of the language can be found in Chapter 10.

Chapter 21

Sources

The Net is broad bazaar of information.

Thoughts, ideas and dreams should be as free as can be.

A redundant, fault-tolerant, flexible, multivendor protocol system for encouraging people to exchange information.

21.1   Language FTP Sources

ftp.cwi.nl (192.16.191.128) This contains the latest sources and documentation for Python, the interpreted, object-oriented language. There is C source that compiles on UNIX machines, LaTeX and PostScript files with documentation and sample programs. Here are some mirrors:

gatekeeper.dec.com	16.1.0.2	/pub/plan/python
ftp.uu.net	192.48.96.9	/languages/python
ftp.wustl.edu	128.252.135.4	/graphics/graphics/sgi-stuff/python
ftp.funet.fi	128.214.6.100	/pub/languages/python
ftp.fu-berlin.de	130.133.1.18	/unix/languages/python
ftp.sunet.se	130.238.127.3	/pub/lang/python
unix.hensa.ac.uk	129.12.43.16	/uunet/languages/python

tp.markv.com (192.122.251.1) A site filled with Python scripts maintained by Lance Ellinghouse.

cambridge.apple.com Apple maintains a research center in Cambridge, Massachusetts staffed by many of the luminaries from the LISP community. This lab is where they did much of the work on Macintosh Common Lisp and Dylan. This server includes information on using these products as well as bug fixes and patches.

ftp.cs.cmu.edu (128.2.206.173) The directory /user/ai/lang/lisp/ contains a large collection of Common LISP code. A great source for many things that you might want to add to an XLISP based agent host. The site ftp.sunet.se is a mirror site. Look through the FAQ for information about a wide range of artificial intelligence algorithms implemented in LISP.

ai.toronto.edu The Gabriel Lisp Benchmarks can be found here stored as /pub/gabriel-lisp-benchmarks.tar.Z. The benchmarks are described in the book "Performance Evaluation of Lisp Systems", by Richard Gabriel.

ftp.cs.berkeley.edu The main directory for dispensing versions of TCL and Tk. John Ousterhout, the developer of these languages, has moved from Berkeley to Sun Microsystems to launch a bigger effort to bring these languages to the Internet. In the future, newer versions of these languages will probably appear at Sun.

harbor.ecn.purdue.edu A good collection of software and extensions written in and for TCL and Tk. Anyone involved in serious development should consider searching through this directory for code that might be of use.

21.2 Cryptography FTP Sources

ftp.csua.berkeley.edu The cypherpunks ftp directory is maintained in directory /pub/cypherpunks by Eric Hughes. This is a great archive that contains a good collection of software, patents, diatribes and government documents about cryptography. The cypherpunks group is defined by a mailing list that links a group of civilians who (generally) believe that cryptography is a liberating technology for people.

garbo.uwasa.fi A large site at the University of Wasa in Finland. The directory /pc/crypto includes several programs for the PC including PGP2.3 and NewDES.

ftp.dsi.unimi.it A nice cryptography collection maintained in the Milan Computer Science department. There is a large selection of source code including raw code for big numbered calculations and more finished code for completed crypto systems. There were more than a half dozen implementations of DES when I checked.

ripem.msu.edu Another large computer science department ftp collection of cryptography information. There are many major and minor papers and documents from the network world of cryptography. There is also plenty of software including RSA's RIPEM.

rsa.com RSA Inc's ftp server. This includes plenty of official information from the company including public versions of a few of their algorithms. RSA's collection of encryption routines, RSAREF, is also available to folks from the U.S. and Canada. A minimally intrusive license is required for noncommercial use.

wimsey.bc.ca Another large collection of software that includes PGP2.6. Only U.S. and Canadians should download software because of the export laws. The rest of the collection is large and multifaceted.

21.3   Other FTP Sources

june.cs.washington.edu An ftp site for papers written at the University of Washington on "Softbots."

oak.oakland.edu The directory /pub/msdos/x_10 contains several good basic X-10 interfaces for a PC computer. Other information can be found in these locations: mrcnext.cso.uiuc.edu in directory /asre and cs.sunysb.edu in directory /pub/386BSD/xten.tg.

ftp.cs.indiana.edu The directory pub/scheme-repository/imp/ contains a scheme based version of Tk in file:STk-2.1.tar.Z. This is the language that Richard Stallman believes would be the best choice for an extension language. Discussion of this can be found in the conclusions to the TCL chapter (section 11.7).

21.4   Mosaic and WWW Pages

http://access.digex.net:/~pcw/pcwpage.html My home page. This will contain the latest reports of fixes, enhancements and changes in the text of the book.

http://tbird.cc.iastate.edu:80/pgp/ A PGP home page with information about PGP.

http://draco.centerline.com:8080/~franl/crypto.html Cryptography, PGP, and Your Privacy. A page with cryptography information with a libertarian bent.

http://www.rsa.com/ RSA Data Security's home page. Plenty of information about their conferences and toolkits.

ftp://ftp.csua.berkeley.edu/pub/cypherpunks/Home.html More information from a group of technical addicts to computers and privacy.

http://digicash.support.nl/company/digicash.html DigiCash's Home page.

http://www.digicash.com/ecash/ecash-home.html The ecash home page at DigiCash.

http://www.commerce.net/ The CommerceNet home page.

http://nii-server.isi.edu/info/NetCheque The NetCheque home page.

http://www.openmarket.com:80/about/ The home page for Open Market Inc., a company devoted to creating a secure place for people to do business on the Net.

http://www.bankamerica.com/ba_tdy.html BankAmerica's home page.

http://www.cybercash.com/ CyberCash's home page.

ftp://ftp.cs.bham.ac.uk/pub/dist/papers/cog_affect/sim_agent.html "For our work exploring architectural design requirements for intelligent human-like agents we need a facility for rapidly implementing and testing out different agent architectures."

http://louise.vfl.paramax.com/iait.html Summary of Unisys's work on Agents. "Unisys, along with other industrial and university collaborators, is developing the Knowledge Query and Manipulation Language, KQML, to support these future information networks. Significantly, KQML supports an scalable architecture for agents including software and other information services. Unisys has demonstrated KQML supporting efficient communication within the ARPA/Rome Lab Planning Initiative (ARPI) supporting initial communication within the

ARPI common prototyping environment (CPE) and subsequently in a demonstration of an intelligent information services architecture.

http://dis.cs.umass.edu/ The home page for the University of Massachusett's at Amherst's Distributed Artificial Intelligence Laboratory.

ftp://ftp.cs.bham.ac.uk/pub/dist/papers/cog_affect/sim_agent.html The location for some draft pages on the Sim_Agent project.

http://vitruvius.cecer.army.mil:8000/fact-sheets/fed.html Information about the Army's Agent Collaboration Environment (ACE). Is this for the secret agents from the Defense Intelligence Agency? No. It's actually an AutoCAD-based assistant for architects and engineers.

ftp://alpha.ces.cwru.edu/pub/agents/home.html Home page for the Case Western Reserve University Autonomous Agent Research Group.

http://www.media.mit.edu/MediaLab/Research.html The MIT Media Lab home page.

http://web.cs.ualberta.ca/~wade/HomeAuto/top.html This page contains a hypertext version of the FAQ compiled for the comp.home.automation newsgroup. You can read plenty about X-10 products including how to modify them to behave differently.

ftp://parcftp.xerox.com/pub/nano/nano.html Ralph Merkle's nanotechnology page. Nanotechnology revolves around making little machines that do tiny jobs. The problem of programming these machines to work cooperatively is quite similar to the problem of getting agents to cooperate.

http://planchet.rutgers.edu/ A home page for the nanotechnology newsgroup, sci.nanotech.

21.5 Newsgroups

Naturally, the Internet and the USENET newsgroups are a great source of information (and disinformation). There are many newsgroups that might be of interest to folks interested in agent-based systems.

comp.lang.tcl Devoted to TCL and Tk. There is plenty of discussion and even some heavy flames when people like Richard Stallman start posting questions about whether TCL could be done better.

comp.lang.lisp A nexus for the LISP community which includes the people working in Scheme and to some extent Dylan.

comp.lang.python For the devotees of this language.

comp.lang.smalltalk A long running newsgroup that explores the original object oriented language and the ways that it can be extended to include all of the needs of autonomous agents. Just remember, these guys probably thought about the problem before many of you were born. This goes for the LISP community as well.

sci.crypt & sci.crypt.research Two newsgroups devoted to cryptography. Sci.crypt.research began because sci.crypt became filled with people discussing the pros and cons of the government's plans for listening in to private conversations. The debate has the intensity of abortion with a strange twist. One side, the FBI, rarely joins in the flame wars and only one or two people seem willing to devote any time to supporting them on the net.

comp.risks This newsgroup is one of the best edited newsgroups on the net. The moderator, Peter Neumann, is one of the funniest guys around. The discussions, though, revolve around the more serious (and occasionally humorous) problems that occur when computers don't do what they're supposed to do. This is often related to the problems of building a secure and trusted network.

comp.sys.mac.programmer.* Information about programming the Macintosh.

gnu.misc.discuss Where to find information about Richard Stallman's latest creations which will, according to him, soon include a fully-featured extensions language that might be appropriate for an agent realm.

cypherpunks This is a mailing list devoted to creating the software that builds private worlds. The group is technically focused, but it can drift from time to time. To subscribe, send mail to "cypherpunks-request@toad.com". For the truly technical.

21.6   Other Sources

Patents

Copies of patents can be purchased for $3.00 (US) by writing to

> Patent and Trademark Office
> Box 9
> Washington, DC 20231

You can also purchase coupons for $3.00 a piece or $150.00 for 50.

Bibliography

[18093]   NIST FIPS PUB 180. Secure hash standard. Technical report, National Institute of Standards and Technology, U.S. Department of Commerce, May 1993.

[Ant90]   H. Van Antwerpen. Electronic cash. Master's thesis, CWI, Netherlands, 1990.

[Ban82]   S.K. Banerjee. High speed implementation of DES. *Computers & Security*, 1, 1982.

[Bat94]   Joseph Bates. The role of emotion in believable agents. *Communications of the ACM*, 37(7):117–121, July 1994.

[BB94]   E. Biham and A. Biryukov. How to strengthen DES using existing hardware. 1994.

[BC86]   G. Brassard and C. Crépeau. Non-transitive transfer of confidence: A perfect zero-knowledge interactive protocol for sat and beyond. In *Proceedings of the 27th IEEE Symposium on Foundations of Computer Science*, pages 188–195, 1986.

[BC87]   G. Brassard and C. Crépeau. Zero-knowledge simulation of boolean circuits. In *Advances in Cryptology-CRYPTO '86 Proceedings*. Springer-Verlag, 1987.

[BC90]   G. Brassard and C. Crépeau. Sorting out zero knowledge. In *Advances in Cryptology-EUROCRYPT '89 Proceedings*. Springer-Verlag, 1990.

[Bet88]   T. Beth. Efficient zero-knowledge identification scheme for smart cards. In *Advances in Cryptology–EUROCRYPT '88 Proceedings*. Springer-Verlag, 1988.

[BFL90]   J. Boyar, K. Friedl, and C. Lund. Practical zero knowledge proofs: Giving hints and using deficiencies. In *Advances in Cryptology–EUROCRYPT '89 Proceedings*. Springer-Verlag, 1990.

[Bih92a]   E. Biham. New types of cryptanalytic attacks using related keys. Technical Report 753, Computer Science Department, Technion–Israel Institute of Technology, Sep 1992.

[Bih92b]   E. Biham. On the applicability of differential cryptanalysis to hash functions. Lecture at EIES Workshop on Cryptographic Hash Functions, Mar 1992.

[Bih95]   E. Biham. On Matsui's linear cryptanalysis. In *Advances in Cryptology–EUROCRYPT '94 Proceedings*. Springer-Verlag, 1995.

[Bin92]   K. Binmore. *Fun and Games: A Text on Game Theory*. DC Heath, Lexington, Massachusetts, 1992.

[Ble86]   Woodrow Bledsoe. I had a dream: AAAI Presidential address. *AI Magazine*, 7(1):57–61, 1986.

[BLR92]   Joseph Bates, A.B. Loyall, and W.S. Reilly. An architecture for action, emotion, and social behavior. In *Proceedings of the Fourth European Workshop on Modelling Autonomous Agents in a Multi-Agent World*. S. Martino al Cimino, Italy, 1992.

[BOGG+90]   M. Ben-Or, O. Gordreich, S. Goldwasser, J. Hstad, J. Kilian, S. Micali, and P. Rogaway. Everything provable is provable in zero-knowledge. In *Advances in Cryptology– CRYPTO '88 Proceedings*. Springer-Verlag, 1990.

[Bra93] S.A. Brands. An efficient off-line electronic cash system based on the representation problem. Technical Report CSR9323, Computer Science Department, CWI, Mar 1993.

[Bra94] S. Brands. Untracable off-line cash in wallet with observers. In *Advances in Cryptology–CRYPTO '93*. Springer-Verlag, 1994.

[BS91a] E. Biham and A. Shamir. Differential cryptanalysis of DES-like cryptosystems. In *Advances in Cryptology–CRYPTO '90 Proceedings*. Springer-Verlag, 1991.

[BS91b] E. Biham and A. Shamir. Differential cryptanalysis of DES-like cryptosystems. *Journal of Cryptology*, 4(1):3–72, 1991.

[BS93a] E. Biham and A. Shamir. *Differential Cryptanalysis of the Data Encryption Standard*. Springer-Verlag, 1993.

[BS93b] E. Biham and A. Shamir. Differential cryptanalysis of the full 16-round DES. In *Advances in Cryptology–CRYPTO '92 Proceedings*, pages 487–496. Springer-Verlag, 1993.

[BSMP91] M. Blum, A. De Santis, S. Micali, and G. Persiano. Noninteractive zero-knowledge. *SIAM Journal on Computing*, 20(6), Dec 1991.

[BW94] Kyle Brown and Bob Whitefield. Sizing up the Smalltalks. *Object Magazine*, pages 59–63, Oct 1994.

[Cha81] D. Chaum. Untraceable electronic mail, return addresses, and digital pseudonyms. *Communications of the ACM*, 24(2), Feb 1981.

[Cha83] D. Chaum. Blind signatures for untraceable payments. In *Advances in Cryptology: Proceedings of Crypto 82*. Plenum Press, 1983.

[Cha85a] D. Chaum. Cryptographic identification, financial transaction, and credential device. U.S. Patent #4,529,870, Jul 1985.

[Cha85b]   D. Chaum. Security without identification: Transaction systems to make big brother obsolete. *Communications of the ACM*, 28(10), Oct 1985.

[Cha88a]   D. Chaum. Blind signature systems. U.S. Patent #4,759,063, Jul 1988.

[Cha88b]   D. Chaum. Blind unanticipated signature systems. U.S. Patent #4,759,064, Jul 1988.

[Cha90a]   D. Chaum. Card-computer moderated systems. U.S. Patent #4,926,480, May 1990.

[Cha90b]   D. Chaum. Online cash checks. In *Advances in Cryptology-EUROCRYPT '89 Proceedings*. Springer-Verlag, 1990.

[Cha90c]   D. Chaum. Returned-value blind signature systems. U.S. Patent #4,949,380, Aug 1990.

[Cha90d]   D. Chaum. Undeniable signature systems. U.S.Patent #4,947,430, Aug 1990.

[Cha92a]   D. Chaum. Achieving electronic privacy. *Scientific American*, ?(?), Aug 1992.

[Cha92b]   D. Chaum. Optionally moderated transaction systems. U.S. Patent #5,131,039, Jul 1992.

[Cr87]   C. Crépeau. A zero-knowledge poker protocol that achieves confidentiality of the players' strategy, or how to achieve an electronic poker face. In *Advances in Cryptology-CRYPTO '86 Proceedings*. Springer-Verlag, 1987.

[CS92]   A. Curiger and B. Stuber. Specification for the idea chip. Technical report, Institute Integrierte Systeme, ETH Zurich, Feb 1992.

[dBB92]   B. den Boer and A. Bosselaers. An attack on the last two rounds
           of MD4. In *Advances in Cryptology–CRYPTO '91 Proceedings*.
           Springer-Verlag, 1992.

[dBB94]   B. den Boer and A. Bosselaers. Collisions for the compression
           function of MD5. In *Advances in Cryptology-EUROCRYPT '93
           Proceedings*. Springer-Verlag, 1994.

[DDG+85]   M. Davio, Y. Desmedt, J. Goubert, F. Hoornaert, and J.-J.
           Quisquater. Efficient hardware and software implementation of
           the DES. In *Advances in Cryptology: Proceedings of CRYPTO
           84*. Springer-Verlag, 1985.

[DGV94]   J. Daeman, R. Govaerts, and J. Vandewalle. Weak keys for
           idea. In *Advances in Cryptology–CRYPTO '93 Proceedings*.
           Springer-Verlag, 1994.

[DH76a]   W. Diffie and M.E. Hellman. Multiuser cryptographic tech-
           niques. In *Proceedings of AFIPS National Computer Confer-
           ence*, 1976.

[DH76b]   W. Diffie and M.E. Hellman. New directions in cryptogra-
           phy. *IEEE Transactions on Information Theory*, IT-22(6), Nov
           1976.

[DJR94]   Bruce Randall Donald, James Jennings, and Daniela Rus. In-
           formation invariants for distributed manipulation. In R. Wilson
           and J.-C. Latombe, editors, *The First Workshop on the Algo-
           rithmic Foundations of Robotics*. A. K. Peters, Boston, MA,
           1994.

[Don95]   Bruce Randall Donald. Information invariants in robotics. *Ar-
           tificial Intelligence*, 72, Jan 1995.

[DT91a]   M.H. Dawson and S.E. Tavares. An expanded set of design cri-
           teria for substitution boxes and their use in strengthening DES-
           like cryptosystems. *IEEE Pacific Rim Conference on Commu-
           nications, Computers, and Signal Processing*, Mar 1991.

[DT91b]   M.H. Dawson and S.E. Tavares. An expanded set of S-box design criteria based on information theory and its relation to differential-like attacks. In *Advances in Cryptology–EUROCRYPT '91 Proceedings.* Springer-Verlag, 1991.

[Ebe92]   H. Eberle. A high-speed DES implementation for network applications. In *Advances in Cryptology–CRYPTO '92 Proceedings.* Springer-Verlag, forthcoming, 1992.

[ElG85a]   T. ElGamal. A public-key cryptosystem and a signature scheme based on discrete logarithms. *IEEE Transactions on Information Theory*, IT-31(4), 1985.

[ElG85b]   T. ElGamal. A public-key cryptosystem and a signature scheme based on discrete logarithms. In *Advances in Cryptology: Proceedings of CRYPTO 84.* Springer-Verlag, 1985.

[ER92]   E. Ephrati and J. Rosenschein. Reaching agreement through partial revelation of preferences. In *Proceedings of the Tenth European Conference on Artificial Intelligence*, pages 229–233, Chichester, UK, 1992. Wiley.

[ER93]   E. Ephrati and J. Rosenschein. Distributed consensus mechanisms for self-interested heterogeneous agents. In *First International Conference on Intelligent and Cooperative Information Systems*, pages 71–79, Washington, DC, 1993. IEEE Computer Society.

[Fey93]   C. Feynman. Nearest neighbor and maximum likelihood methods for social information filtering. Technical report, MIT, Dec 1993.

[FFS87]   U. Feige, A. Fiat, and A. Shamir. Zero knowledge proofs of identity. *Proceedings of the 19th Annual ACM Symposium on the Theory of Computing*, 1987.

[FFS88]   U. Feige, A. Fiat, and A. Shamir. Zero knowledge proofs of identity. *Journal of Cryptology*, 1(2), 1988.

[FS90]   U. Feige and A. Shamir. Zero knowledge proofs of knowledge in two rounds. In *Advances in Cryptology-CRYPTO '89 Proceedings*. Springer-Verlag, 1990.

[FT92]   D. Fudenberg and J. Tirole. *Game Theory*. MIT Press, Cambridge, Massachusetts, 1992.

[Gal94]   Thorton Gale. It's finally here: SmalltalkAgents. *MacTech Magazine*, pages 36–46, April 1994.

[GDW]   P. Gmytrasiewicz, E. Durfee, and D. Wehe. A decision-theoretic approach to coordinating multiagent interactions. In *Proceedings of the Twelfth Interantional Joint Conference on Artificial Intelligence*, pages 166–172, Menlo Park, California. American Association for Artificial Intelligence.

[GO91]   G. Garon and R. Outerbridge. DES watch: An examination of the sufficiency of the data encryption standard for financial institution information security in the 1990's. *Cryptologia*, 15(3), Jul 1991.

[Gol93]   O. Goldreich. A uniform-complexity treatment of encryption and zero-knowledge. *Journal of Cryptology*, 6(1):21–53, 1993.

[GQ88]   L.C. Guillou and J.-J. Quisquater. A practical zero-knowledge protocol fitted to security microprocessor minimizing both transmission and memory. In *Advances in Cryptology-EUROCRYPT '88 Proceedings*. Springer-Verlag, 1988.

[GR83]   J.A. Gordon and R. Retkin. Are big S-boxes best? In *Cryptography, Proceedings of the Workshop on Cryptography, Burg Feuerstein, Germany, March 29-April 2, 1982*. Springer-Verlag, 1983.

[Hay90]   B. Hayes. Anonymous one-time signatures and flexible untraceable electronic cash. In *Advances in Cryptology-AUSCRYPT '90 Proceedings*. Springer-Verlag, 1990.

[JJea90]   J.-J. and Myriam Quisquater et al. How to explain zero-knowledge protocols to your children. In *Advances in Cryptology–CRYPTO '89 Proceedings*. Springer-Verlag, 1990.

[Jon89]   Chuck Jones. *Chuck Amuck: the Life and Times of an Animated Cartoonist*. Farrar, Straus and Giroux, New York, 1989.

[Kal92]   B.S. Kaliski. The MD2 message digest algorithm. Technical report, RSA Laboratories, Inc., Apr 1992.

[Kal94]   B.S. Kaliski. On the security and performance of several triple-DES modes. Technical report, RSA Laboratories, in preparation, Jan 1994.

[Kil91]   J. Kilian. Achieving zero-knowledge robustly. In *Advances in Cryptology–CRYPTO '90 Proceedings*. Springer-Verlag, 1991.

[KLP94]   K. Kim, S. Lee, and S. Park. Necessary conditions to strengthen DES S-boxes against linear cryptanalysis. In *Proceedings of the 1994 Symposium on Cryptography and Information Security (SCIS 94)*, pages 15D.1–9, Lake Biwa, Japan, Jan 27-29 1994.

[Knu93]   L.R. Knudsen. An analysis of Kim, Park, and Lee's DES-like S-boxes. 1993.

[Kob87]   Neal Koblitz. *A Course in Number Theory and Cryptography*. Springer-Verlag, New York, Berlin, Heidelberg, London, Paris, Tokyo, 1987.

[KPL93]   K. Kim, S. Park, and S. Lee. Reconstruction of DES S-boxes and their immunity to differential cryptanalysis. In *Proceedings of the 1993 Korea-Japan Workshop on Information Security and Cryptography*, Seoul, Korea, Oct 24-26 1993.

[Lab93]   RSA Laboratories. Pkcs #3: Diffie-Hellman key-agreement standard. Technical Report version 1.4, RSA Data Security, Inc., Nov 1993.

[LL93]   C.H. Lim and P.J. Lee. A practical electronic cash system for
           smart cards. In *Proceedings of the 1993 Korea-Japan Workshop
           on Information Security and Cryptography*, Seoul, Korea, Oct
           24-26 1993.

[LM91]   X. Lai and J. Massey. A proposal for a new block encryp-
           tion standard. In *Advances in Cryptology–EUROCRYPT '90
           Proceedings*. Springer-Verlag, 1991.

[Mae94]   Pattie Maes. Agents that reduce work and information over-
           load. *Communications of the ACM*, 37(7):30–40, July 1994.

[Mat94]   M. Matsui. Linear cryptanalysis method for DES cipher. In *Ad-
           vances in Cryptology–EUROCRYPT '93 Proceedings*. Springer-
           Verlag, 1994.

[Mat95]   M. Matsui. On correlation between the order of the S-boxes and
           the strength of DES. In *Advances in Cryptology–EUROCRYPT
           '94 Proceedings*. Springer-Verlag, to appear, 1995.

[Mer90a]   R.C. Merkle. A fast software one-way hash function. *Journal
           of Cryptology*, 3(1), 1990.

[Mer90b]   R.C. Merkle. One way hash functions and DES. In *Advances in
           Cryptology–CRYPTO '89 Proceedings*, 1990. Springer-Verlag.

[Mer91]   R.C. Merkle. Fast software encryption functions. In *Advances
           in Cryptology–CRYPTO '90 Proceedings*, 1991. Springer-
           Verlag.

[NIS92]   NIST. Proposed Reaffirmation of Federal Information Process-
           ing Standard (FIPS) 46-1, Data Encryption Standard (DES).
           Federal Register, 57(177), Sep 11 1992.

[Nyb91a]   K. Nyberg. On the construction of highly nonlinear permuta-
           tions. In *Advances in Cryptology–EUROCRYPT '92 Proceed-
           ings*. Springer-Verlag, 1991.

[Nyb91b]   K. Nyberg.   Perfect nonlinear S-boxes.   In *Advances in Cryptology–EUROCRYPT '91 Proceedings*. Springer-Verlag, 1991.

[OO90]   T. Okamoto and K. Ohta. Disposable zero-knowledge authentication and their applications to untraceable electronic cash. In *Advances in Cryptology–CRYPTO '89 Proceedings*. Springer-Verlag, 1990.

[OO92]   T. Okamoto and K. Ohta.   Universal electronic cash.   In *Advances in Cryptology–CRYPTO '91 Proceedings*. Springer-Verlag, 1992.

[Ous94]   John K. Ousterhout. *Tcl and the Tk Toolkit*. Addison-Wesley, Reading, Massachusetts, 1994.

[RB92]   W.S. Reilly and Joseph Bates.   Building emotional agents. Technical Report CMU-CS-92-143, School of Computer Science, Carnegie Mellon University, Pittsburgh, PA, 1992.

[Riv90]   R. Rivest. The MD4 message digest algorithm. Technical Report RFC 1186, RSA Data Security, Inc., Oct 1990.

[Riv91]   R. Rivest. The MD4 message digest algorithm. In *Advances in Cryptology–CRYPTO '90 Proceedings*. Springer-Verlag, 1991.

[Riv92]   R. Rivest. The MD5 message digest algorithm. Technical Report RFC 1321, RSA Data Security, Inc., Apr 1992.

[RM93]   R. Kozierok and P. Maes.   A learning interface agent for scheduling meetings. *Proceedings of ACM SIGCHI International Workshop on Intelligent User Interfaces*, pages 81–88, 1993.

[Rob94]   M.J.B. Robshaw.   MD2, MD4, MD5, SHA, and other hash functions. Technical Report Technical Report TR-101, RSA Laboratories, Jul 1994.

[RSA78]   R. Rivest, A. Shamir, and L. Adleman. A method for obtaining digital signatures and public-key cryptosystems. *Communications of the ACM*, 21(2):120–126, Feb 1978.

[RSA83]   R. Rivest, A. Shamir, and L. Adleman. Cryptographic communications system and method. U.S. Patent #4,405,829, Sep 20 1983.

[RZ94]   Jeffrey S. Rosenschein and Gilad Zlotkin. Designing conventions for automated negotiation. *AI Magazine*, page 29, Fall 1994.

[Sch94a]   Bruce Schneier. *Applied Cryptography*. John Wiley and Sons, New York, 1994.

[Sch94b]   Bruce Schneier. Description of a new variable–length key, 64-bit block cipher (Blowfish). In *Fast Software Encryption, Cambridge Security Workshop Proceedings*. Springer-Verlag, 1994.

[Sch94]   Bruce Schneier. The Blowfish encryption algorithm. *Dr. Dobbs Journal*, 20(4), Apr 94.

[Sim84]   G.J. Simmons. The prisoner's problem and the subliminal channel. In *Advances in Cryptology: Proceedings of CRYPTO '83*. Plenum Press, 1984.

[Sim85]   G.J. Simmons. The subliminal channel and digital signatures. In *Advances in Cryptology: Proceedings of EUROCRYPT 84*. Springer-Verlag, 1985.

[Sim93]   G.J. Simmons. The subliminal channels of the U.S. Digital Signature Algorithm (DSA). In *Proceedings of the Third Symposium on: State and Progress of Research in Cryptography*, Fondazone Ugo Bordoni, Rome, 1993.

[Sim94]   G.J. Simmons. Subliminal communication is easy using the DSA. In *Advances in Cryptology–EUROCRYPT '93 Proceedings*. Springer-Verlag, 1994.

[SM93]   B. Sheth and P. Maes. Evolving agents for personalized information filtering. In *Proceedings of the Ninth Conference on Artificial Intelligence for Applications*. IEEE Computer Society Press, 1993.

[Ste90]   Guy L. Steele. *Common Lisp: The Language, Second Edition.* Digital Press, 1990. ISBN 1-55558-041-6.

[TJ81]   Frank Thomas and O. Johnston. *Disney Animation: The Illusion of Life.* Abbeville Press, New York, 1981.

[vOW91]   P.C. van Oorschot and M.J. Wiener. A known-plaintext attack on two-key triple encryption. In *Advances in Cryptology–EUROCRYPT '90 Proceedings*. Springer-Verlag, 1991.

[vSN92]   S. von Solms and D. Naccache. On blind signatures and perfect crimes. *Computers & Security*, 11, 1992.

[Way]   P. Wayner. Mimic functions and tractability.

[Way92]   P. Wayner. Mimic functions. *Cryptologia*, 16(3), Jul 1992.

[Whi94]   James E. White. Telescript technology: Scenes from the electronic marketplace. Technical report, General Magic Inc., Mountain View, CA, 1994.

[Wie93]   M.J. Wiener. Efficient DES key search. Technical Report TR-244, School of Computer Science, Carleton University, May 1993.

[X3.81]   ANSI X3.92. American National Standard for Data Encryption Algorithm (DEA). Technical report, American National Standards Institute, 1981.

[X3.83]   ANSI X3.106. American national standard for information systems–data encryption algorithm–modes of operation. Technical report, American National Standards Institute, 1983.

[XX91]   NIST FIPS PUB XX. Digital signature standard. Technical report, National Institute of Standards and Technology, U.S. Department of Commerce, DRAFT, Aug 1991.

[YLR93]   H.Y. Youm, S.L. Lee, and M.Y. Rhee. Practical protocols for electronic cash. In *Proceedings of the 1993 Korea-Japan Workshop on Information Security and Cryptography*, Seoul, Korea, Oct 24-26 1993.

Chapter 22

Index

Index